W9-DEB-614

9BB
4000

Role Development and Interpersonal Competence

Role Development and Interpersonal Competence

An Experimental Study of Role Performances in Problem-Solving Groups

DAVID MOMENT
Assistant Professor of Business Administration

and

ABRAHAM ZALEZNIK
Professor of Organizational Behavior

HARVARD UNIVERSITY · DIVISION OF RESEARCH
GRADUATE SCHOOL OF BUSINESS ADMINISTRATION
Boston 1963

© COPYRIGHT 1963

BY THE PRESIDENT AND FELLOWS OF HARVARD COLLEGE

Library of Congress Catalog Card No. 63–16486

PRINTED IN THE UNITED STATES OF AMERICA

Foreword

Role Development and Interpersonal Competence presents the results of a series of experimental studies of the performances of individuals in problem-solving groups and the relationship between performance and individual motivation and development. This study attempts to trace through the development issues involved in the variety of work styles individuals establish in their interactions with other persons.

Much of contemporary life in business organizations centers around interpersonal settings. Staff meetings, committees, and task groups are but a few of the settings in which individuals in organizations engage one another. That this process is important both for the individual and for the organization hardly needs emphasis at this juncture in the continuing study of human behavior in organizations. This study attempts to demonstrate and explain that the work styles of executives are a product of the individual's history, and that there is a developmental continuity underlying styles of individual managers' performance in problem-solving settings.

This book is addressed primarily to a professional audience within universities and industry, including researchers in organizational behavior and interpersonal relations, and those responsible for initiating executive development programs.

The theory and findings presented here may result in some uneasy reactions from those responsible for executive development programs. The emphasis on developmental history tends to urge caution in assessing the possibilities of changing behavior of executives, particularly in short-run programs whose participants' sense of need for change is highly variable. The degree to which these programs result in basic changes in the individual's styles of performance is questioned by the authors. They point out that these styles are too deeply imbedded in the individual's character structure to be altered under the conditions of most short-term educational efforts.

The authors, in assessing the application of developmental theory to education for executive responsibility, present challenging parallels between the conditions governing change in the individual's lifetime development cycle and those conditions applicable to the interventions of formal education. While providing few answers, this study opens for fresh exploration some continuing and perplexing issues in executive development.

The results of the research reported in this book are part of a broad research project being conducted at the Harvard Business School under the direction of Professor Abraham Zaleznik. The over-all objectives of the project are to present systematic analyses of individual development and the individual's adaptation to work and interpersonal relations in organizations. The results of the several other specific studies within this project will be reported in separate volumes in the near future.

The financial support for this project came from an allocation of funds contributed by The Associates of the Harvard Business School and from the B. F. Goodrich Company Endowment for Research in Memory of David M. Goodrich. A portion of Professor Moment's doctoral research was supported by a grant to him from the Ford Foundation. We are ever grateful for this generous support of the research activities of the School.

BERTRAND FOX
Director of Research

Soldiers Field
Boston, Massachusetts
June 1963

Acknowledgments

This study owes much to the help of many persons. We hope we have not overlooked any contributor, but if we have it is because the list is long and our memories perhaps short.

Professors Chris Argyris, Raymond Bauer, David McClelland, and Fritz Roethlisberger served us well as critical readers of the completed manuscript. Doctoral candidates in Organizational Behavior and several of our teaching and research colleagues at the Harvard Business School read and reacted to our earlier working papers. We did not always use their help, but we gave much thought to all their comments.

Professor Louis B. Barnes helped us in the early design phases of our study, as well as with the execution of the experimental research programs by which the data were collected. His interest and support continued throughout the entire project.

The 52 persons who participated in the four experimental groups that provided the data were generous in their contribution of time, interest, and confidence. Key persons within the organizations from which they came played an important part in the study by helping us find the participants and by lending their support and approval to our efforts.

Several persons from the Harvard community helped us in various phases of the study. Dr. Norman Bradburn and Miss Linda Perry analyzed the Thematic Apperception Tests. Dr. Lindsey Churchill did the Interaction Process Analysis of the transcripts and tape recordings of the group discussions. Miss Jane Franklin and Miss Jane MacDougall prepared the manuscript and Mrs. Arlene Walter prepared the index.

The Division of Research of the Harvard Business School

provided the support for this study. As researchers, we could not ask for a finer intellectual climate than that provided by the wise research policies of the Division. Our special thanks go to Professor Bertrand Fox, Director of Research, and to Professor Lewis B. Ward, Professor of Business Research. We also are grateful to Miss Ruth Norton, the Secretary of the Division of Research and long-standing friend, who guided the project from manuscript to book in her usual astute and skillful way.

While the fact of co-authorship expresses in itself the interdependence and indebtedness of the individual authors to each other, it to some degree masks the nature of their working relationship over the period of the study. Professor Zaleznik supervised Professor Moment's doctoral dissertation work, upon which Chapters 1 through part of Chapter 7 of this study were based, and contributed the analysis and interpretations contained in the final two chapters. To them, this publication is the culmination of the first phase of a satisfying and productive working relationship.

Although we acknowledge with gratitude the help of the many persons who contributed to this study, we alone accept responsibility for its shortcomings and face the criticisms which it deserves.

DAVID MOMENT
ABRAHAM ZALEZNIK

Soldiers Field
Boston, Massachusetts
June 1963

Contents

Contents

List of Tables and Exhibits

Number

Role Development and Interpersonal Competence

CHAPTER 1
Introduction

IN THE LITERATURE about problems of change in communities, organizations, and groups, it is becoming common to see the expression "change agent" used to refer to the people who have the responsibility for initiating and facilitating change. The role of the change agent is a relatively new concept among people concerned with improving organizational behavior and human relations. In contrast to older concepts of help, where teaching and advising activities were the predominant ways in which help was given, and this was done at arms' length from the client's real world, the change agent conceives of himself as actively intervening in the ongoing life processes of his client systems. The responsibility he feels goes far beyond the processing and transmission of information which he hopes the client can use. His job is to help the client system change itself toward increased competence in problem-solving. In the case of human relations training, the desired outcome is improved interpersonal competence. The change agent's objective is to help the individual clients to change their behavior.

Lasting changes in individual behavior necessarily involve changes in character structure. The individual's orientations toward tasks and persons have to change, not only at the intellectual level, but at the emotional and motivational levels as well. He will see things differently, think differently, and behave differently. These kinds of changes occur throughout the lives of normally developing individuals as a result of their exposure to many kinds of experiences, many if not most of which were *not* consciously planned by an external change agent for the explicit purposes of helping the person to change. When a conscious plan for change is involved, the change agent's problem is to determine when and how to intervene into the natural process of development in such a way as to economize, facilitate, or accelerate the process with a minimum of dysfunctional side effects. Some kinds of interventions can be worse than no interventions; the existing developmental state of the individual determines what he needs for further development as well as the kinds of experiences which could cause him to regress.

The kinds of interventions designed to achieve the goals of human relations training would include traditional teaching through lectures and readings, case method classes where the client plays a more active role, human relations training groups where the participants are even more active in the process, and individual counseling or psychotherapy sessions. In all except the last mentioned kind of intervention, the change agents treat their individual clients as "classes" in both of the ways the term implies; they are classes in the academic sense that they have come together as a group to learn from a shared experience, and they are classes of people in that they are assumed to be similar in the attributes relevant to their being together. The second kind of classification, which includes attributes such as age, education, and career identities, frequently implies that the clients are all somewhere near each other in development and are all equally ready to move toward the same developmental goal.

Persons with experience in human relations training observe that, in fact, the participants bring varying kinds and degrees of readiness for change to the training situation. The variations in the outcomes of such experiences for the individuals can be directly related to the developmental conditions within those individuals upon entering the situation. Some individuals readily accept and understand the experience; others find the experience threatening and their aroused defenses block them off from learning in the desired directions.

For change agents operating in the environments of formally constituted human relations training programs as well as the more natural learning environment of ongoing organizational life, more knowledge and understanding of the developmental processes that occur within individuals and the ways that current experiences are incorporated into those processes are needed. They need to know and understand the developmental conditions which the trainees or clients bring to the situation in order to intervene in ways which will fit into the individuals' growth processes with maximum effectiveness. The individuals' personality systems strive to maintain continuity over time; external interventions for change must fit in to that continuity rather than violate or disrupt it in order for the desired changes to be realized.

One commonly heard idea among change agents is that every experience that their clients encounter provides learning provided that the outcomes are observed, discussed, and understood. But this kind of justification passes too lightly over the fact that many of the clients' learnings bear little relationship to the change agents' objectives and may, in fact, be dysfunctional for some individuals. The individuals' learnings will have to maintain the continuity of their personal developmental histories. They cannot change in ways which deny or introduce marked discontinuities into their accumulated personal integrities. The here-and-now situation can mean to the individual only what his prior developmental history allows it to mean, regardless of the intentions of the change agents. In order to help an individual move toward a goal, especially if the goal is learning for increased interpersonal competence, the prospective helper has to know where in the developmental cycle the individual is starting and the resources he has at his command that will facilitate progress toward the goal. If the goal is improved interpersonal competence, it is relevant to know the existing interpersonal style or role of the individual and how it fits into his current state of personality development, as well as the relevant resources available to help himself change. The motivation to change is, of course, a prime requisite; but motivations are part of the same personality which is the object of change, and thus can quite reasonably be expected to be part of the defensive system which will resist change and lead to the persistence of old behavior patterns. An often encountered example of this pattern is the person who is strongly motivated to change in order to improve his ability to manipulate others. The motivation is certainly there, but it is of such a nature as to block rather than facilitate movement toward increased interpersonal competence.

When human relations training programs are presented to groups, the assumption that the participants are within a workable range of each other in developmental states is an economic necessity. Even if better selection criteria and practices were used, some "waste" would be unavoidable because of the limits of the validity of selection procedures and the cost of finding and bringing together developmentally ideal training groups. Change agents will apparently have to live with this kind of waste to some degree. The question for this present research study is whether or not they can learn to live with it more effectively and can learn to design training experiences more appropriate to the specific developmental states of the participants.

The study reported in the following pages was designed to contribute toward the knowledge necessary for improving learning experiences aimed at improved interpersonal competence. This chapter will present first a brief discussion of the theoretical background of the research questions explored in this study and will follow with a statement of the research questions. The chapter will close with an outline of the organization of the balance of this book.

THEORY: DETERMINANTS OF BEHAVIOR IN
INTERPERSONAL SETTINGS

One assumption necessary for understanding interpersonal behavior is that the here-and-now situation consists of a field of forces that tend to activate behavior. The force field exists within the confines of the actual physical and temporal boundaries of the experienced situation. The situation is primarily social or interpersonal. In more practical terms, the classroom, the training group, the committee, or the task group meeting provide the field of activity. People may contemplate, reflect, analyze, and plan in solitude, but behavior change and interpersonal learning take place in specific encounters with other persons.

Much attention has been given to describing the structure and dynamics of the interpersonal forces active in social situations. The social controls exercised by the face-to-face group, for example, provide one set of external forces demanding a limited range of behaviors from the individual. The person's own needs, such as his need for acceptance from others, provide the internal conditions which predispose the individual to conform to these external demands. Field theory would state that a change in the configuration and strengths of forces acting on an individual will be accompanied by a change in his behavior in a direction and amount which will maintain a reasonable state of equilibrium between the individual and the surrounding field. However, the individual will respond only to those external forces which he is experiencing at the time. His internal condition may be such as to block out, reject, or be insensitive to the cues emitted by the other people in his field, so that from their points of view he is not responding to their force field. Or, a contrasting pattern is found in the case of the individual who overconforms to the here-and-now force field. His behavior changes to accommodate to the particular group in which he finds himself. He knows very well how to get along with people. His concern with getting along and avoiding conflict constitutes a defensive block to his learning just as do the concerns of the insensitive, out-of-field person.

These examples force attention to the limits of the here-and-now force field as a sufficient conceptual model for explaining behavior and learning. They raise the following question:

> How does the behavior of the individual in a social situation relate to his personal developmental history; how does the behavior maintain continuity in the person's character structure over time?

A brief review of some theories and research findings related to the several points of view being brought together in this study, especially those of field theory and of developmental theory, will help describe the conceptual setting in which the research reported here was analyzed and interpreted.

Role Differentiation and Specialization

The small group studies of Robert F. Bales and associates (1953, 1955) provide a basis for understanding certain aspects of the problem-solving group at work. By studying relatively large numbers of groups working on standardized tasks in standardized situations, and by using systematic observation methods, they described the kinds of forces at work in the situation as well as the tendencies within individuals underlying the emergence of particular role structures.

Bales' findings suggested that in the culture of the kinds of groups he studied, work tends to be disruptive of social relations, and that much socially oriented behavior may be seen as maintaining the integrity of the group in the face of the tensions resulting from work. He found that among the groups observed, there tended to be relatively consistent distributions of activities among various kinds of task and social-emotional activities. He found differences in the profiles of activities between satisfied and dissatisfied groups.

Bales interpreted these findings as follows:

> The relations between the amounts can be viewed as the final result of a repetitive series of cycles, each of which consists of: (1) an initial disturbance of the system (precipitated by the introduction of a new idea, or opinion, or suggestion into the group) followed by (2) a "dwindling series of feedbacks" and corrections as the disturbance is terminated, equilibriated, or assimilated by other parts or members of the system . . . [1955, p. 428]

He concluded that:

> *The problem of equilibrium is essentially the problem of establishing arrangements (or an "orbit of activity") whereby the system goes through a repetitive cycle, within which all of the disturbances created in one phase are reduced in some other.* The dilemma of all action systems is that no one disturbance can be reduced without creating another. [1955, p. 433]

Having identified and interpreted the equilibrium problem, Bales then described how groups develop a structure of role relationships which is functionally related to the maintenance of group equilibrium. He found that although groups without an assigned leader tended to have a more equal distribution of participation among members, there did tend to be a process of *quantitative* differentiation among members. When he ranked and aggregated participants on the quantity of activity they produced, he found that the top man was the only one who addressed more comments to the group as a whole than he did to individual members, while all ranks distributed their comments to others in proportion to the amounts that the others spoke. He also found that qualitative differentiation was associated with quantitative differentiation:

High ranking men tend to have more proactive * Attempted Answers in their profiles and to address more acts to the group as a whole than lower ranking men, while low ranking men have more "Reactions," both positive and negative, and address more of their acts to specific individuals. [1955, p. 438]

His findings along with those of other investigators (Blau, 1955; Zaleznik et al., 1958) , confirmed the high degree of association between individuals' participation rates and their statuses as measured independently.

In addition to being observed in action, the individuals in Bales' groups were asked to evaluate each other on several criteria. By comparing the results of the "voting" on quality of ideas, contribution of guidance, liking, and disliking, with the participation rankings in five-man groups, Bales found indications that the roles taken by individuals tended to be specialized in ways which contributed toward the maintenance of group equilibrium. Men who ranked first in participation received the most votes for guidance and ideas, but also received the most choices as being *dis*liked. The men who ranked second on participation received the *most* votes on being liked, but were lower than expected in votes received on guidance and ideas, the expectation being that evaluations on all criteria would be proportional to participation rates. The interpretation of this finding was that the top participators, having done more work in the sense of initiating more instrumental-adaptive activity, disrupted the *social* equilibrium of the system and aroused negative reactions. The second ranking participators, by not being as directive and constricting in their activity, then became the persons upon whom positive feelings were centered, thereby allowing the group to reintegrate itself in the face of the top men's disruptive effects. The unexpectedly high number of "dislike"

---

* When a person starts talking, his first act is a "reaction" to the acts of others. When he continues to talk, his second, third, fourth, etc., acts are "proactive"; he is reacting to his own acts.

votes received by the *lowest* participators was explained as the scapegoat effect; some of the hostility generated by the top men's activities was displaced onto the scapegoats to resolve some of the ambivalence toward the top men.

Bales' findings and interpretations lead to the conclusion that the dilemma of group problem-solving lies in the apparent antithesis between work and affection. Affection is the "cement" which binds groups together. The aggressive activity which produces work tends to disintegrate groups. Yet for group work to be achieved, the group must hold itself together in some way. The processes by which cohesion and work are accomplished are similar in kind to the physiological processes which maintain organisms in a state of *internal* equilibrium while the organism as a whole maintains some form of stable adaptive equilibrium in its interactions with its environment.

Slater's study addressed the problem of role differentiation in small groups (Slater, 1955). Using measures of participation and voting choices received on Ideas, Guidance, Liking, and Leadership, he found that:

> . . . role differentiation in the High [consensus *] groups seems to be bipartite, with an active "task specialist" and a Best-liked man. In the Low [consensus] groups it tends to be tripartite (as well as more extreme), with an active participator who is neither well-liked nor highly rated on task ability, a more passive task specialist who is not well-liked, and a popular individual who is neither active nor highly rated on task ability. [ibid., p. 504]

He also found that role specialization tended to *increase* over time. His groups each met four times. In each succeeding meeting, the likelihood that a man would be top choice on both Ideas and Liking decreased significantly.

---

* Slater divided his groups into High consensus and Low consensus groups on the basis of the degree of agreement among the members on their voting choices. Members of High consensus groups tended to show more agreement in the way they ranked others than did the Low consensus group members.

After their fourth meeting, each member of each group was asked who stood out as leaders over four meetings. Slater calculated the proportion of cases where the top man on leadership choices was also top in choices received on each of the other criteria. The results were as follows (ibid., p. 505) :

> 80% of top men on Leadership were also top men on Guidance
> 59% of top men on Leadership were also top men on Ideas
> 25% of top men on Leadership were also top men on Liking
> (Note: The average number of members in Slater's group was 5.)

He found that although there was no association between leadership and liking, leadership was most highly correlated with those measures which were in turn most highly correlated with liking—receiving interaction and guidance. He concluded that "the chosen leader of a group is perhaps the man who has the highest hypothetical *combined* rating on all possible characteristics related to the group's purposes and needs" (ibid., p. 505) .

When he compared the behavior patterns of idea men and best-liked men, Slater found that the idea men initiated more problem-solving attempts, disagreed more, and showed more antagonism, while the best-liked men initiated more positive social reactions, asked more questions, and showed more tension. He summarized as follows: "The general picture is thus one of specialization and complementarity, with the Idea men concentrating on the task and playing a more aggressive role, while the Best-liked man concentrates more on social-emotional problems, giving rewards and playing a more passive role" (ibid., p. 507) . He also found evidence that the idea men and the best-liked men tended to work together in a complementary team relationship.

Slater used one personality measure, the California F-scale, to relate tendencies toward authoritarianism, or personal rigidity, to role patterns. He found that the best-liked men, whose role was the most specialized and differentiated in his analysis, tended to be higher than the others on the F-scale. Members of low consensus groups, where role differentiation was more extreme, tended to be higher on the F-scale than were members of the high consensus groups. He summarized, "The sharper the role differentiation in the group, or the more specialized the role played by the individual, the greater the rigidity in the personality or personalities involved" (ibid., p. 511).

Confirming and elaborating on the apparent antipathy between task activity and social activity reported in Bales' work on equilibrium, Slater demonstrated how the roles tend to polarize in group processes. He found that role complementarity provides one way for groups to deal with the task-social dilemma while indicating that highly specialized role performance may be an indicator of rigidity in personality. Slater's ideas suggested that effective leaders in problem-solving groups attempt to overcome the situational forces which tend to force role specialization and are relatively free of strong personal predispositions to specialize in role performance.

Persons who approached this suggested ideal of role fusion were the subjects of a study reported by Borgatta, Couch, and Bales, entitled "Some Findings Relevant to the Great Man Theory of Leadership" (Borgatta et al., 1955). The "great men" who provided the focus of the Borgatta, Couch, and Bales study were identified through analysis of their performances in groups as possessing substantial degrees of three qualities: task ability, individual assertiveness, and social acceptability. These men each worked with four different three-man groups. It was found that the great men tended to remain great men in the sessions following the initial one which provided the measures by which they were identified. Sessions in which the great men participated had higher production of suggestions and agreement than sessions which had no great men. Their sessions showed less tension and a higher incidence of solidarity display and tension release than did the sessions lacking great men. Their fusion of qualities remained relatively stable in all the groups in which they participated.

The ideal condition in which an individual can attend to both the task and the social-emotional issues of problem-solving groups was called role flexibility in an early paper by Benne and Sheats (1948). This condition, which they proposed as the objective of training for group leadership, was conceived of as the performance of the two different kinds of roles, task and maintenance,* as they were needed by the group. Group task roles and group maintenance roles were two of three kinds of member roles identified. The third kind, which they called "individual" roles, referred to behaviors which were aimed at satisfying individuals' needs but which had no relevance to the group task or maintenance problems.

The types of needs or motivations underlying "individual" roles were described in a report by Fouriezos, Hutt, and Guetzkow (1950). They identified five such "self-oriented" needs: dependency, status, dominance, aggression, and catharsis. Their research described the relationships between the expression of these needs in decision-making groups and the outcomes for the participants and for the groups. They saw individual behavior in groups as stemming from one or both of two sources: the requirements of the group situation and the needs of the individuals. They found that those groups where the members were observed as expressing more self-oriented needs tended to score lower on satisfaction with the meeting, with the decisions reached, with the way the group operated, and with the leadership of their meeting. Their productivity was lower and their meetings lasted longer. Conflict tended to be higher in the groups where self-oriented behaviors were more prevalent. From an analysis of

---

* The term "maintenance" as used by Benne and Sheats and the term "social-emotional" as used by Bales are roughly equivalent.

the expressed needs and the personal relevance of the agenda, the researchers concluded that ". . . the self-oriented needs estimates reflect personal involvement, arising from the agenda problems, but are relatively uncontaminated by [those] situationally induced motivations which make particular agenda . . . important to the industrial or governmental organizations to which the participants belong" (Fouriezos et al., 1956, p. 360). This conclusion indicated that agenda which the organization regarded as important evoked personal involvement only insofar as the agenda items impinged upon personal needs.

From the brief review presented thus far of selected research and theory on the behavior of individuals in problem-solving groups, it is clear that any effort to improve individual behavior and group behavior will have to take into account the two different kinds of behavioral determinants: the requirements of the situation, which might be called role requisites, and the role-taking predispositions of the individuals as reflected in their current configuration of personal needs. The nature of predispositions toward certain roles and how they relate particularly to human development has been considered in the literature. The following section reviews some of the pertinent ideas.

Individual Predispositions for Role-Taking

The genetic point of view in the study of personality sees the developing defensive system and character structure of the individual as major determinants of role-taking behaviors in interpersonal situations (Freud, 1937, 1959). An individual's developmental experience constrains him to perform only certain kinds of roles. At the same time, he has learned to react emotionally in patterned ways to the behaviors of others toward him. His own behavior pattern tends to evoke patterned emotional and behavioral responses from others; he learns to "train" others to respond to him in certain ways. (Leary, 1957, pp. 91ff.)

As mentioned earlier, Slater found that extremes of role differentiation were found to be associated with rigidity in the personalities of the persons involved (op. cit.). In another publication, he reported:

> In small experimental laboratory groups, subjects showing the greatest tendency toward role specialization, whether in a task or social-emotional direction, also tended to report that one parent (more often but not necessarily the father) was denying and demanding and the other permissive and rewarding. [1961, p. 302]

The F-scale questionnaire, which was used to measure rigidity of personality, tapped into a current internal condition within the individuals at or near the time at which their role behaviors were observed and measured. This and similar findings confirm the view that some psychological conditions within the individual predispose him to taking or avoiding certain roles. The second finding suggests that highly differentiated role performances by the parents somehow predispose the person to adopt extremely specialized roles. The two findings taken together indicate that the psychological condition predicts the performance *and* represents a resultant of earlier developmental experiences.

The processes by which the predispositions for role-taking are acquired were discussed in a comprehensive paper on role theory by Theodore R. Sarbin (1954, pp. 226–227). He differentiated between intentional instruction and incidental learning, corresponding to the difference between planned change and natural growth and developmental processes discussed earlier in this chapter. Some role patterns are taught to the child through intentional programs designed for the purpose. For example, boys and girls are intentionally treated differently by their parents so that they will learn to act like men and women respectively. They are taught by specific persons, who as teaching agents with the ability to reward and punish, teach the child to expect similar responses from other people.

Incidental learning situations include playing games where adopting roles and shifting roles become part of the activity—playing house is an obvious example. But even in athletic games (baseball, football, basketball, hockey, etc.) the activity involves specialized performances from participants differentiated by role. By shifting positions, the children learn to take the roles of others.

Sarbin indicated the importance of imaginative processes in role-taking. These processes allow the person to identify with another person and to try acting as if he were the other. This also opens the door to vicarious identification with heroes with which the person has had no real face-to-face contact. Another role-learning process can be observed in the imitative behavior of children, where they copy the behavior of parents and playmates. Sarbin reported evidence indicating that "the absence of a number of different standard roles, as well as the absence of skill in taking-the-role-of-the-other, retards socialization and leads to invalid role enactments" (ibid., p. 226) and that ". . . the absence of the opportunities for learning to enact roles appropriate to defined positions leads to deviant conduct" (ibid., p. 227).

The point of view toward role-taking which Sarbin presented was mainly concerned with what this present study would identify as cultural determinants—the ways in which a society or subculture transmits to its young the larger group's prescriptions for the behavior patterns appropriate to positions, or statuses, recognized within the structure of the society. The family of origin, the primary group in which the child grows up, is seen as the initial teaching agent, while peer groups, teachers, and relatively distant heroes and role ideals become the carriers of cultural prescriptions at later stages of the child's development. Much valuable research has been done from this point of view, uncovering the effects of social class, mobility, reference groups, family structure, and other sociological variables on such aspects of role-taking as occupational or career choice, values, and aspirations (Parsons and Bales, 1955, esp. pp. 35–131).

Leary's work, briefly mentioned in an earlier paragraph, was concerned with the emotional dimensions of interpersonal behavior and the emotional-interpersonal aspects of personality (op. cit.). These dimensions underscore the idea that patterns of emotional response to other people develop in the growing person within the matrix of culture acquisition processes. For example, the teaching agents described by Sarbin, the parents and siblings of the growing child, come to be invested with strong emotional meanings to the child. They administer the rewards and punishments instrumental to reinforcing the child's behavior in certain directions. Through these activities they become loaded with emotional value to the child. Thus the "objects" who are the agents of reward and punishment during early childhood assume special meaning independent of the rewards and punishments which flow through them.

Murray and Kluckhohn described this process of cathection as follows (Kluckhohn et al., 1956, p. 11):

> . . . certain specific objects, or kinds of objects, may become more or less enduringly attractive or repellent to the subject. In such cases, we say that the object has acquired a *positive value,* or *positive cathexis,* that is, the power to evoke affection and to attract; or that it has acquired a *negative value* or *negative cathexis,* that is, the power to evoke dislike (either antagonism, fear or revulsion). When the object is both liked (valued) and disliked (disvalued) it is said to be *ambivalent.* A positively cathected object is said to have final, or intrinsic value when it is enjoyed for its own sake, and instrumental, or extrinsic value when it merely serves as an efficient means of attaining a final value. In the development of the child the most significant objects are persons—the mother (or mother-surrogate), the father (or father-surrogate), the siblings, and, to a

lesser degree, early playmates. Since the interactive patterns, or themes, that recur and become established in transactions with these significant persons are apt to be repeated
later when dealing with other authorities or with peers,
these are the interpersonal serials which must be most thor-
oughly understood. A binding cathection which prevents
a person from cathecting some other ("more appropriate")
object is called a *fixation*.

The "binding cathection" referred to by Murray and
Kluckhohn is part of the telescoping of time and collapsing
of space inside the person by which he is bound to the past—
not only to his unique personal past, but to the historical past
of his cultural lineages as well. The term relates as well to
the concept of "repetition," or the tendency for individuals
to repeat in the here-and-now relationships and outcomes experienced in the past and usually with some pain and dissatisfaction (Freud, 1922, pp. 22–25). A person who is *not* fully
bound by his primitive cathexes can presumably distinguish
between current situational demands and his own internal
emotional states and can therefore behave "more appropri-
ately." He has more freedom to use his emotions in relation
to the here-and-now situation.

Because infants are dependent upon adults for their survival, the initial interpersonal cathexes tend to revolve
around the dimensions of affection and authority which have
tended to be highly institutionalized in the roles of mother
and father respectively. The initial learning situation is similar in social structure to the effects found by Bales and Slater
in their studies of small groups. There is a tendency for role
specialization along the lines of task (and/or authority)
and social (and/or affection) activities. This apparent polarity between authority and affection is not limited to west-
ern cultures. Nor is it limited to the common bipartite con-
stellation (Slater, 1961). Uncles, for example, can be, and
in fact are in some cultures, sources for affectionate support,
in spite of their maleness. Among American families, mid-

dle-class parents tend to differentiate less strongly in their roles than do working-class parents (Sears et al., 1957). Women can and do wield punishment and authority in some cultures. But regardless of the specific pattern of distribution by which authority and affection are spread among specific persons in the child's environment, that early situation is where the cathexes initially took place and it provides the learned pattern which must ultimately be unlearned if the individual is to become free of his primitive "binding cathexes."

These ideas, emerging from extensive clinical therapy and research, would lead to the expectation that the individual's emotional organization around significant object relationships, learned in the past, would be reflected in his behavior in small group situations. The situational demands of group problem-solving involve problems of decision-making which are heavily loaded with the connotations of authority and involve problems of group cohesion which are heavily loaded with exchanges of affection. At the same time, work itself involves aggressive activity directed toward objects external to the person, creating some problems as to how aggression will be managed by the individual in the group. Affect (i.e., emotional "substance") will abound, whether it be contained within the individual members or be openly expressed.

To these two points of view on the determinants of role-taking predispositions, cultural processes and interpersonal object cathexes, a third point of view may be added. This is the notion that role behaviors and role-taking predispositions are part of the individual's developing or fixed mechanisms of defense. From this point of view, the individual's internal conditions and observable behaviors may be analyzed with respect to the functions they perform to ward off anxiety at the deeper levels of the individual's personality. For example, overvaluing technical competence and overemphasizing technically specialized behaviors can protect a person from anxieties centered around interpersonal relationships.

Conversely, overvaluing sociability and overemphasizing social maintenance behaviors can defend against anxieties related to the interpersonal aggressiveness involved in technical performance. Many observers have written about the defensive aspects of interpersonal behavior (e.g., Leary, op. cit., and Fenichel, 1945, pp. 461–540), but relatively little work has been done to study the developmental correlates of here-and-now defensive interpersonal behaviors.

The theoretical ideas and research findings reviewed so far may be summarized in the form of propositions upon which this present study builds:

1. The cultural setting of problem-solving groups and the requisites of group problem-solving demand individual performances addressed to task and social problems. Task problems tend to demand aggressive and disruptive behaviors while social maintenance problems tend to demand more passive, nurturant, and integrative behaviors.

2. The life experiences of an individual determine his predisposition to take on situationally demanded roles in characteristic manners. These experiences may be analyzed from three points of view:
   a. as culture-transferring episodes;
   b. as events which determine the emotional meanings of persons-as-objects;
   c. as events which determine the forms in which the mechanisms of defense will be manifested in behavior.

3. The interaction between the external role requisites and the internal predispositions for role-taking within the individual determine the actual behavior he will produce in a specific group activity.

4. The outcomes of the interaction between the external demands of the group activity and the individual's predispositions for role-taking may be viewed within the limits of four *extreme* possibilities:
   a. *Both* task-relevant and socially-relevant behaviors will be produced.

    b. Task-relevant behaviors will be produced, socially-relevant behaviors avoided.

    c. Socially-relevant behaviors will be produced, task-relevant behaviors avoided.

    d. Self-oriented behaviors will be produced which have no task or social relevance.

The extreme behavioral outcomes for an individual are graphically represented in Diagram 1.1.

Diagram 1.1

BEHAVIORAL OUTCOMES OF INTERACTION BETWEEN TASK AND SOCIAL DEMANDS AND INDIVIDUAL ROLE-TAKING PREDISPOSITIONS

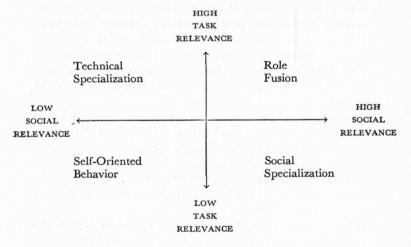

Slater's findings on role differentiation identified the tendencies for individual behavior to be *either* task-specialized *or* socially-specialized. His conjectures as to the requirements of effective leadership and the "great man" findings of Borgatta, Couch, and Bales indicate that the condition of role fusion is approachable by individuals in spite of tendencies toward specialization, and that this condition is actually associated with effective leadership. The Benne and Sheats description of role types identified "individual roles" which had little or

no relevance to either task or social requisites, and the Fouriezos, Hutt, and Guetzkow study of self-oriented needs described the outcomes for the individuals and for the groups
of the expression of these needs.   The behavioral outcome
of strong self-oriented needs with little problem-solving
relevance is indicated as "self-oriented behavior" in Diagram 1.1.

The research questions addressed in this study center
around the typology represented in Diagram 1.1. Some comments about the relationships between the propositions presented above and problems of planned and incidental changes
in individual behavior will help establish the connection between the research questions and the action focus presented in
the opening section of this chapter.

Continuity, Identity, and Change

In discussing certain points which he thought important
for understanding the changes which occur during the process
of natural personality growth, R. W. White stated that
". . . the person is acted upon by a multiplicity of influences
to which he necessarily makes a *selective response . . .*"
(1952, p. 328).   In this sense, the connotation of the idea of
"selection" is more like *screening* than decision-making.
Only certain meanings in the life situations encountered are
admitted to the person by this "screen" of concerns and values.   He does not perceive everything about every situation
he experiences, nor could he possibly do so.   The aspects of a
situation which make an impression on him and influence his
behavior are a function of *both* the nature of the external
reality and of the concerns which he carries with him into the
situation.   The trend of development toward increased personal autonomy and competence may be identified with
changes in the patterns of concerns and predispositions which
individuals carry with them as they encounter new situations.
Concerns and values change with development so that the individual's responses would also change.   White identified and

discussed four trends of personality growth (ibid., pp. 332–356) :

1. The Stabilizing of Ego Identity
2. The Freeing of Personal Relationships
3. The Deepening of Interests
4. The Humanizing of Values

These trends may be used to identify the developmental meaning of the predispositions for role-taking which persons bring to problem-solving situations, and will provide a framework for interpreting the meaning of some of the findings of this study. They provide the basis for adding a fifth proposition to the four presented in the previous section of this chapter:

5. Specific patterns of predispositions for role-taking, when viewed within the context of the individual's developmental history, may be placed conceptually on a continuum ranging between two extreme conditions:
   a. predispositions that are appropriate to the specific phases or stages of development which the individual is experiencing; and
   b. predispositions that may have been appropriate to earlier phases of development, but that represent inappropriate defenses in the face of the current realities of the person's life situation. In this condition, developmental progress is being blocked or constrained by the defensive nature of the predispositions.

An illustration may clarify the meaning of these extreme conditions. Everyone behaves in the bizarre ways characteristic of adolescence when his biological and psychological growth reaches a certain phase. His surrounding culture provides the social identity ("teen-ager," "student," etc.) and, in most cases, the necessary conditions to allow him to "grow out" of the phase (he is not yet expected to carry the responsibilities of an adult). Adolescent behavior is appropriate to the realities of his biological and psychological development.

But when such behaviors persist into the stages of chrono-logical adulthood, and the environment places certain respon-sibilities upon him, the behavior patterns and the predisposi-tions from which they stem are inappropriate.

Proposition number five adds a perspective to the role typology that allows it to be placed in the context of the tem-poral continuity of personality development. For example, if a group member happened to bring a five-year-old child into a meeting, the child's behavior could not be expected to be anything but self-oriented. Similarly, technical and social specialization can be quite appropriate to certain phases of individual development in certain situations. For example, a young engineer or scientist entering a group consisting of older men who have worked together previously is at a phase of career development where technical specialization is appro-priate, and enters a situation where the social maintenance requisites, even if he could respond to them, are relatively un-known to him. On the other hand, social specialization might be a developmentally and situationally appropriate response for an "old-timer" among younger persons who are more "up to date" on the technical requisites for solving a particular problem. These ideas suggest that for any one par-ticular person, the situationally appropriate response *for him* may vary from group to group and from time to time within a given group. The most relevant question, when continued personal development is the objective, is whether the be-havior in both its situational and developmental contexts, manifests openness to continued learning at one extreme, or a defensive, nonlearning response on the other hand.

While White indicates the directions of personality growth in terms of the four trends, Erikson specifies a sequence of developmental crises for the growing person (1959). Ac-cording to his formulations, the outcomes of each crisis for the individual persist within him into his later life tasks and experiences. Erikson plots these crises against the biological time scale as follows (ibid., p. 120) :

Phase	Crisis
I. Infancy	Trust vs. Mistrust
II. Early Childhood	Autonomy vs. Shame, Doubt
III. Play Age	Initiative vs. Guilt
IV. School Age	Industry vs. Inferiority
V. Adolescence	Identity vs. Identity Diffusion
VI. Young Adult	Intimacy vs. Isolation
VII. Adulthood	Generativity vs. Self-Absorption
VIII. Mature Age	Integrity vs. Disgust, Despair

Erikson sees these crises as being interrelated. The elements of each crisis exist in some form before they become "phase-specific." A crisis is phase-specific when the individual is biologically and psychologically prepared and when society places the relevant demands upon him. The critical issues of identity versus identity-diffusion, which Erikson locates as phase-specific to adolescence, provide a strategic nexus among the critical elements of role-taking.

Identity, as the idea is used in this study, refers to the individual's answer to the questions, "Who am I?" and "What am I becoming?" It is clear that at some times some individuals cannot answer these questions, and at some times some individuals could give only confused, ambiguous, vague, searching, hopeful or despairing responses to the questions. Some individuals at some times could answer emphatically with what Erikson calls "negative identity"; they could give clear statements of what they hope *not* to become, projecting a pervading and bitter renunciation of stereotyped others in their view of the world. For this present study, only two of several possible aspects of identity are of interest: (1) the individual's concepts of his own identity in relation to the world of *work* and the world of *people,* (2) the individual's external social attributes in relation to the specific others in group situations.

These brief comments about the ideas of Erikson and White on individual development indicate the importance and complexity of the unplanned changes which take place within individual personalities as they grow. They also indicate that external agents of planned change in individual behavior are not introducing processes which are necessarily new, strange, or alien to the change processes which have existed as long as there have been human societies. The new element is the idea of planned change through the interventions of change agents who use knowledge about man and society to understand, predict, and facilitate change. It is the change agent's belief that positive action can facilitate development. This is in contrast to older but still prevailing views that through the natural random processes of individual exposures to experiences, some persons will go through the "right" sequence and will emerge as competent leaders, in which case the responsibility for contributing to effective group and organizational problem-solving is limited primarily to selecting the "right" people and attending to the technical requisites. The change agent, on the other hand, begins with people, groups, and organizations as they are, for better or worse with respect to interpersonal competence, and intervenes in consciously planned ways in order to help them continue in their own development. The selection of members is by no means overlooked or ignored, but it is resorted to only after the possibilities of change within an existing social system are exhausted.

RESEARCH QUESTIONS AND DESIGN

This chapter began by pointing out some problems encountered by people responsible for training others for increased interpersonal competence. These problems raised the question:

> How does the behavior of the individual in a social situation relate to his personal developmental history; how does behavior maintain continuity in the person's character structure over time?

In order to develop an operational research design which could address this general question, some relevant research findings and theories were reviewed.

Four kinds of behavioral outcomes of the interaction between the demands of group problem-solving situations and individual predispositions for role-taking were described: role fusion, technical specialization, social specialization, and self-oriented behavior. These were proposed as *extreme* possibilities on the assumption that the systematic observation of any individual's behavior in a group problem-solving situation could place him somewhere in relation to these extremes. Although few if any pure types, represented by the extremes, would be expected, it would be possible to "score" each member of a group to the task and social relevance of his behavior.

This fourfold typology provides the structure around which this study was built. Since the questions could be answered only to the extent that the variables implied in the questions could be measured, much of the research design and analysis was devoted to methodological problems. The operational research questions provide the links between the actual measurement operations and the theoretical questions of this study. Once the fourfold typology was decided upon as a way of beginning the exploration, the first problem had to do with the way in which participants could be classified into the four types. This problem was approached by asking the participants to describe and evaluate each other's behaviors along several dimensions thought to be relevant to the analysis of role behavior: quality of ideas, degree of congeniality, demonstrated leadership, guidance, attractiveness as a work associate, and attractiveness as a social acquaintance. Participants were classified into the four types on the bases of others' perceptions of them. The analysis of these data replicated some of Bales' and Slater's work with respect to role differentiation and fusion, but did not constitute a major focus of the study. It provided the basis for the first operational research question:

1. a. What differences, if any, were there among the *behavior patterns* of the four perceived role types?

    b. What differences, if any, were there among the patterns of behavior of *others toward* the four perceived role types?

In addition to identifying the behavioral characteristics of the role types in terms of concrete behavior, the answers to the questions would serve to establish the validity of the typology based on perceptions.

The next major question focused on the relationship between the role types and the measures designed to tap into predispositions for role-taking:

2. What differences, if any, were there among the four role types' orientations toward:
    a. Tasks, and
    b. Persons?

The measures used for this analysis all were designed to indicate current internal states of motivation within the participants.

The third question focused on the social status relationships among the participants, as well as the developmental implications of the same measures used to indicate relative here-and-now status differences:

3. a. To what degree did status differences determine role performances?
    b. To what degree did developmental phases, as measured by age, education, and job success, determine role performances?

In order to confirm the inferred relationships between internal predispositions and observed behavior patterns, and to modify or expand on these interpretations, a fourth question was asked:

4. To what degree were the role types similar to or different from each other in their expressed satisfaction with:
    a. the decision reached by their group; and
    b. the way their group operated?

Finally, in order to illuminate the ways in which the role performances were continuous with the individuals' developmental histories, the study focused upon two different, but not mutually exclusive, relationships between the performances and the individuals' development:

5. a. To what degree could the role performances be characteristics of the current developmental phases of the individuals, as measured by their ages, levels of education, and job success?   (see question 3.b.)

   b. To what degree did the role performances represent patterned defenses arising out of sources of anxiety located in the early family experiences of the participants?

The setting on which this study focused was the small problem-solving discussion group. This is the action setting with which practical questions about the improvement of interpersonal competence are concerned. It was intended that the research situation be as nearly like practical action situations as possible while still maintaining the controls necessary for systematic analytical research.

During the months of May and June of the years 1959 and 1960 a total of four groups took part in experimental research programs that yielded the data for this study. The groups consisted of 13, 15, 11, and 13 participants, and each group participated in one experimental situation. The participants were all adults engaged in business occupations of various kinds, who held positions at varying organizational levels, ranging from technical assistant to company president. They ranged in age from the early twenties to the middle fifties. One group included two female executives.*

As part of each of the experimental programs, each group was shown the same eight-minute filmed human relations problem situation.* Immediately following the film presentation each group engaged in a forty-minute discussion of

* A detailed description of the composition of the groups and the conduct of the research programs will be found in Appendix A.

the problem in an attempt to reach some conclusions about its causes and some practical remedies. Their discussions yielded the behavioral data for this study. Additional information about the participants was obtained from a series of questionnaires completed by each of them.

The main factor which the programs controlled, and hence justified the use of the word "experimental" to describe the groups, was the situation. All of the persons in each group behaved under objectively similar conditions, and all four groups performed the same task under conditions which were as close to constant as possible. Other controls were imposed by selecting the members of the groups. The importance of the situational control is that it enabled the comparison of the behaviors of different persons facing the same situation, a comparison which is impossible by other means.

The data were obtained from systematic observation of the discussion sessions and from questionnaires. The data on role perceptions and satisfaction were obtained from a Post Meeting Reaction questionnaire which was completed by each participant immediately following the discussions. The measurement of behavior was done by using observers' notes and tape recordings of the discussions. The instruments used to assess internal motivational conditions were the Thematic Apperception Test, scored for need Achievement and need Affiliation, and the Individual Preference Study, which scored the participants on their relative preferences for various kinds of rewards available in their current working lives: Self-Actualization, Job-Intrinsic, Belonging, Status, and Economic. These instruments were completed by the participants immediately prior to viewing the film and participating in the discussion group experiences. The data on status attributes and early childhood experiences were obtained from a background information questionnaire. Technical descriptions of the data collecting instruments and methods are contained in the appendices.

The main purpose of this study was to contribute toward

the understanding of role performances and behavior in group problem-solving situations as integral aspects of the processes of individual development. The potential users of this increased understanding are change agents—people whose jobs center about helping individuals, groups, and organizations to increase their effectiveness through improved interpersonal competences. By examining interpersonal behavior within the framework of developmental theory, selected issues and problems in training are highlighted. These issues will be discussed in the final chapter of this book.

ORGANIZATION OF THIS BOOK

The remainder of this book follows the sequence of research questions presented in this introductory chapter. Chapter 2, "Role Specialization and Fusion," presents and analyzes data on perceptions and evaluations of behavior. Chapter 3, "Behavior Patterns," shows the relationships between behaviors produced and evoked and the typology of perceived roles. Chapter 4, "Predispositions for Role-Taking," measures and analyzes the orientations of the four role types toward tasks and persons. Chapter 5, "Social and Developmental Influences," is concerned with the influences of social status and developmental phase on role performances. Chapter 6, "Satisfaction," analyzes and interprets the patterns of expressed satisfaction in relation to role performances. Chapter 7, "Developmental Trends," compares the role types with respect to their current developmental phases and their early childhood experiences. Finally, Chapter 8, "Implications," interprets the findings in relation to the practical problems of responsible agents of change.

CHAPTER 2

Role Specialization and Fusion

As a starting point in the analysis of the many variables with which this study is concerned, this present chapter addresses the problem of making operational the theoretical typology introduced in Chapter 1. In addition, attempts will be made to establish the validity of the operational typology by examining its correlations with some data which were to some degree independent of the data used to establish the typology. Finally, some developmental implications of the analysis will be examined.

The theoretical typology consisted of four possible extreme behavioral outcomes of the interaction between the individual's predispositions for taking roles and the demands of the situation surrounding him. The outcomes were identified in Chapter 1 as (1) role fusion, (2) technical specialization, (3) social specialization, and (4) self-oriented behavior. The theoretical typology originated from the research findings and clinical observations of other workers. It is based on how the subjects of the original experiments and field situations actually reported their perceptions and evaluations of each other's behavior, as well as, in some cases, the researchers' perceptions and evaluations of the subjects' behavior. In this study the operational typology was constructed around the subjects' reports of their perceptions and evaluations of each other.

SOURCE OF DATA

Immediately following the problem-solving discussions, each participant completed a Post Meeting Reaction questionnaire and identified the persons in their groups who they thought stood out as "best" or "most" on certain kinds of performances and evaluations.* The participants had not been advised beforehand that they would be asked for these evaluations. Individuals were scored on the number of other people who chose them on each of the criterion questions.

The performance criterion questions were as follows:

(Who do you think) presented the *best ideas* . . . ?
. . . did the most to *guide the discussion?*
. . . added most to the *congeniality and friendliness* of the discussion?
. . . stood out as *leaders* . . . ?

In addition to these performance questions, two social attractiveness questions were included for the two groups made up of persons who had not known each other prior to the discussion: †

Which of the people . . . do you think you would *enjoy working with?*
. . . do you think you would *like to know better socially* . . . ?

INTERRELATIONSHIPS AMONG CRITERIA

It was found that if a person scored high (i.e., ranked among the top half in his group) on choices received on any one criterion, it was more likely that he would score high than he would score low on any other criterion, with two exceptions where no associations were found. The degrees of association among choices received on the six criteria are shown on Table 2.1.

* A copy of the Post Meeting Reaction questionnaire form is included in Appendix C.
† See Appendix A for the composition of the groups.

Table 2.1

DEGREES AND DIRECTIONS OF ASSOCIATIONS AMONG PMR
CHOICE QUESTIONS, MEASURED BY MUTUAL
PREDICTIVE VALUES *

	GUIDANCE	CONGE-NIALITY	LEADER-SHIP	"WORK WITH"	"KNOW SOCIALLY"
IDEAS	.44(+)	.12(+)	.50(+)	.26(+)	.00
GUIDANCE		.28(+)	.42(+)	.05(+)	.14(+)
CONGENIALITY			.17(+)	.00	.20(+)
LEADERSHIP				.33(+)	.27(+)
"WORK WITH"					.26(+)

* See Appendix B for the explanation of the Mutual Predictive Value (MPV) index. An index of .00 indicates no relationship between the variables, while 1.00 indicates perfect correlation. A plus sign (+) indicates that a high score on one variable tends to occur along with a high score on the other variable. A minus sign (−) indicates that a high score on one variable tends to occur along with a *low* score on the other variable. The higher the numerical value of the index, the greater the utility of any one of the two variables for predicting to the other.

The associations among the various scores may be partially explained by "halo effect." A person who was perceived and evaluated as good, or outstanding, on one attribute tended to be evaluated as outstanding on other attributes as a result of a general, over-all attribution of "goodness" to the person. This effect has been found in many sociometric studies (e.g., Selltiz et al., 1960, pp. 351–352, and Hovland, 1958, pp. 148–149).

The six criteria may be organized in relationship to each other on the basis of differences in the kinds of processes to which they refer. Ideas, guidance, and congeniality may be considered to be relatively *specific components* which combine to yield an over-all performance pattern which is evaluated in a more *general* manner in the leadership and liking questions. Table 2.2 presents a reorganization of the correlations according to these assumptions. It is here that evidences of role differentiation become apparent.

The degrees of association may be assumed to be measures

Table 2.2

DEGREES OF ASSOCIATION AMONG COMPONENTS OF ROLE
PERCEPTIONS AND RESULTANT EVALUATIONS, MEASURED
BY MUTUAL PREDICTIVE VALUES

		GENERAL EVALUATIONS		
		LEADERSHIP	"LIKE TO WORK WITH"	"LIKE TO KNOW SOCIALLY"
SPECIFIC COMPONENTS	IDEAS	.50	.26	.00
	GUIDANCE	.42	.05	.14
	CONGENIALITY	.17	.00	.20

of the relative importance of the specific components as co-determinants of the general evaluations. It appears in Table 2.2 that ideas, guidance, and congeniality were important *in that order* for determining the leadership evaluation. Although the ordering remained intact for determining the "work with" evaluation, the strengths of the effects were diminished considerably. The ordering was completely reversed under the "know socially" evaluation. The clearest reversals took place with the ideas and congeniality components, which showed the lowest degree of association (.12) between themselves of all the pairs of *components* on the earlier Table 2.1. Although perceived quality of ideas was of importance for a high evaluation on leadership, it was less important for social attractiveness as a potential work associate, and was of no importance as a basis for wanting to know people socially. Congeniality was the least important of the three components for high evaluation on leadership, was of no importance for desirability as a work associate, but was the most important of the three in relation to desirability as a social acquaintance.

ROLE TYPOLOGY

The relatively low degree of association between choices received on ideas and on congeniality, and the indication that they tended to work with each other in some way as specific elements determining general evaluations, led to their use as the basis for the operational role typology. It was predicted that persons scoring high on both criteria would approximate the theoretical role fusion type, that persons high on ideas but low on congeniality would approximate the technical specialization type, that persons scoring low on ideas but high on congeniality would approximate the social specialization type, and that persons scoring low on both criteria would approximate the self-oriented behavior type. Since the theoretical typology was proposed as representing *extreme* outcomes, and the operational typology was based on arbitrary dichotomization of continuous rankings, the operational types must be viewed as including persons who varied in the degree to which they approached the extreme conditions. The operational typology represents tendencies of individuals in terms of *direction* only, and does not imply that the individuals classified as any one type were similar to each other in the degree to which they approached the extreme condition. The resulting distribution of cases among the operational typology is indicated in Table 2.3.

Table 2.3

NUMBERS OF PARTICIPANTS RECEIVING HIGH AND LOW CHOICES
ON IDEAS AND CONGENIALITY

	LOW CHOICES RECEIVED ON CONGENIALITY	HIGH CHOICES RECEIVED ON CONGENIALITY	TOTAL PERSONS
HIGH CHOICES RECEIVED ON IDEAS	10	15	25
LOW CHOICES RECEIVED ON IDEAS	15	12	27
TOTAL PERSONS	25	27	52

The operational types were given different names from the four theoretical extreme conditions for two important reasons. The first reason was indicated above; the operational types merely approximate tendencies, while the theoretical types represent extremes. Secondly, the operational typology was constructed as a predictive device; its construction was based upon reported perceptual data only. Its empirical meaning in terms of actual behavior patterns and conditions within the individuals has yet to be discussed. In other words, at the stage of analysis discussed so far, the degree to which the operational types are related to the theoretical expectations or empirical realities is unknown. The names given to the operational types, along with their theoretical and empirical derivations, is summarized on Table 2.4.

Table 2.4

DERIVATION OF THE ROLE TYPOLOGY

| | EMPIRICAL APPROXIMATION: CHOICES RECEIVED ON: | | NUMBER OF | NAME GIVEN |
THEORETICAL EXTREMES OF BEHAVIORAL OUTCOMES	IDEAS	CONGENI- ALITY	CASES IN CLASS	OPERATIONAL ROLE TYPE
Role Fusion	High	High	15	Star*
Technical Specialization	High	Low	10	Technical Specialist
Social Specialization	Low	High	12	Social Specialist
Self-oriented Behavior	Low	Low	15	Underchosen†

* The name "Star" was derived from the usages of sociometric researchers. It connotes a central position and a large number of choices received, and refers to the star-shaped appearance of a sociogram. In this study, Stars tended to receive high choices on *all* criteria, hence the additional connotation of versatility seems justified.

† The Underchosen participants constituted a residual category. They were the persons who remained after the Stars and Specialists were identified. Hence they might turn out to be a fourth type, which could be characterized by (1) not being noticed; (2) a mixture of various kinds of roles which were not noticed; or (3) manifesting self-oriented behavior. They and the other types were to some extent artifacts of the analytical operations. For example, if a new group consisting of the 15 Stars were selected and the same procedures repeated with them, most of them would be classified Specialists and Underchosen, while if the 15 Underchosen participants made up a new group, the same classification scheme would identify some Stars and Specialists among them.

Of the 15 Stars, 12 also received high choices on guidance and leadership. Of the 15 Underchosen, 11 also received low choices on guidance and leadership. These 23 extreme cases were analyzed separately, but no associations were found in that analysis which were not also found in the following analysis of the four role types.

Role Types, Leadership, and Social Attractiveness

The relationships between the role types and choices received on the other PMR (Post Meeting Reaction questionnaire) items are shown in Tables 2.5 and 2.6. These tables are in the format which will be used for most of the later analysis. The statistical meaning of this format is explained in Appendix B. It is necessary to know how the tables were constructed in order to understand the findings and their meanings. Table 2.5 will be interpreted in detail as an example.

Individuals were scored high or low on the various measures used in this study. Their high or low scores were determined by their ranking, in relation to the other members of their particular group, on their absolute, or raw, scores. In the case of the sociometric data, the raw scores were the number of times a person was chosen by others on the particular question. The raw scores on each question were listed in the order of their magnitudes. They were then divided as near to the middle as possible. Individuals whose scores were in the upper half were scored high and those in the lower half were scored low. Approximately 50% of the participants were in each class. In some instances the division point included more or less than 50% in each of the two classes. This happened when there were ties in raw scores at the middle of the rankings.

Table 2.5 indicates that 48% of the 52 persons were scored high in choices received on guidance and that 44% were scored high in choices received on leadership. If an individual's role type was of *no* importance in determining the number of choices he would receive on guidance and leadership, then it would be expected that about 48% of each type would be high on guidance and that about 44% of each type would be high on leadership. However, the results indicated that 87% of the Stars scored high on leadership. The Technical Specialists were divided in about the same proportions as were the entire 52. Fewer Social Specialists and Underchosen were high on guidance and leadership than would be expected if there had been no relationship between the role types and the number of choices received on guidance and leadership.

Table 2.5

ROLE TYPES AND PMR CHOICES RECEIVED ON GUIDANCE
AND LEADERSHIP: PERCENT OF CASES
HIGH ON CHOICES RECEIVED

		PERCENT HIGH CHOSEN	
ROLE TYPE	NUMBER	GUIDANCE	LEADERSHIP
Total	52	48%	44%
Stars	15	87	87
Technical Specialists	10	50	50
Social Specialists	12	33	17
Underchosen	15	20	20

Role Types vs. Guidance: $X^2 = 14.8$, $.001 < p < .01$
Role Types vs. Leadership: $X^2 = 18.2$, $p < .001$

The findings indicated on Table 2.5 confirm Slater's suggestion that "the chosen leader of a group is perhaps the man who has the highest hypothetical *combined* rating on all possible characteristics related to the group's purposes and needs" (Slater, 1955, p. 505), as well as the role fusion aspects of "great man" theory (Borgatta et al., 1955). In addition to confirming the findings indicated earlier on Table 2.2, which illustrated the relationships between specific components and general evaluations, the analysis by role type brings out the low "value" of perceived congeniality *alone* as a component of perceived leadership. The Social Specialists and the Underchosen shared about equally as low likelihoods of being seen as leaders, although the perceived congeniality apparently gave the Social Specialists a slight edge over the Underchosen on guidance. The hypothesis that role fusion tends to be a requisite for leadership was confirmed. In addition, it was learned that in these particular experimental groups, consisting of professional and executive employees,* technical specialization (as measured) tended to be of more value to the groups than did social specialization (as measured). Finally, it appears that perceived congeniality, in the absence of good ideas, gave the Social Specialists no clear advantage over the Underchosen, who were seen as neither being congenial nor having good ideas, in terms of leadership contribution.

The relative degrees of social attractiveness of the four role types is indicated on Table 2.6. For approximately half of the experimental population it was possible to differentiate between attractiveness as a work associate and attractiveness on a purely social basis, since these participants had not known each other before the experimental sessions. This differentiation could not be made for the other groups, whose members actually were work associates before and after the experimental sessions.

The most interesting indication on Table 2.6 is that perceived congeniality *and* quality of ideas worked together as determinants of social attractiveness, with respect to *both* task-related sociability ("work with" and actual friends on the job) and pure, nontask related sociability. In the new groups, all of the Stars were among the top half in choices received on ". . . would like to know better socially." In both the new and natural groups, the Stars were more likely

* Many of the previous studies of role patterns in small groups used college students as subjects. This was true of Bales' and Slater's work. The "great man" study involved enlisted men in the Air Force (Borgatta et al., 1955, p. 569).

Table 2.6

ROLE TYPES AND SOCIAL ATTRACTIVENESS:
PERCENT OF CASES HIGH ON CHOICES RECEIVED

ROLE TYPE	NEW GROUPS *			NATURAL GROUPS *		AGGREGATE	
	NUMBER	"...WOULD ENJOY WORKING WITH"	"...WOULD LIKE TO KNOW BETTER SOCIALLY"	NUMBER	"...AMONG [MY] BETTER FRIENDS"	NUMBER	"KNOW SOCIALLY" AND ACTUAL FRIENDSHIPS
Total	24	37%	58%	28	50%	52	54%
Stars	6	67%	100%	9	67%	15	80%
Technical Specialists	4	50%	25%	6	50%	10	40%
Social Specialists	8	25%	50%	4	25%	12	42%
Underchosen	6	17%	50%	9	44%	15	47%
		Stars vs. others, Fisher's Exact p = .10	Stars vs. others, Fisher's Exact p = .02		Stars vs. others Fisher's Exact p = .17		Stars vs. others Chi² = 5.8, .05 > p > .02

* Among the four experimental groups, two were "new groups," in that the participants had not known each other before the experimental sessions, while the other two, the "natural groups," consisted of persons who normally worked together on their jobs. In the new groups, the sociometric questions assessed feelings derived from the experimental situation only. In the old groups, the sociometric question assessed feelings that had existed before the experiments. Details on the composition of the groups will be found in Appendix A.

than any of the other types to be chosen as enjoyable work associates. The implication is that task activity, the production of ideas in this case, does *not* detract from social attractiveness when combined with perceived congeniality, as would be the case if task activity were inherently incompatible with social attractiveness. This could mean that among older working people, in contrast to the college students who were the subjects of the studies reported by Bales and Slater (1955), affection and respect for competence tend to become fused into a generalized social attractiveness. Where technical competence was found in addition to perceived congeniality, the likelihood that the person would be socially attractive increased.

Table 2.6 also yields some insights into the consequences of the two kinds of specialization. In these cases, where good ideas or congeniality each occurred in the absence of the other, the subjects tended to receive inverse evaluations on the omitted dimension. The participants in the new groups expressed less preference for a Social Specialist as a work associate than for a Technical Specialist. They saw the Social Specialists as barely more attractive than the Underchosen as work associates. On the other hand, Technical Specialists were even less desirable than the Underchosen as purely social friends. In the natural groups, where friendship choices represented actual conditions rather than imagined conditions, the Social Specialists were even less attractive than the Underchosen. In the aggregated column, where those receiving high "know socially" choices among the new groups were combined with those receiving high choices as friends among the natural groups, the differences among the Specialists and Underchosen tended to wash out, but the outstanding social attractiveness of the Stars remained.

In summary, Tables 2.5 and 2.6 indicated that those persons who were perceived as tending toward role fusion also tended to be evaluated highly as demonstrating leadership *and* tended to be seen as socially attractive. Of the remaining three types, the Technical Specialists tended to be the most attractive as work associates while the Social Specialists tended to be most attractive as purely social acquaintances or friends. The Underchosen tended to be the least attractive as work associates, but tended to be as attractive as the Social Specialists, and more attractive than the Technical Specialists, as purely social acquaintances.

The Effects of Time

Slater's groups each met four times. He found that role differentiation *increased* over time (1955, pp. 504–505). This was expressed in the decreasing percentages of cases where the top man on ideas was also the top man on liking from the first through the fourth meetings. Although this present study does not have directly comparable data because the four groups each met only one time, the fact that two of the groups contained people who had worked together for as long as several years, while the other two groups had not worked together before the experiment, gives an indirect basis for comparison. Role perceptions in the natural groups may be assumed to reflect the effects of social structures which had been developed over time, while role perceptions in the groups of strangers were necessarily the consequences of only the one 40-minute discussion experience. Analyzing the relationships between choices received on ideas and choices received on congeniality, which was $MPV = .12(+)$ for the aggregated 52 cases from the four groups, it was found that there was *no* relationship $(MPV = 0)$ for the "new" groups, and an association of $MPV = .23(+)$ for the "old" groups. This indicated that there was a tendency for the ideas and congeniality perceptions to go together in the old groups, while the perceptions were independent of each other in the new groups.

A similar conclusion results from the analysis of ideas and liking. In this present study, liking would be measured by friendship choices received in the old groups and "would like to know better socially" choices received in the new groups. Between leadership and liking, the degree of association was lower for the "older" groups, but in neither the old nor the new groups were the two measures *negatively* associated. In both the old and the new groups, people perceived as standing out as leaders tended to be liked although the effect was stronger in the new groups $(MPV = .27(+))$ than in the old groups $(MPV = .12(+))$. The findings suggest the possibility that with older, more experienced subjects, role differentiation might actually *decrease* over time in the life of a group.

There are logical reasons why it would be expected that role differentiation would tend to decrease over the life of a natural work group and over the life of an individual. One reason concerns the natural processes of selection that take place as members enter and leave the group. If role fusion means greater competence for working in groups, then those persons who had or were acquiring this competence would tend to remain in the group, while less competent persons would tend to be driven out, both by the natural internal processes of the group, and by the external evaluations of organizational superiors. Secondly, as the group grows older, so do its members. Under the external (to the individual) demands of the group and the organization, persons who wanted to remain in the system would have to change in the direction of role fusion in order to continue to be part of the system.

SUMMARY AND DEVELOPMENTAL IMPLICATIONS

The major purpose of this chapter was to describe the construction of the operational role typology. The analysis of the Post Meeting Reaction data in relation to the typology demonstrated to some extent the validity of the typology; the Stars did appear to represent the condition of role fusion while the specialists did appear to deserve the names given them. Little could be learned as to the degree to which the Underchosen represented the condition of self-oriented behavior.

Since the analysis so far has replicated some of Bales' and Slater's earlier work, it is of interest to compare the findings of this study with their findings. Their work with college students highlighted role differentiation. Role fusion, while hypothesized by them, was treated as a relatively rare occurrence. In the "great man" study, the authors chose 11 out of 126 subjects as fusion types on their assumption "that only about the top tenth of the total sample would satisfy the criterion of 'greatness' " (Borgatta et al., 1955, p. 570). In this present study, 29% (15 out of 52) were placed in the Star category, and 12 of the 15 had received high choices on all of the questions other than those around which the typology was constructed (ideas and congeniality). Role fusion may have been more prevalent in this present study than it was in the previous researches cited. The analysis confirmed that this was an appropriate assumption.

Important differences in methodology between this and the other studies prevent the definite conclusion that role fusion was more common among the subjects of this study than among the subjects of the previous studies. However, the differences between the population studied in this research and those who were the subjects of the prior researches contain developmental implications which will have relevance to the theme of role development toward which the later chapters of this book converge.

The subjects of this present study were all adults, employed in relatively responsible positions in the middle and upper managerial levels of their organizations. Their daily lives included a commitment to working careers, involving an attainment of responsible social roles through marriage, parenthood, and/or community participation as well as through membership in a purposeful, working organization. It may be assumed that these individuals had, by and large, attained a higher level of personal development toward maturity than had the college students or military recruits who were subjects of the previous studies.

The condition of role fusion, when viewed within the context of individual development rather than as a purely here-and-now condition, could represent an outcome of a sequence of events occurring outside and inside the individual. It could represent something that persons learn over their lives. This viewpoint would account for the possible differences in the occurrence of role fusion between younger persons experiencing the status of student and the older working persons who took part in this present study. It also suggests that an analysis of the relative developmental stages of the subjects of this study might demonstrate the relationships between developmental phases and role performances. This will provide the focus of later chapters.

The next step in this analysis is to describe the behavioral correlates of the *perceived* role types. This is the subject of the next chapter, where the first of the major research questions will be addressed.

ed
task,
to the
get done.
mong per-
sfer informa-
sis and evalua-
ion of sentiments
exercise of direct-
se processes, tensions

OF BEHAVIOR MEASURES

	MEASURES RELATED TO RESOLUTION OF PROBLEMS	
LEM	IN ACTION	IN CONTENT OF COMMUNICATION
nance	Participation	
uity: xchange	Interaction	
ommunication of Sentiments: A. Social-Emotional Expressions		Social Acts
2B. Influence		Ask Acts
3. Tension Management	Tension Release	
1. Aggression Management	Interruption	Competitive Questions
2. Exchange of Sentiments A. Positive	Personal Recognition	Agreement
2B. Negative		Disagreement

er-
ersonal
Relations
(Inter-
personal
Activities)

CHAPTER 3

Behavior Patterns

THE ANALYSIS in this chapter searches for pa[tterns of]
behaviors which could be associated with th[e ...]
is assumed that the behaviors provided the [...]
perceived and evaluated by the others. T[...]
pares an outcome—role perceptions by ot[hers ... pre-]
ceding series of events—the subject's beh[avior. Ac-]
cording to Leary's formulation of the i[...]
other persons' behaviors toward an indi[vidual are ex-]
pected to form a patterned response (Le[ary ...].
Therefore, a second behavioral variabl[e ...]
havior patterns of others toward the su[bject. In inter-]
personal situations, others' behaviors a[...]
as outcomes of a particular person's b[ehavior ...]
that the behavior of others toward [...]
rather than random, that behavior [...]
been *evoked by* the person in the [...]

The analysis will take place arou[nd the typol-]
ogy developed in Chapter 2: Stars, Techni[cians, So-]
cial Specialists, and Underchosen.

The measurement and analysis of actual behaviors posed
methodological problems which are dealt with in detail in
Appendices B, D, and F. The meanings of the findings and
the validity of the interpretations which may be attached to
them are constrained by the research operations. For this
reason, it is necessary to introduce a minimal operational
framework at this point.

Role Development and Interpersonal Competence

individuals toward others. In addition, the same five interpersonal measures were applied to the behaviors received by
individuals from others. The theoretical organization of the
behavior measures is shown on Table 3.1.

The kinds of problems with which behaviors were assum[ed]
to be concerned were abstracted from the requisites of [...]
social, and interpersonal activities. Continuity refers [...]
necessity for activity to go on in order for work to [...]
Dominance describes the distribution of activity [...]
sons. Exchange describes activities which tran[...]
tion from one person to another. The anal[...]
tion of approval and disapproval require the communica[...]
of approval and disapproval as well as th[...]
ing influences. Concurrently with the[...]

48

THEORETICAL ORGANIZATION

Table 3.1

	KIND OF PROB[LEM]
LOCUS OF PROBLEM	
Group Process (Task and Social Activities)	1A. Continuit[y]
	Domi[nance]
	1B. Conti[nuity]
	E[xchange]
	2. C[...]

tent of [...]

These ten measu[res ...]

* The operational derivations of thes[e ...]
pendix D. The scoring systems are described in A[p-]
liabilities are also contained in Appendix F.

are built up which must be released in some manner for the processes to continue.

These problem-solving processes are instrumented by humans whose personality systems are involved. A parallel set of problems related to the maintenance and enhancement of their personality systems arises around the activities necessary to perform problem-solving work. The distribution of activity among persons involves acts of aggression, in that the scarce commodity of attention is, in some cases, taken away from one person by another through interruption. Ideas are evaluated and criticized, and the people involved in these maneuvers may feel that their personal competences are being attacked and need defending. Approval and disapproval of ideas involve an enhancement or a lowering of the esteem of the person who originated the ideas. The identification of ideas with persons addresses attention to the person, as well as to the idea.

It is the pattern of distribution of behavioral attention to these various kinds of problems which make up role patterns in this study. The various kinds of behavior which were measured had to be originated with individuals. If there were no role specialization, the origination of the behaviors would be expected to be distributed equally among all of the participants, and there would be no differences in the proportions of persons of each perceived role type who were classified High on the measures.

The measures concerned with *continuity* were participation and interaction. An individual's score on participation was the number of 12-second time intervals during which he spoke,* and was intended to be an index of the amount of time during which he *dominated* the group's attention. Interaction was the proportion of the number of intervals during which the subject spoke *and* others spoke ("shared" intervals) to the subject's participation score. Interaction was

---

* He would receive one "count" on participation regardless of the length of his comments within the time interval.

intended to be an index of the amount of social *exchange*. Persons low on interaction tended to deliver long comments when they participated; they tended *not* to share intervals of time with others. Persons high on interaction tended to be involved in more spontaneous interchanges. Persons low on interaction and high on participation could also be called high on proaction, the tendency to continue talking once started.

Participation, as it was measured in this study, was an index of over-all activity. It would be expected that the amounts of particular kinds of behavioral activities, such as asking questions, joking, showing agreement, and showing disagreement, would tend to vary with the total amount of activity, or participation, produced by an individual. This tended to be the case in this study, as indicated by high degrees of correlation between participation and the absolute amounts of other behaviors measured. In order to factor out the effects of individuals' over-all activity rate on the quantities of particular behaviors produced by them, their scores on these other behavior measures were expressed as ratios of the absolute amount of the particular behavior measured to their total participation rates. For example, if person A talked during 80 intervals, and hence received a participation score of 80, while he showed agreement during 10 intervals, his agreement ratio score would be 10/80, or .125. If person B's participation score was 20, and he showed agreement during 5 intervals, his agreement ratio score would be 5/20, or .25. Thus, although A showed more agreement as measured in absolute counts, 10 to 5, B's tendency to show agreement was higher, .25 as compared to .125.

The behavior measures concerned with the *communication of sentiments* were the social acts ratio and the ask acts ratio. Both were derived from the Bales Interaction Process Analysis system.* The social acts ratio was the propor-

---

* The IPA system consists of 12 mutually exclusive scoring categories in which Total IPA Acts = Expressive Acts + Instrumental Acts. The Social

tion of the individual's total acts which were classified into the IPA Social-Emotional categories: Shows Solidarity, Shows Tension Release, Agrees, Disagrees, Shows Tension, and Shows Antagonism. The measure was intended to be an index of the degree to which the subjects' behaviors were socially and emotionally expressive, in contrast to instrumental task behaviors involving the exchange and evaluation of information. The ask acts ratio was the proportion of the person's total instrumental task acts (asking *and* giving information, opinions, orientation) which fell into the "ask for" categories. This measure was intended to be an index of the degree to which the individual expressed openness to influence, in contrast to the expression of unilateral influence which would be reflected in the absence of ask acts.*

The final group process behavior measure was *tension release,* the proportion of the person's total acts which were classified under IPA category 2, Shows Tension Release. Joking was the predominant behavior counted in this category. Tension release was intended to be an index of the degree to which the person resolved conditions of social tension by joking. Or, inversely, low joking was an index of the seriousness manifested by the subject.†

The interpersonal behavior measures concerned with *ag-*

Acts Ratio was therefore complementary to the Task Acts Ratio, in that the

Social Acts Ratio $\dfrac{\text{(Social Emotional Acts)}}{\text{Total Acts}}$ plus the Instrumental (Task) Acts

Ratio $\dfrac{\text{(Instrumental Acts)}}{\text{Total Acts}}$ had to be equal to 1.00. Therefore, persons classi-

fied High on their Social Acts Ratio were automatically the same people who would be classified Low on their Instrumental Acts Ratios. Although the later analysis refers to the Social Acts Ratio, this may be understood to mean the same as the complement of the Instrumental Acts Ratio.

* Under the IPA system, Ask Acts + Give Acts = Total Instrumental Acts.

$\dfrac{\text{Ask Acts}}{\text{Instrumental Acts}} + \dfrac{\text{Give Acts}}{\text{Instrumental Acts}} = 1.00.$

† Tension Release Acts are included in Social-Emotional Acts in the IPA system. The fact that these two measures differentiated among the role types in *different* ways in the later analysis, in spite of their built-in interdependence, adds significance to the empirical differences in the behaviors of the role types.

gression management were Interruption, as a behavioral manifestation, and competitive questions, as an intellectual manifestation. Interruption was the ratio of the number of times the subject successfully interrupted others to his participation score. It was intended to be an index of *aggression in action*. Competitive questions were those questions asked of others which evoked a defensive response from the others. The measure used in this study was the ratio of the number of such events to the person's participation score. It was intended to be an index of *aggression in content*, or intellectual aggression.

The interpersonal behavior measures concerned with the *exchange of sentiments* were agreement and disagreement in content and personal recognition in action. Agreement and disagreement were ratios of the occurrences of these kinds of events to the individual's participation score. They were intended to be indices of the degree to which the person intellectually communicated positive and negative personal evaluations to others. Personal recognition involved those events where the speaker referred to specific others directly by name or as "you" in contrast to impersonal, indirect comments addressed to no one in particular or to the group in general. This index, expressed as a ratio to the person's participation score, was assumed to be related to the degree to which the speaker behaviorally bestowed individual, personal recognition to others, manifestly identifying the "other" in the action situation as a specific person, and thus personalized his exchanges while contributing to the esteem of the personally-addressed others. (In the two groups who had not known each other prior to the experiments, the participants' names were printed on cards placed in front of them during the discussion and while they completed the PMR's. Hence it was possible for the strangers to address each other by name if they wished.)

The received behavior measures corresponded to the produced interpersonal behavior measures, except that *at-*

tempted interruption from others was used rather than *successful* interruptions. All of the received behavior measures were expressed as ratios to the *receiver's* participation score.*

GROUP PROCESS BEHAVIORS PRODUCED

The relationships between the perceived role types and *group process behaviors* produced are shown in Table 3.2.

Table 3.2

ROLE TYPES AND GROUP PROCESS BEHAVIORS PRODUCED

PERCENT HIGH ON PRODUCED BEHAVIORS

ROLE TYPE	NUM-BER	PARTICI-PATION	INTER-ACTION	SOCIAL ACTS	ASK ACTS	TENSION RELEASE
Total	52	48%	48%	48%	38%	52%
Stars	15	80	33	40	47	60
Technical Specialists	10	30	30	30	20	70
Social Specialists	12	33	75	83	50	50
Underchosen	15	40	53	40	33	33

$.05 > P_x > .02$ * $.05 > P_x > .02$ TS vs. U
$.10 > P_x > .05$

$.10 > P_x > .05$ S + SS vs. TS + U
$.20 > P_x > .10$

* P_x = probability derived from Chi Square analysis.

The Stars tended to dominate the group discussions while being relatively low in interaction. They tended to be like the Underchosen participants on social-emotional expressivity, low but not extreme. They were moderately high on joking. Proportionally more of them expressed openness to influence than was the case for the population as a whole. *They were like each of the three other types in some respects, standing out by themselves on participation only.*

It is of interest to notice the kinds of differentiation patterns on Table 3.2, with respect to the differences between

* See footnote in Appendix A for correlations between the individuals' Participation scores and behaviors of others *toward* them.

high and low idea men, between high and low congeniality persons, and between the two kinds of specialists. High participation differentiates the Stars from the three other types. Interaction differentiates the Social Specialists (High) from the Stars and Technical Specialists (Low) $(.02 > P_x > .01)$. Their levels of social-emotional expressivity differentiates the specialists from each other $(.02 > P_x > .01)$. Openness (ask acts) differentiates the types receiving high choices from those receiving low choices on congeniality $(.20 > P_x > .10)$. On tension release, the high congenials were located between the extremes. A list of conditions found to be associated with receiving high ideas and congeniality choices and with specialization reads as follows:

—Perceived quality of ideas was associated with proactive (speech-like) explanation (indicated by low interaction).*

—Congeniality was associated with openness to influence and a *moderate* amount of joking.

—Social specialization was positively associated with social-emotional expressivity while technical specialization was negatively associated with social-emotional expressivity.

The Technical Specialists' pattern was characterized by the extremity of their behavioral tendencies. They were in one of the extreme positions on *all* five of the measures. They were the most likely type to be *withdrawn* both in participation and in interaction. Although they were the type most likely to be jokers (high on tension release), they were the *least* likely to be high in expressivity (social acts). This contrast is especially interesting because tension release acts were operationally included within the social acts

---

* Appendix G contains an intercorrelation matrix which shows the correlations of the individuals' scores on each variable with their scores on each other variable. These correlations may be referred to in order to test some of the results of the role typology analysis and to test hypotheses that do not involve the role types. For example, the correlation between ideas and participation was .53, the correlation between ideas and interaction was − .26.

category. This would indicate that there was a tendency for the low proportion of expressive behaviors which they did generate to be predominantly joking, to the extent that it tended to exceed the proportion of joking behaviors of those who were more expressive. As a result, a second order of specialization is indicated for the Technical Specialists. Their repertoires of expressive behaviors tended to be withheld during the discussions, but what they did express tended to be limited to joking. Finally, they were the least likely type to demonstrate openness to influence by asking questions of the others. *Closed withdrawal, with a tendency to stay in the group by joking, would characterize the way in which the Technical Specialists related themselves to the groups' processes.* Although in many contexts joking might be associated with congeniality, it is relevant to notice that within the over-all pattern of the Technical Specialists' behaviors joking was associated with *low* choices received on congeniality. One inference could be that their joking served to relieve *their own tensions* rather than serving an integrating function for the group. Another interpretation would be that joking was used by them as a legitimate vehicle for expressing aggression or hostility.

Polarity between technical and social specialization was reflected in the opposition of the positions of the Social Specialists compared to the Technical Specialists on interaction, expressivity, and openness to influence (ask acts). The Social Specialists were the type most likely to be high on these three measures. Although they, too, were likely to be relatively limited in their participation, when they did participate it tended to be spontaneously reactive, social-emotionally expressive, and expressive of openness to influence, compared with the other types. On the tension release measure, the distribution of highs and lows among the Social Specialists was proportionally similar to the population as a whole. In their case, as with the Stars, congeniality was associated with a *moderate* mix of joking, in contrast to the strong likelihoods for Technical Specialists to be jokers and for the Underchosen participants to be serious. *The Social Specialists' relationships to the groups' processes may be characterized as socially and emotionally reactive and expressive, open to influence, and with a tendency to be limited in the amount of their participation.*

The Underchosen participants were more likely to be high in participation than were the Specialists, but were still far below the Stars' tendency to dominate in this respect. On interaction, the Underchosen participants were more likely to be high than the idea men, but less likely than the Social Specialists. They were like the Stars on social-emotional expressivity, mixed toward the low side. They tended to be closed to influence, although this was not as strong a tendency as with the Technical Specialists. The Underchosen participants were the most likely to be serious (low or tension release). This measure was the only one of the group process behavior measures on which the Underchosen participants held an extreme position. On all the other measures they were between the other types or like one of the other types. *The Underchosen participants apparently related themselves to the groups by participating and interacting seriously, tending to be relatively indistinguishably mixed on expressivity and openness.*

In summary, the following tendencies were noted in the production of group process behaviors by the role types:

—The Underchosen participants tended to be serious.
—The Social Specialists tended to be socially and emotionally reactive and expressive, to express openness to influence, and to joke moderately.
—The Technical Specialists tended to be closed and withdrawn, and to relate themselves to the groups' processes by joking.
—The Stars tended to be the dominant participants, to explain their ideas at length, to express openness to influence, and to joke moderately.

INTERPERSONAL BEHAVIORS PRODUCED

The relationships between the perceived role types and *interpersonal behaviors produced* are shown in Table 3.3. Eight of the ten extreme positions on the five interpersonal behavior measures were held by the Social Specialists and the Underchosen participants. The Stars and Technical Specialists were close to the population's proportion of highs on most of the measures, but each of them held an extreme position on one measure. The interpersonal behavior measures did not differentiate among the role types as strongly as did the group process behavior measures.

The Stars were even closer to the population proportion than were the Technical Specialists on all of the interpersonal behavior measures other than personalness, being no more than 5% different from them. This would suggest that the Stars and the Technical Specialists were mixed in their production of interpersonal behaviors in about the same proportions as the entire population, except for the differentiating factor of *personalness* (*identifying the other as a unique person*), *which differentiated the Stars from all of the other role types* ($.05 > P_x > .02$).

The Technical Specialists fell within 10% of the population proportion of highs on all of the interpersonal behavior measures, which means that their distributions were displaced by no more than one case in either direction from the proportional expectancy. They were the type most likely to be high on disagreement, although this does not substantially differentiate them from the Stars. The only substantial difference in interpersonal behavior, between the Stars and the Technical Specialists, was on personalness.

The Social Specialists may be described as behaving politely and agreeably, but tending to be impersonal, as were all of the types except the Stars. The Social Specialists were the type most likely to be low on interruption ($.20 > P_x > .10$), competitive questions ($.20 > P_x > .10$),

Table 3.3

ROLE TYPES AND INTERPERSONAL BEHAVIORS PRODUCED

ROLE TYPE	NUMBER	PERCENT HIGH ON PRODUCED BEHAVIORS				
		INTERRUPTION	COMPETITIVE QUESTIONS	PERSONALNESS	DISAGREEMENT	AGREEMENT
Total	52	44%	48%	38%	50%	44%
Stars	15	47	53	60	53	40
Technical Specialists	10	50	50	30	60	50
Social Specialists	12	25	25	33	42	67
Underchosen	15	53	60	27	47	27
		SS vs. others, $.20 > P_x > .10$	SS vs. others, $.20 > P_x > .10$	Stars vs. others, $.05 > P_x > .02$	SS vs. others, $.70 > P_x > .50$	U vs. SS $.05 > P_x > .30$
		U vs. SS $.20 > P_x > .10$	U vs. SS $.10 > P_x > .05$		TS vs. others, $.50 > P_x > .30$	

and disagreement $(.70 > P_x > .50)$, and were the most likely to be high on agreement (compared to Underchosen, $.05 > P_x > .02)$. They were the only type that was more likely to be high on agreement than on disagreement.

The Underchosen participants were the type most likely to behave *aggressively* (high on interruptions: $.20 > P_x > .10$, compared to Social Specialists) and compete intellectually (high on competitive questions: $.10 > P_x > .05$, compared to Social Specialists). They were the *least* likely to be high on agreement $(.05 > P_x > .02$, compared to Social Specialists), and they were more likely to be high on disagreement than they were to be high on agreement. The difference between their proportions high on agreement and disagreement (20%) was greater than the corresponding difference for the Stars (13%) and the Technical Specialists (10%) although in the same direction.

In summary, the following tendencies were noted which tended to differentiate among the interpersonal behaviors of the four role types:

—The Underchosen participants tended to be relatively aggressive, competitive, and critical.
—The Social Specialists tended to behave politely and respectfully.
—The Technical Specialists' interpersonal behaviors were mixed in about the same proportions as in the total population, but tended slightly to be high in disagreement.
—The Stars' interpersonal behaviors were even more like the population proportions, except that they were the only type that tended to be high in personalness.

PATTERNS OF INTERPERSONAL BEHAVIORS EVOKED

A comparison of the role types on received behaviors, shown on Table 3.4, yields some fairly clear differences among the role types. From the point of view of a participant, this kind of analysis might have as its underlying question, "What can I infer from the way people behave toward me as to their perceptions and evaluations of me?" A possible expectation, drawn from cultural prescriptions, might be that politeness and agreement would indicate feelings of liking and respect. The actual behavioral data taken from the four experimental groups do not agree with this expectation. Those who ultimately received the highest evaluations, the Stars, did not receive a polite and respectful pattern of behaviors from others. Those who received *low* evaluations of liking and respect, the Underchosen participants, were likely to have received a polite pattern of behavior from others. Feelings of liking and respect apparently were communicated through willingness to disagree and compete intellectually.

Table 3.4

ROLE TYPES AND BEHAVIORS RECEIVED

PERCENT HIGH ON RECEIVED BEHAVIORS

ROLE TYPE	NUM-BER	INTER-RUPTION ATTEMPTS	COMPETI-TIVE QUES-TIONS	PER-SONAL RECOG-NITION	AGREE-MENT	DISAGREE-MENT
Total	52	48%	37%	46%	50%	52%
Stars	15	47	47	40	53	60
Technical Specialists	10	70	40	80	40	60
Social Specialists	12	42	25	50	42	42
Underchosen	15	40	33	27	60	47

TS vs. others, $.20 > P_x > .10$ $.10 > P_x > .05$ S + TS vs. SS + U $.30 > P_x > .20$

S vs. SS $.30 > P_x > .20$ TS vs. U $.50 > P_x > .30$

The Stars stood out from the other types only on competitive questions received $(.50 > P_x > .30)$, although the effects were slight. They were just as likely to receive disagreement as were the Technical Specialists, but were more likely to receive agreement. They may be described as more likely to have evoked *intellectual* competition and support, but less likely to have evoked *behavioral* aggression and recognition than were the Technical Specialists.

The highest degree of differentiation was evidenced by actions received by the Technical Specialists. They were the most likely type to be high on interruption attempts received $(.20 > P_x > .10)$ and personal recognition received $(.10 > P_x > .05)$, both of which measures referred to the *actions* of others rather than the verbalized *content* of their comments. In the content categories, there was more likelihood that they would be high on disagreement received than on agreement received (they were the type least likely to be high on agreement received), while their receipts of competitive questions were in line with the proportion of highs in the entire population. The perceived high quality of their ideas, in the absence of an accompanying impression of congeniality, was associated with the relatively high receipts of *behavioral* aggression and support, measured by interruption and personal recognition, along with an imbalance of intellectualized negative sentiments in the direction of expressed disagreement.

The Social Specialists received a relatively polite pattern of behaviors. They were likely to be low on interruption received, were the least likely to be asked competitive questions $(.30 > P_x > .20$, compared to the Stars) and were the least likely to receive disagreement. They were just as likely to receive disagreement as they were to receive agreement. They tended to receive more personal recognition than did the Stars or the Underchosen participants.

The Underchosen participants were the only type which was more likely to evoke agreement than they were to evoke disagreement. They were also the type most likely to receive agreement. At first glance this is paradoxical. If they were the most likely type to be high in agreement received, how was it that they did not receive high choices on quality of ideas? In clinical retrospect the writer recalls that in these groups, as well as in other discussion groups, it was not unusual for a person to present ideas which were at such a high level of abstraction and generality as to be unassailable, yet which were not relevant to the solution of the problems facing the group. Such ideas would not only be unapproachably generalized, but would tend to invoke unquestionable and undiscussible sources of external authority, such as references to the morally right thing to do, justice, efficiency, etc. Since such comments could not be debated, and/or were perceived to be task-irrelevant, the alternative reactions would be for the others either to ignore the comments or to dispose of them by agreement. The facts that the Underchosen participants were the most likely type to be *low* on personal recognition received $(.10 > P_x > .05)$ while high in agreement received would confirm the clinical interpretation of the tendency of their ideas.

In summary, the evoked behavior patterns differentiated among the four role types in the following ways:

—The Underchosen participants tended to evoke polite condescension.
—The Social Specialists tended to evoke polite recognition.
—The Technical Specialists tended to evoke behavioral aggression and recognition along with the intellectual aggression.
—The Stars tended to evoke intellectual competition and aggression.

Interpretations of Behavior Patterns

The interpretive descriptions which concluded each of the preceding three subsections yield the following over-all behavioral descriptions of the four role types in relation to each other:

1. The Stars tended to be dominant, proactive, open, and personal, and tended to evoke *intellectual* competition and aggression from others.
2. The Technical Specialists tended to be withdrawn, bland,

closed, joking, and critical, and tended to evoke *behavioral* aggression and recognition and intellectual aggression from others.

3. The Social Specialists tended to be passive, reactive, expressive, open, polite, and respectful, and tended to evoke polite recognition from others.

4. The Underchosen participants tended to be serious, aggressive, competitive, and critical, and tended to evoke polite condescension from others.

The relativity of the above descriptions is an important qualification. The most aggressive of the behaviors observed in these groups would seem mild when compared to other kinds of situations. The most expressive of the observed behaviors would seem bland when compared to the proceedings of some groups. The word "tendency" has been used to express the idea that statistical associations were found which differentiated among the role types. These associations were not in the people who participated in the discussions, but were in the analysis process. The likelihood of finding all of the descriptive properties analytically ascribed to each role type in one specific person would be low.

With these qualifications in mind, it is possible to come to some conclusions about the validity of the role typology and of the concepts of role specialization and role fusion. These conclusions will be based on the nature of the *patterns* associated with each type, rather than the differences in position on each measure. The patterns of the population's proportions of highs on each measure, shown in the top row of each of the tables, are the basis for comparison.

One characteristic of the idea of roles is that the behaviors which are *excluded* from the patterns are just as important in identifying the patterns as are those which are included. One way of looking at the behavior measures used in this study is that, although they by no means covered all kinds of behaviors which could have been counted, they did cover a range of behaviors which may be considered to be required for solving external task problems and for resolving problems in social and interpersonal relations. The resolution of all the problems that appear in group problem-solving situations requires behavioral attention to all of them. Role specialization would be manifested by either an imbalance of attention toward certain kinds of problems, or avoidance of certain kinds of problems, or both. From this point of view, each of the tables which related the role types to the behavior measures represented a distribution of attention by the role types to the various kinds of problems confronting the groups (see Table 3.1 for the theoretical organization of the behavior measures in relation to kinds of problems).

The Stars were expected to manifest a fusion of whatever role behaviors were required of them to be perceived as *both* productive of good ideas and adding to the congeniality and friendliness of the discussions. The importance of these qualities in relation to the perception of leadership was shown in Chapter 2. In the Stars' behaviors there were no indications of tendencies to *avoid* any kinds of performances. They stood out on two attributes only, participation and personalness. In both instances, their high positions may be just as easily ascribed to *avoidances by the others* as to any positive efforts on their part. Their low position on interaction was a result of the lengths of their comments rather than avoidance of exchange (the number of shared intervals [exchange events] was correlated .94 with participation). Whether they dominated the discussion as a result of the active avoidances of others, or because of their own aggressiveness, it is safe to conclude that they were the most *active* type and that their activities were *varied* to a greater extent than were the others'. Activity and variety, and an absence of avoidance, are attributes which may be ascribed to the Stars with confidence. In clinical terms, the Stars seemed to be highly involved, direct, and open in their behaviors.

The behavior patterns of all of the other types indicated tendencies toward avoidance and/or excess along certain

lines. Of all of the role types, the Social Specialists originated the behavior pattern most consistent with the expectations built into their role title. Their pattern indicated that
they may have been trying to avoid hurting people and that
they tended to support people by agreeing to a greater extent
than did the other types. Their relatively high positions on
interaction, expressivity, and openness would indicate sociable behavior modes.

The Technical Specialists, rather than producing behavior patterns which would confirm their title, tended to
avoid the behaviors associated with sociability. It will be
recalled that the perceptions and evaluations of them by
others conformed to this pattern. They were respected for
their ideas but were not particularly attractive socially. They
were more likely to be evaluated as standing out as leaders
than were the Social Specialists and the Underchosen, indicating that their avoidance of sociable behaviors did not dis-
qualify them from respect for leadership. It should be emphasized that there was *no* evidence that they were *anti*-social.
There was little difference between them and the Stars on
aggressive and competitive behaviors, and, in fact, the Underchosen participants were more likely to be aggressive and
competitive than were the Technical Specialists. In addition to avoidance of sociable behaviors (i.e., behaviors which
the Social Specialists tended to produce), the Technical Specialists were differentiated from the others by their high
tendency toward joking. It may have been that they did not
know any way to relate themselves to the others socially other
than by joking, and that this joking was, for them, a socially
legitimate form in which to express aggression.

The Underchosen participants are the type requiring the
most cautious interpretation because their role type was not
defined by positive attributes as were the others. Rather,
they were defined by the fact that others did *not* tend to
choose them. The fact that their participation and interaction were not extremely low would indicate that they gave

others some opportunity to see, hear, and evaluate them, so that it would not be justifiable to assume that they were not noticeable. The fact that they occupied extreme positions on several measures would rule out the idea that they were a mix of persons similar to the other three types, differing only in that they were not as prominent. Their behavior pattern, involving seriousness, aggressiveness, and competitiveness, and evoking patronizing, nonreactive behavior from others, suggests a role involving evaluating others' ideas but not initiating acceptable original ideas. They would be uncommitted in their groups in that their own ideas and competence were not at stake in the discussions. They, like the Social Specialists, could be described as reactive, but the difference would lie in the nature of the reaction, critically aggressive in the case of the Underchosen and expressively supportive in the case of the Social Specialists. It will be recalled that this difference did not increase the likelihood that the Social Specialists would be named as leaders, and actually the Underchosen were slightly more likely to be so evaluated.

Summary

The analysis of the behavioral patterns associated with the role types confirmed that the Stars tended to produce a pattern involving high activity and a broad variety of behaviors. The Social Specialists tended to give more behavioral attention to problems concerning the communication of sentiments and affective support of others, while the Technical Specialists tended to avoid these kinds of behaviors. The behavior pattern of the Underchosen suggested that they were relatively uncommitted to their groups, and that their behavior tended to be at the service of personal needs with low task and group relevance.

The behavioral findings may be restated in terms of ways in which the behavior patterns of the role types represented their handling of aggression and affection and their emotional relationship to the groups' processes. It seemed clear that the behavior patterns of the specialists represented avoidances; avoidance of aggression by the Social Specialists, and avoidance of interpersonal expressivity by the Technical Specialists. These patterns indicated differences in kinds of commitment to the group situation. The Social Specialists manifested commitment to the group as a group, while the Technical Specialists demonstrated commitment to the task (ideas) dimensions of the groups' processes. The impressive intellectual "armor" of the Technical Specialists may have tended to prevent the others from directly assaulting them intellectually and from directly "reaching out" to include them. Instead, the Technical Specialists tended to receive *behavioral* aggression and recognition. Hence, the Technical Specialists were involved in the exchange of aggression, but there is some evidence that they tended to prevent or deflect direct intellectual challenges.

The Social Specialists, on the other hand, could have defended themselves against aggression by avoiding aggressive behavior themselves. They behaved like "nice guys" and were treated like "nice guys." It seems likely that they maintained their social commitment to their groups by avoiding strong intellectual commitments to ideas that might prove to be disruptive or place themselves on one or the other side of an aggressive debate.

The Underchosen participants, although active in the production of aggressive behaviors, were not engaged with by the others; they tended to evoke condescension rather than aggression from the others. Their behaviors were seen as being not particularly useful to the group; they received few choices on the PMR questionnaire. This might imply that they brought relatively high levels of anxiety to the situations and had not been able to deal with the anxiety in ways which might engage them with either the social or task requisites of the group problem-solving processes.

In terms of contemporary clinical theory, Rogers' concept

of congruence is suggested by the tendencies indicated in the Stars' behavior patterns (Rogers, 1961, pp. 282–283). Their external behaviors tended to express openly their internal feelings, and they communicated honest involvement. They let the others know where they stood, manifesting neither strong avoidances nor excesses in their behaviors. They actively engaged themselves with the others, allowing the others to engage them and their ideas directly. Their particular mode of aggressiveness did not prevent others from being directly aggressive toward them. The implications are that they were not particularly anxious in the group situations, or that they could manage their anxieties through task and socially relevant behaviors.

These interpretations and speculations impute certain motivations to the role types, especially with respect to their handling of aggression and affection. The next step in this analysis is to look at the internal conditions of the role types as assessed by certain measures of motivation and to find out the nature of the consistency between internal conditions and behavior patterns. The internal predispositions for role-taking are the subject of the next chapter.

CHAPTER 4

Predispositions for Role-Taking

THE PREVIOUS CHAPTER analyzed the relationships among three kinds of variables: (1) the ways that individuals behaved toward others, (2) the ways that others behaved toward them, and (3) the ways that others perceived and evaluated their behaviors as indicated by the role typology. It was assumed, prior to the analysis, that the behavior patterns produced by the individuals systematically evoked behavior patterns from the others, and that the role perceptions were a result of the produced behavior patterns. The findings tended to confirm these assumptions, and the interpretations of the findings attempted to explain the specific interpersonal and group dynamic processes involved, as well as their developmental implications.

The role typology originally represented patterns of perceptions and evaluations. It was predicted that the role typology would also represent behavior patterns. This prediction was confirmed in terms of identifiable tendencies. This present chapter will proceed on the assumption that the role types represented perceptions, evaluations, *and* behavior patterns. These three kinds of variables investigated in Chapter 3 will be collapsed conceptually into a single variable, role performance. The analysis will proceed in the direction of exploring the determinants of the role performances.

For the purposes of this study, behavior in the experimental situations was conceived to be influenced by two sets of forces. One set consisted of the external demands of the situation. The other set of influences was the internal motivational conditions which predisposed the individuals to take on particular roles in response to the external demands. Each person was assumed to have certain concerns, including current life goals and situationally evoked motives, which would interact with the external demands of the situation to determine his role performances.

The patterns of concerns indicated by the individuals as they completed two different paper-and-pencil instruments, the Thematic Apperception Test (Test of Imagination) and the Individual Preference Study, constituted their measured predispositions for role-taking. Technical details about these motivation measurement instruments, including their theoretical backgrounds and empirical correlates, are provided in Appendix E; the tests appear in Appendix C. A minimal explanation of the theoretical relationships among the several separate measurements will provide the background for the analysis and interpretations in the following pages.

MOTIVATION MEASURES

The motivation measures used in this analysis relate to three kinds of concerns, needs, or motives, at two levels of consciousness. The theoretical organization of the motivation measures is shown in Table 4.1. The separate motivation measures refer to internal states of the individuals. Combinations or patterns of these measures made up their predispositions for role-taking, as they were operationally constructed.

The Belonging Preference, Status Preference, and Job-Intrinsic Preference measures were three of the five scores derived from Zaleznik's Individual (or Executive) Preference Study questionnaire. The other two measures available from this questionnaire, Self-Actualization Preference and Economic Preference, were not used in the study. They

Table 4.1

MOTIVATION MEASURES RELATED TO EACH CONCERN
AND LEVEL

CONCERNS:	CONCERNS WITH PERSONS		CONCERNS WITH TASK AND SELF-ESTEEM
	AFFECTION	OTHERS' ESTEEM	
LEVELS:			
Conscious, Deliberate, Planned, Related to Current Life Goals.	Belonging Preference	Status Preference	Job-Intrinsic Preference
Preconscious or Unconscious, Situational, Spontaneous, Related to Persistent Needs.	need Affiliation	need Achievement ⟷	need Achievement

were considered to be concerns which were less relevant to experiences available in the experimental group situation than were the other three. The scoring method distributed a constant number of points among the five categories for each person.* The degree to which the individuals preferred or rejected one or more categories was reflected in their relative scores on the remaining categories. Thus, although the Self-Actualization and Economic Preference categories were not used directly in this study, they indirectly influenced the scores on the measures which were used.

Need Affiliation and need Achievement scores were derived from a standardized content analysis method applied to the Thematic Apperception Test by a trained scorer (McClelland et al., 1953). These scores measured the amounts and kinds of affiliation and achievement content found in imaginative stories written by the participants around themes

* See Appendix E for a theoretical interpretation of the Preference Study and a scheme for adjusting scores to reflect relative preferences and rejections. These adjustments were made in order to be able to compare scores among different individuals.

suggested to them by a series of ambiguous pictures. The high or low classification to which each participant was assigned related his score to the others in his group, whose stories were written under the same external conditions.*

The scoring tendencies of the role types on the various measures of motivation are shown on Table 4.2.

Table 4.2

ROLE TYPES AND MOTIVATION MEASURES

PERCENT HIGH ON MOTIVATION MEASURES

ROLE TYPE	NUM-BER	NEED ACHIEVE-MENT	NEED AFFILIA-TION	BELONG-ING PREFER-ENCE	STATUS PREFER-ENCE	JOB-IN-TRINSIC PREFER-ENCE
Total	52	48%	44%	58%	52%	50%
Stars	15	60	47	73	47	33
Technical Specialists	10	60	30	50	50	60
Social Specialists	12	33	42	67	58	67
Underchosen	15	40	53	40	53	47

S + TS vs. SS + U
.20 > P_x > .10

S + SS vs. TS + U
.10 > P_x > .05

TS + SS vs.
S + U
.10 > P_x > .05

TS vs. U
.30 > P_x > .20

.70 > P_x > .50

On Table 4.2 certain motivation patterns show up which seem to be associated with the underlying dimensions of the role classification. *The Stars and Technical Specialists (the "idea men") tended to be high on need Achievement (.20 > P_x > .10). The persons who received high choices on congeniality (the Stars and the Social Specialists) tended to be high on Belonging Preference (.10 > P_x > .05). The specialists, both Technical and Social, tended to be high on Job-Intrinsic Preference (.10 > P_x > .05) and tended slightly to be low on need Affiliation (.50 > P_x > .30).* There was

* A discussion of the methods for scoring nAch and nAff and some of the findings reported by researchers using these measures appears in Appendix E.

little indication of differentiation on Status Preference, although there was a slight tendency for the Social Specialists to be high on this measure.

The first two of these findings lend additional validity to the original expectations behind the construction of the role typology. The idea men contributed most toward the group's task, an effect that would seem to follow from high motivation to achieve. The congenial members contributed toward the group's warmth and friendliness, an effect which would follow from high motivation toward belonging to a group. The association between role specialization, technical *or* social, and Job-Intrinsic Preference does not fit neatly into any simple prior expectations. The facts that the Stars tended to be the *lowest* and the Social Specialists tended to be the *highest* on this measure further confuse matters. The finding does make sense if it is assumed that Job-Intrinsic Preference measures a tendency toward a relatively *narrow, specialized, and rigid conception of work.* Slater found that his well-liked (social) specialists were the *most* specialized role and that they tended to score high on the F-scale, a purported measure of *personal rigidity* (Slater, 1955, p. 511). The relatively low scores of the Technical Specialists on need Affiliation seem consistent with their role performance. The fact that the Underchosen participants tended to be the highest on need Affiliation does not agree in any commonsense way with their performances, which tended to be nonsocial or possibly a bit antisocial. This finding becomes especially interesting when combined with the fact that the Underchosen participants tended to reject belonging rewards on the preference study.

The foregoing analysis of motivation measures taken one at a time confirms some relatively obvious expectations about the relationships between motivation and behavior. The findings indicate that in some, if not most, respects the participants' performances were directed toward satisfying their personal needs. However, the findings also indicate that there were some effects which did not fit obvious explanations. The Job-Intrinsic Preference and need Affiliation measures did not follow an obvious pattern. The results on the motivation measures suggest that they might be combined, rather than dealt with singly, to yield more comprehensive descriptions of individuals' concerns in the experimental situations. Orientations toward task and orientations toward persons represent one way in which such combinations might be made, and move closer conceptually to the notion of predispositions for role-taking.

The findings may be reorganized by referring to the theoretical meanings of the measures shown on Table 4.1. The measures concerned with affection may be used to construct categories reflecting orientations toward persons. The measures concerned with task and self-esteem may be similarly combined to yield orientations toward task. Table 4.3 shows how the classes of orientations were constructed. Since Status Preference was not found to discriminate among the role types (see Table 4.2), it was not included in the construction of the classes of orientations.

An important characteristic of the orientation classes is

Table 4.3

CONSTRUCTION OF ORIENTATION CLASSES
FROM MOTIVATION MEASURES

ORIENTATIONS TOWARD TASK			ORIENTATIONS TOWARD PERSONS		
SCORE ON NACH	SCORE ON J–I PREF.	ORIENTATION CLASS	SCORE ON NAFF	SCORE ON BELONGING PREFERENCE	ORIENTATION CLASS*
High	High	Task-Achievement	High	High	Unconflicted
High	Low	Diffuse Achievement	High	Low	Conflicted
Low	High	Task Oriented	Low	High	Socialized
Low	Low	Disinterested	Low	Low	Disinterested

* The descriptive names given to the classes of Orientations Toward Persons have deliberate theoretical meanings which are explained later in the text.

that they each combine measures of two levels of motivation, conscious or manifest, and unconscious or latent. Need Achievement and need Affiliation are assumed to measure latent motivations. Job-Intrinsic and Belonging Preferences are assumed to measure conscious concerns. These assumptions are based upon the design of the measurement instruments and the scoring procedures (Appendix E).

Orientations Toward Task

The categories of task orientation theoretically represent different personal resolutions of a potential means-ends dichotomy and represent different ways of relating oneself to work and to time. Under the content analysis system from which the need Achievement scores were derived, the achievement and success imagery was not differentiated as to means. Competition against external standards of performance and the overcoming of obstacles were the main kinds of themes identified as containing achievement imagery. Recognition by others and the nature of the accomplishment were not differentiated in the scoring, although either element could have been developed in the imaginative stories written by the participants.

The items going into the Job-Intrinsic Preference score related to doing a job well, or being challenged by a new assignment, where references to recognition by others and interaction with others were excluded from the statements.* The items indicated experiences wherein the enjoyment was a purely personal matter, and the referent was task accomplishment, or the anticipated involvement in or completion of a unit of work during *relatively short periods of time.* Job-Intrinsic Preference may be interpreted as objectifying the discrete unit of work as a desirable and immediate end in itself.

* In Appendix E the Preference Study is broken down to show all of the statements used to indicate each one of the five preferences. On that listing the items used to indicate Job-Intrinsic, Status, and Belonging experiences may be inspected.

Table 4.4. shows the relationships between orientation toward task classes and the role types. This table was constructed in a different manner from earlier tables involving the role typology. Here the percentage figures add to 100% when read horizontally by rows. The four orientation classes contained 27%, 21%, 23%, and 29% of the total cases. The tendency of a role type to be associated with or away from an orientation class is indicated by differences between the percentage distribution of the role type among the four orientation classes and the percentage distribution of the total 52 cases among the orientation classes. For example, about twice as many Stars were diffuse achievement oriented as would be expected by chance; 40% of them were in this class compared with only 21% of the entire 52 people.

Table 4.4

ORIENTATIONS TOWARD TASK: PERCENT OF CASES IN
EACH ORIENTATION CATEGORY, BY ROLE TYPE

ORIENTATION TOWARD TASK

		TASK-ACHIEVE-MENT-ORIENTED	DIFFUSE-ACHIEVE-MENT-ORIENTED	TASK-ORIENTED	DIS-INTER-ESTED	
NACH CLASS		High	High	Low	Low	
J–I PREF. CLASS		High	Low	High	Low	
	Total cases					
Number	52	14	11	12	15	
Percent		27%	21%	23%	29%	100%
Stars	15	20	40	13	27	100%
Technical Specialists	10	40	20	20	20	100%
Social Specialists	12	17	17	50	17	101%
Underchosen	15	33	7	13	47	100%

Reading Table 4.4 one row at a time yields the following findings:

1. Stars tended to be diffuse-achievement-oriented
   ($.05 > P_x > .02$) and *not* to be task-oriented
   ($.30 > P_x > .20$).
2. Technical Specialists tended to be task-achievement-oriented ($P_x = .30$).
3. Social Specialists tended to be task-oriented
   ($.05 > P_x > .02$).
4. Underchosen participants tended to be disinterested
   ($.10 > P_x > .05$) and tended *not* to be diffuse-achievement-oriented ($P_x = .10$).

The modal orientation was different for each of the role types. Three interesting effects stand out. First, although both the Stars and the Technical Specialists tended to be high on need Achievement, the Technical Specialists tended to indicate a higher concern with work as an end in itself, as reflected by their Job-Intrinsic Preference scores. Stating this inversely, *the Stars tended to give evidence that they did not identify achievement with objectified and immediate task accomplishment.* They were more likely to "generalize" their measures of achievement; finite "work" was not an end in itself, as it would seem to be to a Technical Specialist.

The second effect is indicated by the facts that although both the Technical Specialists and the Social Specialists tended to be oriented toward immediate and discrete tasks, as measured by their relatively high scores on Job-Intrinsic Preference, the Technical Specialists also tended to be high on need Achievement, while the Social Specialists tended to be low. This, when added to the finding that there was a slight tendency for the Social Specialists to be high on Status Preference (Table 4.2), would suggest that *the task-orientation of the Social Specialists was more closely identified with recognition by others than with pure achievement for the sake of self-esteem.* The task-achievement orientation of the Technical Specialists tended to identify work with self-esteem, rather than with esteem from others.

This impression may be checked by inspecting the need

Achievement and Status Preference scores of those participants who scored *high* on Job-Intrinsic Preference. These results are shown in Table 4.5. Of the six Technical Spe-

Table 4.5

COMBINATIONS OF TASK-ORIENTED CASES WITH ACHIEVEMENT
AND STATUS ORIENTATIONS, BY ROLE TYPE

(Number of Cases in Each Cross-Classification)

	TASK-ACHIEVEMENT-ORIENTED		TASK-ORIENTED		
J–I PREFERENCE CLASS	High	High	High	High	
NACH CLASS	High	High	Low	Low	
STATUS PREFERENCE CLASS	High	Low	High	Low	Total
Stars	2	1	0	2	5
Technical Specialists	2	2	1	1	6
Social Specialists	1	1	4	2	8
Underchosen	4	1	0	2	7
Total	9	5	5	7	26

cialists who were high on Job-Intrinsic Preference, four were also high on need Achievement. The same effect is found with the Underchosen participants; seven of them were high on Job-Intrinsic Preference, and five of these seven were also high on need Achievement. In both cases, there was a tendency for need Achievement and Job-Intrinsic scores to vary together. This may be inferred to represent a tendency for both the Technical Specialists and the Underchosen participants to identify achievement with discrete units of work. To a person in whom this identification was extreme, social processes would seem to be unrelated to or distractive from their concepts of achievement.

Of the eight Social Specialists who were high on Job-Intrinsic Preference, six were *low* on need Achievement. Four of these six were high on Status Preference. This leads to the inference that in an extreme case of social specialization in these groups, work would be valued as a means toward

attaining the esteem of *others,* rather than a contribution toward self-esteem. Table 4.6 compares the specialists who
were high on Job-Intrinsic Preference as to their preferences
for status rewards, highlighting the difference discussed
above.

Table 4.6

TASK-ORIENTATION AND STATUS PREFERENCE
AMONG THE SPECIALISTS

JOB-INTRINSIC PREFERENCE	High	High
STATUS PREFERENCE	High	Low
Technical Specialists	3	3
Social Specialists	5	3

Finally, the fact that 80% (12 out of 15) of the Underchosen participants were either high on *both* nAch and J–I
Preference (5 cases) *or* low on *both* measures (7 cases)
stands out. In only three cases did they differentiate between
task and achievement in their scoring pattern. Consequently, *the extremity of their inferred tendency to identify
immediate objective task accomplishment with more general
achievement distinguishes the Underchosen participants.* In
this respect they were similar to the Technical Specialists,
who also tended to identify achievement with discrete tasks.

From these findings, and the interpretation of their meanings in extreme cases, a clinical description of the role types'
orientations toward task may be ventured. Persons who
embodied the *extremes* of the indicated orientations would
view work in their lives in different ways, and these views
presumably would be reflected in their behaviors. With regard to task activities, the extreme Star would feel that
achievement was a *process* over a *long period of time,* where
attention to discrete units of work was only one of the important aspects. The extreme case of the Technical Specialist would feel that achievement meant getting discrete
tasks done. The extreme case of the Social Specialist would

view work as a means of obtaining the respect and affection of others. The extreme case of the Underchosen participant would agree with the Technical Specialist that achievement meant getting discrete tasks done, but he would be different in that he would tend to feel ambivalent toward achievement. These descriptions will be elaborated upon when orientations toward persons are added to the analysis.

Orientations Toward Persons

When the role types were analyzed with respect to the motivation measures taken one at a time, it was found that the congenial types (Stars and Social Specialists) tended to score high on Belonging Preference and that the Specialists (Technical and Social) displayed a slight tendency to score low on need Affiliation. Table 4.7 presents the data once more. The relatively high position of the Underchosen participants on need Affiliation along with their low position on Belonging Preference was noteworthy when their behavior pattern was recalled. They tended to behave as if they were uncommitted to either the task or the group, featuring a tinge of self-oriented aggressiveness in the behaviors they produced, and a tone of polite condescension in the behaviors they re-

Table 4.7

ROLE TYPES AND MOTIVATION MEASURES
CONCERNED WITH INTERPERSONAL NEEDS

		PERCENT HIGH ON MOTIVATION MEASURES	
ROLE TYPE	NUMBER	NEED AFFILIATION	BELONGING PREFERENCE
Total	52	44%	58%
Stars	15	47	73
Technical Specialists	10	30	50
Social Specialists	12	42	67
Underchosen	15	53	40
		TS vs. U .30 > P_x > .20 TS + SS vs. S + U .50 > P_x > .30	S + SS vs. TS + U .10 > P_x > .05

ceived from others. These actual behavior patterns do not seem to be consistent with their tendency to indicate a relatively high need for affiliation, but do seem to be consistent with their relatively low preference for (or high rejection of) belonging rewards.

There is an accumulation of clinical research in psychology and psychiatry around the theme of unconscious needs for affection coupled with a defensive denial of such needs at the manifest, conscious, behavioral level (e.g., White, 1948, pp. 431–443). This tendency would be represented in the data of this study by a high score on need Affiliation and a low score on Belonging Preference. The combination of need Affiliation and Belonging Preference scores into classes of orientations toward persons is based upon variants of these dynamics; it was assumed that congruence or incongruence between conscious desires and unconscious needs would be as important a variable as would be the magnitudes of the desires taken singly. The classes of orientations toward persons, which were introduced earlier in Table 4.3, are as follows:

NEED AFFILIATION SCORE	BELONGING PREFERENCE SCORE	ORIENTATION CLASS
High	High	Unconflicted
Low	High	Socialized
High	Low	Conflicted
Low	Low	Disinterested

The reason for the use of the title "conflicted" to apply to those scoring high on need Affiliation and low on Belonging Preference was explained above. Persons scoring high on both need Affiliation and Belonging Preference are called unconflicted with the expectation that this pattern, where the manifest concern is congruent with the latent concern, would be associated with less defensive interpersonal behaviors. Those scoring low on both measures could similarly be called unconflicted, but since the relative level of their scores would indicate relatively less concern with affectionate personal relationships they are called disinterested, indicating low concern as well as lack of conflict. Finally, those indicating low latent concern but high manifest concern with affectionate personal relationships are called socialized to indicate a predisposition for social relationships free of strong personal needs for such relationships. Theoretically, the socialized would also be unconflicted. Table 4.8 presents a cross-classification of the role types with the four orientations toward persons. This table is intended to be read in the same manner as Table 4.4, which was explained earlier.

Table 4.8

ORIENTATIONS TOWARD PERSONS: PERCENT OF CASES IN
EACH ORIENTATION CATEGORY, BY ROLE TYPE

		ORIENTATIONS TOWARD PERSONS				
		UNCON-FLICTED	SOCIAL-IZED	CON-FLICTED	DISIN-TERESTED	
nAff class		High	Low	High	Low	
BELONGING PREFERENCE		High	High	Low	Low	
CLASS	Total Cases					
Number	52	12	18	11	11	
Percent		23%	35%	21%	21%	100%
Stars	15	33	40	13	13	99%
Technical Specialists	10	0	50	30	20	100%
Social Specialists	12	33	33	8	25	99%
Underchosen	15	20	20	33	27	100%

Orientations toward persons do not present as clean a differentiation among the role types as did orientations toward task, where each role type tended to stand out on a different orientation. With regard to their orientations toward persons, the Stars tended to be unconflicted and socialized, which is to say that they tended to be high on Belonging

Preference. In their case, the orientation analysis has added nothing to what could be said about them from analyzing their positions on the motivation measures taken separately. On the other hand, the Technical Specialists tended not to be unconflicted ($P_F = .05$ *), tended to be socialized ($P_F = .15$), and indicated a slight tendency toward conflictedness ($P_F = .23$). Although it was previously found that they tended to be low on need Affiliation, the orientation analysis adds to this the fact that all (three) of them who were high on need Affiliation were also low on Belonging Preference. This, coupled with the absence of the expected (two) unconflicted cases, leads to the interesting conclusion that the Technical Specialists tended to contain a mixture of orientations toward persons: wanting but not needing, needing but not wanting, or indicating relative indifference. Their orientations toward persons tended to be incongruent; 80% of them were in orientation classes where wants were out-of-line with needs ($.10 > P_x > .05$).

The Social Specialists, in addition to repeating the finding that perceived congeniality tended to go along with high Belonging Preference, stand out in their tendency not to be conflicted ($P_F = .17$). The Underchosen participants tended away from being socialized ($P_F = .09$) and tended slightly toward being conflicted and disinterested ($P_F = .34$). These findings accompany the facts that they were the type most likely to be high on need Affiliation, and that their behavior patterns indicated their tendency toward having problems working with people. Not to be forgotten is the obvious fact that they were Underchosen; they tended to receive few if any choices of any kind from the other participants.

The findings about the role types' orientations toward persons do not give indications of providing conclusively clear explanations of the various role performances. The assumed, or predicted, relationship between conflicted ori-

* P_F = Fisher's Exact probability.

entations and conflicted performances was not clearly confirmed, but neither was it denied. However, the indications will be used, along with the results of the analysis of orientations toward task, in constructing descriptions of how hypothetical extreme cases of the role types would view their worlds of work and people.

SUMMARY

There were 52 different patterns of motivative concerns brought to the experimental situations by the 52 participants. Since only five of an infinite number of possible measures were used in this study to describe patterns of motivation, it is not surprising that the orientations toward task and orientations toward persons analyses did not yield as clear-cut differentiations among the four types as might be desirable in a study of this kind. The distributions of the orientation types among the four role types can suggest theoretical interpretations which would be consistent with both the perceived role typologies and the behavior patterns found to be associated with the role types. These interpretations have to be qualified by the facts that the participants were scored relative to each other and that there were probably many kinds of motivations which were not measured which actually influenced behaviors and perceptions in the experimental groups.

With these qualifications and limitations clearly understood, clinical-descriptive models of extreme types may be constructed. These descriptions are not intended to represent real people. They will be more like caricatures, where analytical tendencies have been extrapolated to their extremes. They might realistically be expected to describe conditions which could exist within any person from time to time, but which would really vary in form and intensity over time. Anyone will experience his world at certain times as would the extreme Star, or as would the extreme Technical Specialist, Social Specialist, or Underchosen participant.

The Stars tended to be diffuse-achievement-oriented. They did not tend to identify achievement with the objectified form of the task exemplified by the Job-Intrinsic Preference Items. Under these conditions, the person's definition of task is broadened to include the nonobjectifiable elements of group problem-solving such as teaching, learning, influencing, and interacting. This is consistent with the Stars' orientations toward persons. They tended to be socialized and unconflicted toward persons, more likely to prefer belonging experiences (or less likely to reject them) than were other types. They had the lowest proportion of persons in the conflicted and disinterested orientations of all the types, 26%.

The extreme state of these tendencies would view the world of work and people as an ongoing, interesting process. This ambiguous, but real, process would be seen as the medium in which achievement takes place. People and task would be inseparable elements of the process. Thus, getting a discrete unit of work done would not be as important as maintaining the continuity of the process involving work and people. With this orientation, interpersonal communication would be seen as the means of achievement; an otherwise excellent but uncommunicated or uncommunicable idea would be of little value. On the other hand, the communication of affection in social relations would be included as part, but not all, of the process; task-less communication would be accepted as being of value to continuity, but not as a valuable end in itself.

The achievement orientation of the Technical Specialists tended to go along with task objectification, as indicated by their tendency to score high on Job-Intrinsic Preference. They were just as likely to be socialized as they were to be conflicted and disinterested in their orientations toward persons. None of them was unconflicted in his orientation toward persons. Their likelihood of being conflicted was, as with the Underchosen participants, a little higher than the population's proportional expectancy. As was the case with their interpersonal behavior pattern, there is no evidence of antisocial or counterpersonal tendencies in their orientations toward persons, but their behavior pattern of relative withdrawal from the groups would tend to confirm the task-objectification interpretation.

A person experiencing the extreme conditions of the Technical Specialists' tendencies would view individual work as the means to achievement. Excellence of ideas, whether they were socially accepted or not, would be the major value. The communication of ideas would not be as important as excellence of individual achievement. Pressures to communicate would be felt as deterrents to excellence. People would be seen as an entirely separate kind of problem from task achievement; at best leaving you alone, and/or approving of your ideas; at worst interfering with task productivity and creativity.

The Social Specialists tended to be task oriented, which was contrary to what would be expected from the theoretical task-social dichotomization discussed by Bales and Slater (Bales, 1955, and Slater, 1955). Their low need Achievement and slight tendency to prefer status rewarding experiences differentiates their orientation toward task from that of the Technical Specialists. This combination suggests a dynamic of task accomplishment as a means of earning esteem from others, and/or the lack of the identification of task with self-esteem ("pure" achievement) which characterized the Technical Specialists. The Social Specialists' orientations toward persons were similar to the Stars', except that there were fewer conflicted and more disinterested among the Social Specialists. They tended to be high in Belonging Preference, as did the Stars.

The extreme Social Specialist would view people as the most important object in his working world. Being a well-liked and respected member of a warm and friendly group would be his most important goal. In his working world, affection and recognition are rewards for good work; work is important for its social value. People and tasks would be seen as separate things, but related in that in order to be accepted by people one has to work and reward the work of others with affection and esteem. It would be important to him to avoid upsetting and antagonizing other people. This would limit his work efforts to noncontroversial, emotionally supportive performances and issues. To him, many issues in his working life would be seen as requiring choice between human and task values, and he would choose to accept human values at the expense of task excellence.

The identification of achievement with an objectified task was inferred for the Underchosen participants from the finding that they tended to be high on both, or low on both, need Achievement and Job-Intrinsic Preference. Their distribution of cases among the orientations toward persons was the most even of all the types, but they were the only type which was more likely to be conflicted or disinterested than to be unconflicted or socialized. They were the type most likely to be high on need Affiliation and were the type most likely to be low on Belonging Preference. They were the only type which was more likely to be high on need Affiliation than they were to be high on Belonging Preference. Their profile suggests a tendency toward a conflicted orientation toward persons.

A person embodying the extremes of these tendencies would appear to be a disenchanted Technical Specialist. He would see achievement as a result of individual task performance, but would not be sure that he wanted to play the game. He might see Technical Specialists as "eager beavers," would envy them while he resented them, and would try to deflate them or interfere with their success by criticizing. He would have to get involved with people, and would use task logics to express his mixed admiration and dislike for them. He would not commit himself by initiating ideas, but would wait until others committed themselves, then criticize them. He would be drawn strongly to groups, but their behaviors toward him would reinforce his somewhat bitter views toward people. He would react by an over-aggressive insistence upon the importance of task accomplishment, but could not separate his feelings about work from his feelings about people. His latent need for affiliation, coupled with a behavior pattern which trained people to repudiate or ignore him, would result in an overloading of interpersonal emotion onto task efforts.

These descriptions of four kinds of extreme orientations toward the working world, while suggested by the tendencies found among the four role types, look very much like a series of fleeting moods which any person would experience from time to time. The actual research operations by which the data in this study were collected tapped into relatively instantaneous conditions. The behavior patterns themselves were contained within the short time period of forty minutes, which was not a sizable sample out of the life histories of the participants. These operational realities suggest that the "fleeting mood" idea might usefully illuminate the actual findings and the clinical-descriptive interpretations extrapolated from them. This interpretation, as well as the looseness of the typology, would justify extrapolating extreme conditions from rather weak tendency findings because it would account for the variability caused by continual mood fluctuations among the participants. For example, those perceived as Stars most likely were experiencing a wide variety of moods among themselves, and within any one of them over time. The analytical findings would indicate modal tendencies around which their moods would fluctuate.

An evident problem in using the "mood" analogy is that it connotes a pervasive emotional tone to the experiencing process, while one of the major differences among the four extreme orientations described was in the degree and kind of emotional involvement. For this reason, the idea of *modes of experiencing*, rather than moods, would be more appropriate.

The Stars' indicated mode of experiencing could be called a *process orientation*. Interest, involvement, and personal caring become invested into a total, ambiguous process of working and living with people. Interpersonal communication becomes the way that a person experiencing the process-oriented mode would connect himself to the world around him. Process orientation is a *verbal* mode; it would be difficult for a person with underdeveloped verbal skills to experience this orientation.

This kind of experience is in sharp contrast to the *task-oriented* mode suggested by the Technical Specialists' orientations. They were relatively nonverbal (their participation and interaction rates were low) compared to the Stars. The description of their extreme orientation pattern suggested that work in their hands and ideas in their minds would provide their connections with the world around them. Either physically competent activities, such as involved in skilled arts and craftsmanship, and/or intellectual activity, rather than verbal activity, would characterize this mode. Other people would be experienced as audiences or as interferences to these activities.

The *social* mode of experiencing would exude a glow of affection onto the surrounding social situation. Peace, tranquility, interpersonal warmth, understanding, and acceptance would be the desired external conditions to a person experiencing this mode. He would inject affection to subdue any symptoms of disagreement, hostility, or conflict. He would feel upset if there were trouble out there which could not be controlled by his giving affectionate support. The feeling of disturbance would overpower his consideration of the logical aspects of the disturbing issues. He would rather not work than hurt people. He would rather see the group engaging in purely social, integrating activities than in work of a socially disruptive nature. He would attempt to steer work efforts away from potentially controversial issues.

The *uncommitted* mode of experiencing, suggested by the

extremes of the Underchosen participants' orientation, would feature heightened awareness of self. External events would be interpreted in terms of their possible interpersonal meanings. Task work by others would be felt as bids, on the part of the others, for interpersonal dominance and group leadership. Support received from others would be overinterpreted as bids for affectionate pairing. Criticisms from others would be felt as punishment. While the *social* mode would feature sensitivity to external, social disturbances, the uncommitted mode would be sensitive to interpersonal dominance, affection, and hostility, as these effects impinged upon the self.

These various modes of experiencing represent conditions which could have occurred within *all* of the participants from time to time. They represent a synthesis of the internal motivational tendencies of the four role types which would be consistent with their behavioral tendencies and the perceptions and evaluations which others had toward them. They suggest that the Stars, for example, while probably experiencing all four modes before, during, and after the experimental situations, tended to fluctuate in their orientations and behaviors around the process-oriented mode. Similarly, the Technical Specialists centered around the task mode, the Social Specialists around the social mode, and the Underchosen participants around the uncommitted mode. This kind of explanation leaves open the possibility, and suggests the probability, that the Underchosen participants might have experienced and behaved according to different modes in different group situations. Similarly, each of the other types of performance was "fixed" only in terms of the research operations applied in this study.

Developmental Implications

This chapter started out to investigate the predispositions for role-taking which were characteristic of the various role types. Because of the limitations of the measurement methods and the lack of absolutely clear differentiations in the findings, the analysis has proceeded through several conceptual levels, moving some distance away from a strict interpretation of the data. The operational levels were (1) motivation measures, (2) orientations toward task and toward persons. From the findings at the operational levels, analysis moved in a clinical direction, using the ideas of (3) emotional conditions, (4) fleeting moods, and, finally, (5) modes of experiencing. This final construct, modes of experiencing, implies the existence of patterned and integrated emotional, cognitive, and motivational elements within the character structures of the exemplified types. When characteristic behavior patterns are added to these descriptions of internal conditions, the resultant is an integrated, consistent picture of role performances, where the external manifestations of the internal conditions, observable interpersonal behavior, are but one part of the individual's current condition in relation to his environments.

Particular modes of experiencing are relevant to more than interpersonal behavior in specific situations. They contain orientations toward time and personal identities which extend considerably beyond the here-and-now confines of particular situations such as the experimental problem-solving groups. They include, for example, general concepts of self in relation to occupation or career and in relation to significant others such as past and current family members. Those relatively limited aspects of the characteristic modes which engage with particular situational demands are what is here called "predispositions for role-taking."

The clinical descriptions of the hypothetical extreme modes of experiencing suggested some characteristics of developmental stages. Process orientation was suggestive of the "generativity" and "integrity" outcomes of the crises which Erikson described as phase-specific to the Adulthood and Mature Age phases of development (Erikson, 1959, p. 120. See Chapter 1 of this present book). The task-oriented mode suggested autonomy, industry, isolation, and self-absorption, outcomes of some of the earlier phases described by Erikson (ibid.). The social mode of experiencing suggested the "intimacy" outcome laden with residues of the earlier inferiority, guilt, shame and doubt, and perhaps even mistrust outcomes. The uncommitted mode of experiencing suggested the mistrust, shame and doubt, guilt, inferiority, isolation, and self-absorption outcomes on Erikson's scheme.

Similar interpretations may be undertaken with reference to White's four growth trends (White, 1952, pp. 332–356). Three of these trends, The Stabilizing of Ego Identity, The Freeing of Personal Relationships, and The Humanizing of Values, seem to have direct relevance to the modes of experiencing which were described earlier in this chapter (see also Chapter 1). The process orientation would represent relatively advanced progress in all three of these directions. Task orientation would represent movement in the fourth direction, The Deepening of Interests, but might indicate slower movement to date in the other three directions. Social orientation would represent movement toward The Humanizing of Values, but at the expense of parallel development along the other direction. The uncommitted mode of experiencing suggested blockages or slow progress along all four directions.

These interpretations, while highly speculative at this stage of the analysis, provide some expectations against which the findings to be presented in the next chapter may be compared. In that chapter, the social and developmental correlates of the four role performance patterns will be presented and interpreted. The analysis will be restricted to the here-and-now attributes of age, salary, and education level, as they represent indicators of relative social status in the group situation, *and* as they represent indices of current developmental phases. The earlier, historical family experiences of the four role types will be analyzed in a later chapter.

CHAPTER 5

Social and Developmental Influences

In order to maintain continuity in the analysis of various combinations of the several variables with which this study is concerned, interpretation has proceeded in a cumulative manner.

At this point, the investigation addresses the kinds of social and developmental influences which were associated with the role performance patterns represented by the role types. The analysis will begin by examining the effects of three factors: age, salary, and education level. These results will then be elaborated upon through the use of indices which combine these three factors with others according to three theories relating external social influences with individuals' internal predispositions.

The age, salary, and education level of a participant in the experimental groups indicated several things about him as an individual. The position of the individual on the three attributes, relative to the positions of the other members of the group in which he participated, was expressed as High or Low. His relative age, salary, and education level indicated several things about him *in relation to the others.* These relational attributes would then be expected to indicate something about the social influences acting upon the person in the group. For example, the effects of relative age as a *social influence* would be reflected in a tendency for younger people to defer to older people in the discussion and for older people to expect this deference. Salary and education level, while not as visible as age, represent socially valued achievements to which status is attributed. These attributes become revealed in manner of dress and speech, as well as in more subtle behavioral cues which express self-confidence. It was quite common for participants in the experimental groups to talk about their personal experiences, and in the course of such comments much was revealed about the individuals' social status attributes. As with age, relative salary and education levels would be expected to determine a deference pattern.

In addition to revealing relative statuses, these attributes also imply differences in developmental experiences. The effects of relative age as an indicator of *developmental history* would be reflected in a tendency for older people to behave in a "more mature" manner because of the greater opportunity they have had, in terms of absolute time, to have experiences and to learn from their experiences. To the degree that salary measures success, higher salaried persons would be expected to be more competent. Persons with more education would be expected to be more knowledgeable than persons with less education. Hence the status indicators could acknowledge real differences in the distribution of resources and abilities in the groups.

These two effects could tend to influence behavior in the same direction; older people would be deferred to because of the cultural prescription of showing respect for age, *and* they would be deferred to if, in fact, their ideas were more appropriate (that is, "more mature") than the ideas of the younger persons. The assumption with which the following analysis starts is that the two kinds of effects, status and experience, will be observed as if they were a single effect. The theoretical difference in these effects will be used in interpreting the actual findings. The intuitively acceptable ideas that chronological age does not necessarily indicate development ("maturity"), that salary does not necessarily measure competence, and that education does not necessarily increase competence, along with the actual findings of the analysis, force attention to the two ways in which relative age, salary, and education level may be interpreted.

THE EFFECTS OF AGE, SALARY, AND EDUCATION

The relationships between the role typology and three indicators of social and developmental influences—age, salary, and education—are shown in Table 5.1.

Table 5.1

ROLE TYPES AND SOCIAL-DEVELOPMENTAL INFLUENCES

ROLE TYPE	NUMBER	PERCENT HIGH ON SOCIAL-DEVELOPMENTAL INDICATORS		
		AGE	SALARY	EDUCATION LEVEL
Total	52	58%	46%	54%
Stars	15	80	80	67
Technical Specialists	10	30	50	70
Social Specialists	12	50	25	42
Underchosen	15	60	27	40

$$.10 > P_x > .05 \qquad .30 > P_x > .20$$
$$.01 > P_x > .001$$

The Stars tended to be the highest on age and salary, and tended to be high in education. This pattern appears to be consistent with the expected effects of both social influence (deference to status) and developmental history (experience and education develop competence). Salary may be interpreted in two ways. In one respect, it is an indicator of success. This interpretation says that the Stars tended to be the most successful in their regular jobs. It is not surprising that they were also successful in the small group experiments. The second interpretation of salary, which would have developmental as well as social implications, would hold that salary was a reward for performance. If the Stars felt relatively more satisfied with their rewards, and hence their career success, then they would be expected also to feel more self-confident than the others, to feel that a condition of fair balance existed between the world's evaluation of their worth and their own estimates of their value, and to have little cause for anxiety about their status or identity.

The Technical Specialists tended to be the youngest, were mixed on salary, and tended to have the most education. Their education and salaries were both disproportionately high for their ages; they were relatively "overpaid" and "overeducated" when compared to the other types along their actual age scales. Here the effects of social influence and developmental history appear to be working in opposition to each other. Their technical competences would be indicated by their education level and their relatively high salaries, compared to their ages. But their relative youth would indicate relative inexperience, compared to the other types.

The Social Specialists were mixed in age, tended to be low in salary, and tended slightly to be low in education compared to the other types. Compared to the Technical Specialists along the age scale, the Social Specialists were "underpaid" and "undereducated." According to the "success" interpretation of salary, they were relatively less successful in their careers than were the Stars and Technical Specialists. This description also applies to the Underchosen participants. There is some possibility, indicated by the results on Table 5.1, that the Underchosen participants were slightly more extreme in their relative lack of success than were the Social Specialists, since they tended to be older, but their salaries did not tend to be much higher.

In the above descriptions, only the Stars tended to be *in line* on all three of the social-developmental indicators. They tended to be high on *all* of them. The other three types tended to be *out of line* on the three indicators, in that their positions were not consistently proportional, and yielded patterns which showed culturally incongruent relationships between age, relative success or reward, and education. The behavior patterns of these other three role types, it will be recalled, featured extremes of excesses and avoidances. Their imputed modes of experiencing featured "either-or" orientations toward tasks and persons. The perceptions of the specialists were constructed from "either-or" evaluations along the task and social dimensions. These combinations of findings suggest that the congruence or incongruence (in- or out-of-lineness) among the social-developmental indicators might be an important determinant of internal motivational conditions and behavior patterns. Uncertainty about one's status and identity would be cause for personal anxiety. Three theories involving *combinations* of social-developmental indicators might be useful for integrating these findings.

SOCIAL STATUS INDICES

The four status indices developed in the Zaleznik, Christensen, and Roethlisberger *Prediction Study* were used in this present study to investigate further the social influences on motivation (Zaleznik et al., 1958, pp. 66–74). These four indices were constructed from six status factors: salary, age, seniority, education, ethnicity, and sex. For this study the indices were constructed in the same manner as described in the *Prediction Study* (ibid.), with the exception that experience was substituted for seniority as a more relevant factor for the two groups whose members had not formerly worked together.

The four indices, and their operational derivations from the six status factors, were as follows:

Social Status   = the sum of a person's scores * on age, seniority or experience, education, ethnicity, and sex.

---

* See Appendix D for a description of the methods used to score individuals on the various status factors.

Total Status	=	Five times the person's salary score plus his Social Status score.
Reward-Investment Index (R–I)	=	Five times the person's salary score *minus* his Social Status score.
Congruity-Ambiguity (C–A)	=	The sum of the differences between each social status factor score and each other social status factor score, disregarding sign. This score was then converted by means of an inverted scale so that a high score would mean that factors tended to be more in line than would a low score.

The individuals in each of the four groups were ranked within their groups on their scores on each of the four indices. The rankings were dichotomized as near to the medians as possible. Individuals above the dichotomization point were classified as high on the index, and persons ranking below the dichotomization point were classified as low on the index. By these operations, a score which was classified as high in one group could have been classified as low in another group. The referent for the high or low classification was the group in which the person participated.

The status factors going into the construction of these indices represent some of the attributes of individuals that are socially evaluated in the wider culture. The particular factors selected were thought to be relevant to behavior in social situations involving work groups, based on the findings of prior field researches (e.g., Zaleznik et al., 1958, pp. 43–45, 48–50, 56–63).

The Social Status index is intended to be a measure of the degree to which certain given attributes (ethnicity and sex), attained attributes (age and seniority or experience), and achieved attributes (education) realize the culture's standards for social evaluation. The assumption is that the more a person realizes these values, the higher the social status

which is ascribed to him in our culture. The persons classified as high in their groups would tend to be evaluated as
higher in social status than those classified as low.

The status factors included in the Social Status index were
not directly relevant to task performance if the logics of
problem-solving are applied to the group situations. Indirectly, individuals' feelings of their own, and others', task
competences could be related in their implicit evaluations of
social status factors. In the Total Status index the factor of
salary has been added, weighted as equal in value to all five
of the social status factors. The assumptions underlying this
operation were that salary reflects the degree to which the
individual has been rewarded by, or through, his organization for relevant performances, and that salary level carries
achieved status connotations in the culture.

The Reward-Investment index intends to measure the condition of balance or imbalance between the individual's job
status reward, measured by his salary level, and his social investments, measured by his social status factors. The Theory
of Distributive Justice holds that when an individual's social
investments exceed his job status rewards, relative to the R–I
condition of the others with whom he works, he will experience a feeling of injustice which will have behavioral consequences. Persons whose R–I balance is favorable relative
to the R–I condition of those with whom they work will feel
favored and/or guilty about the condition, and will reflect
the condition in responsible behavior.

The Congruity-Ambiguity index intends to measure the
degree to which individuals' social status factors were in- or
out-of-line with each other. The theoretical condition of
Social Certitude would obtain when a person was at the same
relative level on all of his social status factors; if he ranked
first, or last, or in the middle on one factor, he would rank
at the same position on all factors. Under this condition he,
and the others in the group, would be relatively certain of
his status. The opposite condition, a condition of ambiguity,

would obtain where a person was out-of-line on his social status factors. He, and the others in his group, would be uncertain of his social status. From this point of view the R–I index may be accepted as another measure of in- or out-of-lineness; in this case the social status factors are reduced to a single measure and compared with salary level. The high and low classes of R–I condition then indicate the direction of the discrepancy. The high R–I's would tend to be relatively higher on salary than on social status, and the low R–I's would tend to be relatively lower on salary than on social status. The theoretically expected behaviors associated with out-of-lineness measured by the R–I and/or C–A indices would be in the direction of bringing the factors into line where possible, compensating for out-of-lineness, or tending to reduce or avoid the anxiety that goes with uncertainty by joking.

ROLE TYPES AND SOCIAL INFLUENCES

In a preliminary analysis of the relationships between the status indices and their component measures, it was found that Social Status and the C–A index tended to vary with age, and that Total Status and the R–I index tended to vary with salary. Table 5.2 shows the associations between the status indices and the role types. The rank orderings of the types on Social Status, C–A index, and age are in virtual agreement. This is also true of Total Status, R–I index, and salary. Education is also shown on this table in order to give full presentation to those status components which turned out to be relevant to role patterns, and which may be considered to be important theoretical indicators of stages of development during an individual's lifetime. The factors of ethnicity and sex are not shown separately because they were not found to be of predictive value in relationship to the status indices or in relationship to the role types.

On Table 5.2 it can be seen that the Stars tended to be high on all of the status indices and factors and were espe-

Table 5.2

ROLE TYPES AND STATUS INDICES

PERCENT HIGH ON SOCIAL DETERMINANTS

ROLE TYPE	NUM-BER	SOCIAL STATUS	TOTAL STATUS	R-I INDEX	C-A INDEX	STATUS FACTORS		
						SALARY	AGE	EDUCATION
Total	52	44%	50%	54%	50%	46%	58%	54%
Stars	15	60	73	93	60	80	80	67
Technical Specialists	10	30	60	50	30	50	30	70
Social Specialists	12	33	17	25	42	25	50	42
Underchosen	15	47	47	40	60	27	60	40

$.3 > P_x > .2$ $.01 > P_x > .001$ $.01 > P_x > .001$ $.30 > P_x > .20$

$.05 > P_x > .02$ $.5 > P_x > .3$ $.10 > P_x > .05$

cially high on salary in relation to their social status, as measured by the R–I index. In addition, they and the Underchosen participants tended to be more in line in their social status factors, as measured by the C–A index, than were the specialists.

The specialists of both kinds tended to be out of line. The Technical Specialists tended to be "too young," or "overeducated," or "overpaid," or all three, from the point of view of distributive justice, and tended to be ambiguous from the point of view of social certitude. The Social Specialists likewise tended to be ambiguous, but in their case this was a resultant of the likelihood that they would be low in salary. They tended to be underrewarded in relation to their social status, which itself tended to be low and relatively ambiguous.

The Underchosen participants were close to the population proportion on Social Status, Total Status, and age, and although they tended to be low on salary in relation to social status, as measured by the R–I index, as well as low on salary itself, their social status factors were just as likely to be in line as were the Stars'.

THEORETICAL INTERPRETATIONS

Since the major focus of this study is on individual behavior rather than group behavior, it will be useful to restate the three social theories of motivation derived from the *Prediction Study* (ibid.) in forms appropriate for the understanding of the ways in which social influences determine internal motivational conditions and behavior. For this purpose the three theories will be relabeled. The Theory of External and Internal Rewards becomes the *Reinforcement of Competence,* the Theory of Distributive Justice becomes *Justification,* and the Theory of Social Certitude becomes *Identity Reinforcement.*

Reinforcement of Competence yields the simplest explanation for what went on in the experimental groups. Persons who had been rewarded for competence by their organizations continued to behave in the same manner in the experimental situations. They were confident of their competence and thus did not have to assert themselves by behaviors irrelevant to group problem-solving. The evidence supporting this explanation is that the rank ordering of the role types on their likelihood of being chosen as standing out as leaders (see Table 2.5, Chapter 2) was identical to their rank ordering on their likelihood of being high in salary (Table 5.2).*

* From the fact of prior social organization for two of the groups, it might be expected that in those groups perceived leadership would correspond to formal leadership on the job, which would be related to salary level. This raises the question of whether or not the association between salary and choices received on leadership for the entire population of 52 cases was a result of the two natural groups only. The correlations between salary and choices received on leadership for the four groups were as follows:

Groups		Number of Cases		Pearsonian r	
All			52		.48
1	natural groups	13		.59	
2		15		.76	
1 + 2			28		.55
3	new groups	11		.51	
4		13		.33	
3 + 4			24		.40

Justification theory adopts a complementary viewpoint with respect to individuals' needs to assert their value. Persons whose salary rewards were high in relation to their social status, compared to the similar index for the persons with whom they were interacting, would feel it necessary to justify their rewards by behaving more responsibly and more competently, and by being more active (ibid., pp. 54–55). This explanation would fit the data (R−I index vs. participation and leadership) on the Stars, Social Specialists, and Underchosen participants, but the Technical specialists were too low in participation and interaction to fit the theoretical odering of the types on the R–I index. Perhaps their avoidance of sociable behaviors on the supposition that they were irrelevant to problem-solving was their mode of justification and their way of carrying feelings of responsibility.

Identity Reinforcement is related to the discussion of the writings of R. W. White and Erik Erikson, cited earlier (see Chapters 1 and 4). The Congruity-Ambiguity index, borrowed from the *Prediction Study* for use here, is a measure of the degree to which the individual has reason to feel certain about his social identity. This index does not measure feelings or sentiments, but does measure the in- or out-oflineness of social attributes around which sentiments of social identity may form. The Stars and Underchosen participants were, according to this theoretical view, more likely to have achieved some degree of social certainty than were the specialists, although the salaries of the Underchosen participants tended to be out-of-line on the low side. The Technical Specialists were the least likely type to be high on the C–A index. The specialists' behavior patterns may be interpreted as their different ways of behaviorally attempting to achieve increased certainty of their identities. The Social Specialists evidenced a clearly identifiable pattern of sociable behaviors,

---

Although the association was stronger for the natural groups, salary and perceived leadership were also positively associated in Groups 3 and 4, where the participants were removed from their regular organizational social structures.

while the Technical Specialists tended to avoid sociable behaviors while behaviorally identifying themselves as task experts. The quantitative differences among C–A index scores do not account for the qualitative differences in role perceptions and behavior patterns. Competence Reinforcement and Justification Theory, in combination with Identity Reinforcement, might help in accounting for the qualitative differences.

The Stars' social attributes were patterned toward certainty and high status. They tended to be high in social status, their salaries tended to be high, and their status factors, including salary, tended to be in line, in comparison with the other role types. Not only would these conditions tend to result in feelings of confidence and competence, but they would also tend to carry with them social obligations. People who are recognized and rewarded for their competences are expected to exercise their competences, and thus justify their social positions (Homans, 1950, pp. 140–141). To the extent that they were successful in their activities in the experimental groups, and felt that others were listening and reacting to them, the social debt along with situational confidence would increase and lead to proaction, limited only by interruption by others or by increasing guilt feelings about dominating the discussions. Joking, allowing others to interrupt, exaggerating a point so as to invite joking and interruption, and asking questions, while providing variety in their behaviors, also provided them with convenient ways out of the proactive dilemma. While these processes went on, identity was being confirmed or enhanced. The reactions of the others reinforced and encouraged a continuation of activities expressing competence. Finally, the justice of the reward condition was kept in line by their relative openness to others along with their high activity rate.

The Technical Specialists, tending to be low in social status but relatively high in salary, and tending to be young and highly educated, were out-of-line in their social attributes. While those attributes on which they were relatively high, salary and education, should carry with them the social obligations of position, their relative youth should call for deference toward older persons. Such conflicts could be resolved by withdrawal into low participation and interaction and by avoidance of sociable behaviors. Such tendencies were observed. Their tendency to be high in joking could reflect a means of resolving the anxieties built up in them by the awkwardness of their position. Their ideas stimulated reactions (they tended to be high in receiving interruption, personal recognition, and disagreement) which could tend to reinforce and call for more of the same behaviors from them. By these processes, their identity as task experts would emerge and would continue to reinforce the processes of justification and confidence in a specialized competence.

The Social Specialists tended to be low in social status and low in salary, but high enough in age to yield low congruence and low rewards in relation to social status, compared to the other types. Salary, age, and education levels were the factors which differentiated their social attributes from those of the Technical Specialists. They were underrewarded, relative to the others, which could have led to their feeling less confident in their task competences. Their relative deprivation of rewards did not lead to manifestations of complaints, as suggested in the development of the Theory of Distributive Justice in the *Prediction Study* (op. cit., p. 54), but may have resulted in their avoiding task responsibility (low participation, low in the aspects of group work involving instrumental activity and criticism), another direction of behavior suggested by the *Prediction Study*. Task activity would not be expected to be rewarding to them as they had little reason to feel competent in this kind of activity, judging by their relative lack of success. Either by avoidance of task activity or by positive emphasis on social activities, or both, they established their identity as congenial persons. Although this identity did not result in high evaluation as leaders, it expressed a legitimate value and role in terms of the wider culture. Their behavior patterns dovetailed with those of the Technical Specialists in that one type provided what the other type avoided. The Technical Specialists were evaluated as performing a more task-relevant role, as reflected in their higher likelihood of being chosen as leaders, but the Social Specialists were evaluated as more attractive for purely social acquaintance.

The Underchosen participants ("Uncommitted") tended to be mixed in social status, low in salary, and low in education. Their social status attributes were as likely to be in line as were those of the Stars, but at a slightly lower level. In age they were mixed in a proportion similar to that of the population. Although their salaries tended to be low, they were more in line with their social status than was the case with the Social Specialists, as indicated by their positions on the R–I index. On the two dimensions of Congruity-Ambiguity and Total Status, their location in relation to the other types is shown on Table 5.3.

Table 5.3

LOCATIONS OF ROLE TYPES ON TOTAL STATUS
AND CONGRUITY-AMBIGUITY

	TOWARD AMBIGUITY	TOWARD CONGRUITY
HIGH TOTAL STATUS	Technical Specialists	Stars
LOW TOTAL STATUS	Social Specialists	Underchosen (Uncommitted)

The inferred dynamics of the Underchosen participants' variety of Competence Reinforcement would picture them as questioning their competence in relation to the others and thus being *unwilling to initiate* task activity. Their R–I condition would put them in the position of slight relative deprivation of rewards and hence less obligated or responsible. Their mode of seeking identity was one of reactive aggression, competitiveness, and criticism, compared with the others' behavior patterns. They engaged in more activity (participation) than did the specialists, and though they were relatively mixed in the expressive *content* of their comments, their position on interruption, competitive questions, and their disagreement-agreement imbalance indicated that they tended to express aggression indirectly, in their *behaviors*. Of all the types, they achieved the least social identity (they tended to be underchosen on all perceptions and evaluations). The nonreactive pattern of behaviors which they received would confirm their relative lack of social identity They behaviorally called attention to themselves, but they were the type least likely to receive personal recognition from the others. Social identity was denied them in that they did not receive external validation of any special competences.

In the cases of the Stars and the Specialists, certain patterns of reward, in terms of validations of social identity, may be seen in the data. According to these interpretive theories, the Underchosen participants had the least likelihood of obtaining satisfaction from the experimental group discussions. In order to illuminate further the interpretations made up to this point, some data on the internal consequences of the group experiences for the participants will be introduced. The following chapter will examine and interpret the extent to which the four role types expressed satisfaction with the groups' decisions and processes.

CHAPTER 6

Satisfaction

THE PREVIOUS CHAPTER closed with the suggestion that role perceptions were an indicator of the degree and kind of social identity achieved by the participants in the experimental group situations. It would be expected that if this were true, then the satisfactions indicated by the role types should be consistent with the identity rewards they received. The data analyzed so far in this book have been limited to here-and-now attributes of the individuals in the experimental group situations; their perceptions of each other, their behaviors toward each other, concerns and motives active within them at the time, and their social status and developmental attributes at the time. The data to be introduced in this chapter will be drawn from the same temporal and spatial field; it was their expression of the degrees of satisfaction they derived from the experimental group situations. To the degree that the here-and-now measurements were adequate for the explanation of the behaviors and the internal conditions of the participants, the satisfaction data should be consistent with the data presented so far.

In particular, it would be expected that the satisfactions expressed by the four role types should bear some discernible relationship to the *rewards* which the four role types received in the here-and-now situation. These situational rewards could have been of two operationally separable kinds: (1) gratifications derived from the behavioral processes, and (2) gratifications derived from having left impressions on the others. The behavioral rewards would include the "profits" received by the individuals during the process of social exchange (Homans, 1961, pp. 30–82). The "commodities" exchanged would include esteem, help, and affection. The analysis of behaviors produced and received, in Chapter 3, dealt with this kind of exchange. The analysis of the perceptions and evaluations of others, in Chapter 2, dealt with the final balance of the behavioral transactions insofar as the final impressions measured the external outcomes, for the individuals, of the exchange process.

SOURCES OF DATA

Each participant in the four experimental groups was asked, on the Post Meeting Reaction questionnaire, to indicate his satisfaction with the *"decision* or conclusion reached" and with "the way this group *operated"* on an eight-point scale running from 1, Very Dissatisfied, to 8, Very Satisfied. The format and context within which these questions appeared are reproduced below and the entire PMR questionnaire will be found in Appendix C.

Specimen of PMR Questionnaire Page Containing
Satisfaction Questions

A. In many groups there are wide differences in how satisfied each member is with the *group decision* or conclusions. Some members will like it, some will not.

Please indicate how satisfied *you* are with the *decision* or conclusion reached in this meeting by circling the appropriate number on the following scale.

Very							*Very*
Dissatisfied							*Satisfied*
1	2	3	4	5	6	7	8

B. In many groups there are wide differences in how satisfied each member is with the way the group *operates*.

Please indicate how satisfied *you* were with the way this group operated by circling the appropriate number on the following scale.

Very   *Very*
Dissatisfied   *Satisfied*
1   2   3   4   5   6   7   8

SATISFACTION WITH THE GROUPS' DECISIONS

The relative degrees of satisfaction with their groups' decisions expressed by the four role types are shown on Table 6.1.

Table 6.1

ROLE TYPES AND SATISFACTION WITH GROUP DECISION

ROLE TYPE	NUMBER OF CASES	PERCENT HIGH ON SATISFACTION WITH DECISION
Total	52	62%
Stars	15	87
Technical Specialists	10	50
Social Specialists	12	58
Underchosen	15	47

Stars vs. others
$.02 > P_x > .01$

The fact that stands out most strongly on Table 6.1 is that 87% of the Stars (13 out of 15 cases) were high on satisfaction with the decision $(.02 > P_x > .01)$. It is tempting to explain this finding with the idea that because the Stars were high participants, and would tend to identify themselves with the group product, they attempted to protect their self-esteem by calling the decision good. The correlation (Pearsonian r) between participation and satisfaction with decision was −.04, and was −.06 between participation and satisfaction with operations, indicating that participation and satisfaction were almost completely independent of each other.* It was not the Stars' dominance of the discussions which led to their satisfaction with the decision. Their mix of satisfaction with group operations was close to the population's proportion, indicating that their high satisfaction with the deci-

* See intercorrelation matrix, Appendix G.

sion was not just a result of a halo of over-all good feelings, although the two kinds of satisfaction correlated .44 with each other.

A clue to the findings on satisfaction with the decision may lie in the nature of the groups' decisions or conclusions in relation to the inferred modes of experiencing discussed in Chapter 4. The questions around which the groups' discussions took place (see Appendix A) had to do with evaluating the behavior and decision of a person in the filmed case and suggesting action alternatives for him. Compared with engineering problems, investment alternative problems, or other types of more easily objectifiable business problems, the human relations problem presented in the case lacked easily communicable external standards for evaluation, such as costs, rates of return on investment, or any other traditionally recognized quantitative decision criterion. Because of this lack, it is not unusual for some business people and students to think of human relations problems as "nonsubstantive." The problems cannot be easily objectified according to the usual kinds of task logics. In the discussion of internal motivational conditions, it was concluded that of all the four types, the Stars showed the least evidence of concern with task objectification. The Social Specialists were the only other type who were assumed to objectify some *relationship* between tasks and persons, although it was inferred to be a dichotomous "either-or" relationship. For the Technical Specialists and the Underchosen participants it was inferred that tasks and persons were unrelated to each other in their modes of experiencing. These last two types were the least likely to be satisfied with the groups' decisions, while the Social Specialists were more likely to be satisfied with the decisions, though considerably less likely than were the Stars. The conclusion is that those persons who felt most comfortable with ideas which were not easily objectifiable in the usual sense tended to be the most satisfied with the groups' decisions, while those persons who could tolerate only concrete, easily objectifiable forms of decisions or conclusions tended to be the least satisfied with the groups' decisions. It was implied in Chapter 4 that the Stars gave the least evidence of task-objectification while the Technical Specialists and Underchosen participants gave the most evidence of task-objectification and tendencies to separate persons from task accomplishment.

An alternative, but not inconsistent, interpretation of the findings on satisfaction with decision would relate to the identity reinforcement process discussed in Chapter 5. A frequent explanation of the higher satisfaction of *some kinds of people* with participative problem-solving than with hierarchical, or authoritarian, problem-solving is that identification *with* the group product, attained through participation (or ego involvement), enables a person to feel more satisfied with, and committed to, the product than if it were imposed upon him by external authority.* In this study there was no operational measure of identification *with* the decision, but there were measures of social identification attained *through* task and social activities. These were the quantities and patterns of choices which were used to identify the role types. Chapter 5 concluded that the Underchosen participants attained the least social identity, the Stars attained the most social identity, and the Specialists were socially identified in specialized ways consistent with the titles conferred upon them in this study. Those who attained the greatest degree of social identity were the most satisfied with the decision, while those who attained the least social identity were the least satisfied with the decision. In the absence of quantitative measures of the differences between the degrees of social identity attained by the Technical and Social Specialists, the

---

* Vroom, 1960, p. 60:

". . . participation in decision-making has positive effects on attitudes and motivation . . . Authoritarians and persons with weak independence needs are apparently unaffected by opportunity to participate in making decisions. On the other hand, equalitarians and those who have strong independence needs develop more positive attitudes toward their job and greater motivation for effective performance through participation."

higher likelihood of satisfaction for the Social Specialists may be related to the higher value of social identity to them, if the interpretation of their mode of experiencing is valid.

SATISFACTION WITH THE GROUPS' PROCESSES

The relative degrees of satisfaction with their groups' operations expressed by the four role types are shown on Table 6.2.

Table 6.2

ROLE TYPES AND SATISFACTION WITH GROUP OPERATIONS

ROLE TYPE	NUMBER OF CASES	PERCENT HIGH ON SATISFACTION WITH OPERATION
Total	52	50%
Stars	15	47
Technical Specialists	10	40
Social Specialists	12	50
Underchosen	15	60

U vs. TS
$.50 > P_x > .30$

Conceiving of the groups' processes, or "the way (the) group operated," as capable of gratifying group participants, the findings on satisfaction with group process indicate that gratifications other than social identity must have been involved. The Underchosen participants, who were the least rewarded with a social identity, in terms of both choices received and behaviors received, were the type most likely to be high in satisfaction with their groups' operations, although the differentiation among types was relatively weak. When it is recalled that the Underchosen tended to be low in salary compared with the others and that their behaviors tended to be more aggressive, competitive, and critical than the others, one aspect of the Hawthorne effect * comes to

---

* The term "Hawthorne effect" has been used by various writers to describe the finding reported in *Management and the Worker* by Roethlisberger and Dickson (1939) that the experiments inadvertently increased the satisfac-

mind. If their low salary level indicates that their jobs provided them with less autonomy than the others, and that the experimental group was, to them, an opportunity for interaction which they lacked in their jobs, then the act of participating would in itself be rewarding. This explanation would hypothesize something like a need for expression, interaction, or interpersonal communication, which, when not satisfied in the normal everyday life of the person, would be an active determinant of behavior in social situations which legitimized personal expressivity. Clinical examples of this effect would include the housewife, deprived of interaction with adults during the day, who can talk for hours about nothing (from the husband's point of view) on the telephone, and who would expect lively conversation from her husband upon his return home from work. Similar effects are found in New England town meetings as well as committee meetings in general, where persons who are deprived of normal interaction opportunities are often perceived as talking for the sake of hearing themselves. Their usual environmental returns are so scant, relative to those available to others, that they will seek to make up the deficit in situations which provide the opportunity to do so.

These examples, though extreme, are consistent with the finding that the R–I index, salary, and education were all inversely correlated with expressed satisfaction with group operations.* These three indices are such that the higher their value, the more likely it is that the person's job involved high interaction opportunities. The role types which tended to consist of persons of higher job status, the Stars and Technical Specialists, tended to be lower in satisfaction with the groups' operations than did the Social Specialists and the Underchosen participants.

---

tion and productivity of the girls in the relay assembly room. This increase in morale and productivity was attributed to the attention given to the girls by the researchers, and the opportunity given them to be heard and to exercise some control over their own working conditions.

* See Intercorrelation Matrix, Appendix G.

Although the Technical Specialists were the type least likely to be high in satisfaction with operations, their proportion of highs was displaced by only one case (out of ten) from the population's proportion. Their inferred tendency to objectify task, and an accompanying impatience with ambiguous situations, would account for the slight tendency for them to be dissatisfied with operations. The lack of clear authority and procedural structures in the groups would tend to lead to dissatisfaction in persons who needed such structure.* This effect was reported in the Vroom study on the effects of personality types on the consequences of opportunities to participate (Vroom, 1960). Although the Underchosen participants were inferred to relate themselves to task logics in a manner similar to that of the Technical Specialists, the relatively low job status of the Underchosen participants, and its consequence in the form of an imputed need for expression, would, in their case, be a stronger determinant of their satisfaction than would a need for structure.

The Stars and Social Specialists were as close as they could possibly be to the population's proportion of highs on satisfaction with the groups' operations. From this it may be inferred that the attributes which in other respects differentiated between them, and between them and the other types, made little difference regarding their satisfaction with group operations. For the Stars, who were relatively high status people, it may be inferred that the experience was not unlike other situations which they commonly encountered. Although the Social Specialists were similar to the Underchosen participants in their low job status, they, unlike the Underchosen participants, attained some degree of social identity in the experimental groups. This would suggest that the identity reinforcement process is related to expressive needs. The Underchosen participants, deprived of identity, were expressive in their *actions* (aggression, competition, and criti-

* See Table A.11 in Appendix A for the F-scale results on some of the participants.

cism) , and tended to express more satisfaction with the process than did the others. The Social Specialists, expressive in the *content* of their comments, were not deprived of identity, and showed no identifiable tendency in their satisfaction with the process.

Summary

Although satisfaction with group process showed little quantitative differentiation among the role types, the fact that the Underchosen participants were *not* low, as would be expected if social identity were the main factor involved in this kind of satisfaction, called for an interpretation which would augment the minimum framework provided by the particular internal motivational conditions measured and by social and developmental influences. The interpretation was a hypothesis of expressive needs, which in the case of the Underchosen were presumably activated by their relative deprivation of normal opportunities for expression and by their relative deprivation of social identity.

The interpretation of the expressed satisfactions with the decision confirmed the utility of the idea of modes of experiencing developed in Chapter 4. The Stars' relatively high satisfaction with the decision, or, equally plausible, the relatively low satisfaction of the other types with the decision, was the strongest differentiating tendency found in the satisfaction data.

The findings regarding satisfaction with the groups' decisions were explainable in relation to the here-and-now variables analyzed in earlier chapters of this book. The unexpected results on "satisfaction with operations" called for the invention of a new variable, a hypothetical need for expression, which was bound to imputed personal historical experiences of relative deprivation. In order to conceive of such a need, it was necessary to consider the experiences of the participants *outside* the experimental groups, and in the participants' past histories. The need for this kind of explanatory device emphasizes the necessity for thinking of here-and-now events as parts of individuals' ongoing developmental processes.

This theme of developmental continuity will form the basis for the next chapter in this book, where the findings will be summarized around the idea of developmental trends. Additional data on the early family experiences of the four role types will be brought in to illuminate further the processes of development, and to understand further the relevance of situational role performances to individual development.

CHAPTER 7

Developmental Trends

THE TWO PRECEDING chapters identified two types of internal states of individuals that seem to be associated with role patterns in the experimental situation. The first type of internal state, *orientations toward task and persons,* concerns essentially how persons conceive for themselves the interrelationship between work and persons in a social reality. The second type of internal state is related to how individuals experience positions within the social reality as determined by status and status congruence. These two internal states act as systems of motivation and are related, but the sense in which they interact is not too clear.

In this chapter the focus shifts to an attempt, by way of further explanation of the role types, to examine how an individual's role pattern can be understood in terms of the continuities and trends in his personal development. Whereas previously the discussion was limited to events and experiences in the "here-and-now," the task at this point in the study is to link the past and the present. The theoretical orientation outlined in the introductory chapter indicated the view that the explanation of individual behavior requires a historical orientation.* What the person does today is re-

* One of the major hypotheses in the psychoanalytic theory of personality is the genetic or developmental hypothesis. Freud, Abraham, and more recently Erikson have shown how individual development proceeds according to a timetable whose main dimensions are first the biological changes in the body zones as centers of instinctual excitation and second the life tasks imposed by the culture within a matrix of changing object relationships. The way in which phase-specific developmental problems are dealt

lated to his past and represents continuity in his personal development. In other words, a role pattern adopted by an individual in a work setting may best be understood in the light of his personal history, his characteristic conflicts, and the modes by which he seeks to resolve conflict. In this sense, a role pattern can be viewed as an integral part of the individual's character structure and system of ego defenses.* These aspects of personality are formed early in life and are at the basis of the analysis of personal history.

An individual's style of interpersonal behavior, called a role type in this study, can be relevant to the reality situation with which he is engaged, and it can be related to his characteristic methods of managing anxiety. All behavior probably has both elements in it, but in some cases the behavior may be more nearly directed toward maintaining the system of defenses than it is to dealing with the reality in a need-satisfying way.

In what sense are the role types identified in this study a part of the defensive system of the individual? Are there identifiable early developmental trends which at least suggest the genetic correlates of the role types? Presumably, the more the here-and-now behavior is rooted in the individual's defensive structure, the less free he is to behave flexibly depending on his intentions and the nature of the situation. The more fixed the behavior, based on early life experiences, the more difficult it becomes for the individual to learn, to maintain a path of continuing growth, and to act in ways designed to assure need gratification.†

---

with has prophetic significance for the individual's character formation as well as for his capacity to work and to love. (Freud, 1910, 1952; Abraham, 1927, Chapters XXIII–XXV; Erikson, 1950; Erikson, 1959)

* W. Reich and Anna Freud have illuminated the ways in which behavior can be understood within the framework of the individual's character structure and system of ego defenses. (Reich, 1949, 1961; Freud, A., 1937, 1954)

† Slater offers suggestions on the nature of defensive patterns of Task and Social Specialists. The Social Specialists may need to be liked and will have acquired skills over a lifetime aimed at securing affection from others. "Avoidance of conflict and controversy may be a felt necessity for this type

The data to be utilized in this chapter come from two sources: (1) the personal history questionnaires completed by each of the participants in the study; (2) the imaginative stories written to a series of ambiguous pictures.* The chapter will be organized into three main parts: (1) a review of the role types; (2) an analysis of role specialization as a developmental trend; (3) an analysis of role-taking as an aspect of the ego defenses.

REVIEW OF ROLE TYPES:
PATTERNS OF BEHAVIOR AND MODES OF INVOLVEMENT

A review of the role types, establishing them as totalities, is necessary prior to the introduction of new data on developmental trends which may explain their origins. The following descriptions of the entities designated as "Stars," "Technical Specialists," "Social Specialists," and "Underchosen" are clinical inferences and are stated from within an internal frame of reference.

The Stars: Involvement with Process

The mode is one of felt *interdependence*:

> People need each other to get work done and to live full lives. The fullness of life is measured by achievements. Communicating with people is the ultimate achievement process. Something new is created through talking and working with people. The ultimate achievement is the creation of new and better resolutions of social and technical problems.
>
> Although there are standards of excellence for individ-

---

of person—hence, his behavior will show nothing that could be a source of disharmony. . . . The Task Specialist, on the other hand, may assume this role only because of an unwillingness or inability to respond to the needs of others. A compulsive concentration on an abstract problem will serve as an intellectual shield against the ambiguity of human feelings." (Slater, 1955, pp. 512–513)

* The analysis of the imaginative stories supplements the personal history data by indicating the existence of particular types of conflict, anxiety, and modes of dealing with the affect aroused under such conditions.

uals' contributions, real resolutions of problems are tested in the communication process. The value of experience and education is not intrinsic to them; it comes about through personal learning from them. External rewards and success are measures of the validity of those learnings.

Satisfaction comes from engagement in the social-technical process in a way that balances progress toward improvement with the disruptions of change. Conflict is intrinsic to change. Satisfaction involves the management of conflict, both interpersonal and intrapersonal, rather than absence or avoidance of conflict on the one hand, or being carried away with either of the conflicting extremes on the other hand.

The external observer sees the behavior of the person experiencing involvement with process as spontaneous, energetic, and varied. His behavior clearly communicates his feelings. He also communicates his confidence in himself; he will unapologetically defend his positions, but he will also change his position in accordance with what he is learning in the process. He acknowledges in his behavior that he is communicating with specific people, rather than thinking out loud about ideas separated from people. His behavior says that the other persons as individuals, as well as sources of ideas, are bound up in the problem-solving process.

Other people are drawn to the person experiencing involvement in process because he maintains behavioral contact with them. Even his open disagreements with them communicate caring rather than indifference or hostility. He lets them know where they stand with him, but expresses openness to learn from them. Although he tends to dominate the group's activities, he can be depended upon as a source of both technical and personal support. Consequently, he is respected for his ideas, seen as an important positive social influence, liked, and seen as an outstanding leader.

His maintenance of contact with others leads them to react to him without fear of his withdrawing. He can accept aggression and criticism without deviating from the task into self-defense. People want to talk to him. He lets them and helps them express themselves by giving them immediate and open feedback while maintaining contact with them and openness to hear from them.

The Technical Specialists: Involvement with Task

The mode is one of felt *independence*:

The excellence of an individual's endeavor is measured by standards within one's self. Excellence of ideas, of designs, and of technical execution are the goals of achievement. Committees, groups, and people in general are at best mediocre in the quality of their performances. The excellent, beautiful, self-contained *integrity* of ideas is the valued goal of achievement. People need each other for social and personal support, but they get in the way of each other when it comes to achieving excellence. Therefore, it is of utmost importance not to mix work with the pleasures of sociability. There is a time to work and a time to love, but they are *different* times.

The process of formal education is in itself exciting and rewarding. In that setting, excellence may be pursued without the need to compromise with social mediocrity. This pursuit is of value to the outside world; high salaries are paid and impressive titles are given for good technical specialization. Older people, with more experience, seem to have compromised their personal standards with social mediocrity to achieve their kind of tainted success. As long as the "administrators" do not interfere with or discourage the pursuit of technical excellence, they can be tolerated and may even be helpful by protecting the pursuit from interference by others, and may help by explaining its importance to them.

Satisfaction is derived from the achievement of a clear, unambiguous plan or from the completion of a definite project. It is also satisfying to spend time with people as long as the purpose is purely social. Confusion and ambiguity are frustrating. Goals and procedures should be clearly agreed upon for the experience to be satisfying.

The outside observer sees the behavior pattern of the person experiencing involvement in task as sporadic, tense, and withdrawn. When he disagrees with others he will do it in an ambiguous, joking manner. Other than the joking, he talks "shop" and engages in few sociable gestures. He does not talk directly to people, but works on their ideas as if they were detached and floating in space. While others talk, he sits and waits thoughtfully. When he does talk, he explains his ideas at length.

The other members of the group see him as being distant but brilliant. He would be satisfactory as a leader, but others would not want to try to get close to him personally. Although he jokes, he does not seem to help pull the group together socially. It is difficult to tell how he feels about people and their ideas.

This behavior pattern causes others to try to include him socially out of respect for his ideas, but makes it difficult for them to talk with him directly about his and their ideas. To overcome the social distance he is apparently establishing, the others reach him through interrupting and criticizing. His joking would tend to increase the felt social distance between himself and the others, rather than bring them closer together.

The Social Specialists: Involvement with Persons

The mode is one of felt *dependence*:

People need each other for support. Feeling lonely, disliked, and disrespected by people is the worst thing that could happen to a person. Living together in harmony is the ultimate value. One must work hard and do a good job in order to be accepted by others. But work should not be allowed to interfere with harmony, respect, and affection.

One learns from experience that being close and friendly with people is more important than career success. Having friends and being friendly are necessary to support and encourage a person through periods of disappointment and hardship.

Satisfaction is derived from being liked and accepted in the group. Argument and conflict are frustrating and make for an unhappy experience.

The person experiencing this condition would be observed to be somewhat reserved and quiet during the group discussions. When he does enter into the discussion, it is in open, spontaneous reaction to the others. He is polite and respectful and expresses emotional support to individuals and to the group. He rarely interrupts, disagrees, or asks competitive questions. His comments are short, and tend to be positive reactions to others' comments rather than initiations of new ideas.

The others in the group see him as a nice guy. They are polite to him in return. He tends to get personal recognition for his contribution and is seen as contributing to the congeniality of the group. His ideas are not seen as particularly useful, nor would the others particularly care to have him as a leader. They tend to like him, but strictly in a social context. They would not like to work with him.

The Underchosen: Involvement with Self and Detachment

The mode is one of *counterdependence*:

In this condition, the person tends to feel somewhat rebellious, bitter, cynical, critical, defensive, and competitive. He sees and interprets what is going on in the group in terms of its interpersonal meanings for himself. He is somewhat detached from what is going on and he is carried away with his concern for his self-esteem. He is experiencing the most sensitivity and self-awareness of the four role types. He sees task and social activities as an arena for interpersonal competition. Hence he cannot get involved in either the task or the social systems of activities for their own sake, but observes them and sees people scoring competitive points against each other and against himself. He feels a strong conflict between wanting to achieve and display intellectual excellence, and a fear of failing and making a fool of himself. The safe ground is the role of critic. This means that he does not initiate many ideas, but uses his abilities to criticize the ideas initiated by others. He is apt to impute competitive, or otherwise impure, motivations into the behaviors of others.

His response to disappointment or discouragement is to devalue a formerly valued pursuit. If he feels that he has failed at an endeavor, he will protect his esteem by concluding that it was not a worthwhile activity in the first place. If he succeeds, he concludes that this is proof of the mediocrity of his competitors. If he loses at others' games, he wins at his own. If he wins at others' games, he also wins at his own.

An observer would see the behavior of a person in this condition as serious, aggressive, competitive, and critical. He rarely agrees with anyone and often asks questions which cause the other person to justify defensively his position. While his rate of participation would indicate that he was involved in the discussion, the things he says and does indicate that he is maintaining a critical distance from the events while welcoming the chance to express himself.

The others do not see him as being very useful to the group. They tolerate his expressivity and even tend to indicate agreement with him. They tend to avoid giving him personal recognition. They tend to react to him as a critical person rather than to his ideas.

The foregoing quasi-clinical descriptions of the four role types set the stage for the exploration of the two types of developmental trends: (1) role specialization as a trend specific to a phase in development; (2) role patterns as an aspect of the ego defenses.

ROLE SPECIALIZATION AS A DEVELOPMENTAL TREND

Role specialization by individuals over long periods of time may be conceived of as a condition of incompleteness. The distinction between a developmental phase and a pathological condition is the difference between movement toward completeness and rigidity, or lack of change. In the condition of normal personality development described by R. W. White and others (e.g., White, 1952, pp. 332–356) growth involves cyclical processes of differentiation and integration involving all levels of personality—intellectual, emotional, and striving. When this process becomes frozen, blocked, or unduly constrained, the person may be described as engaged in pathological trends.

The Technical Specialists provide a convenient example for following these processes through the findings of this study. They tended to be young and highly educated, compared with the others. From this combination it may be assumed that their formal education was quite recently completed, or was still in process. One aspect of most kinds of formal education is that differentiation is built into the structure and function of the institution and its relationship to the person. The student learns to separate problems into parts, and his curriculum reflects this analytical separation. The higher the level of the course offerings, the more limited and specialized their scope. Professional education labels the graduate as not only specialized by profession, such as law, medicine, engineering, physics, or chemistry, but subspecialized down to a single narrow aspect of his field. The degree to which he will integrate his recognized specialization into a condition of involvement appropriate to resolving the conflicting social realities which he will face in his career is left open, to be resolved through his own personality development processes. (Kubie, 1960, pp. 141–168) He has not formally learned to objectify the relationships between task logics and social and personal realities, nor would it be possible to "teach" this kind of objectification as course *content*, since it is basically an *experienced* resolution involving one's feeling, knowing, and wanting processes.

When the young person enters the practice of his occupation, it is usually in a capacity that is specialized in relation to the organization. He is rewarded for the exercise of competence in his specialty up to certain limits. For promotion to higher status levels, social competence is required. Even at that point, social competence is expressed in ambiguous terms, such as "leadership ability" or "ability to get along with people," a language strikingly different from the relatively crisp and clean criteria for evaluating technical achievements. These desired social qualities may be objectified in the content of executive training courses of the Dale Carnegie type, or other "how to" orientations, but this is still quite a distance from objectifying the *experiential* aspects of personality development.

The young person learns to perform a specialized role, and sees in his environment external standards for evaluating his technical performance but only vague, ambiguous hints of the need for other kinds of competences essential to achieve success in his career. In the face of a group problem-solving situation, inherently ambiguous to even more experienced persons, the Technical Specialist initially sees few alternatives other than to exercise technical competence. Eventually he will recognize social realities, or else he will be excluded from interpersonal work situations. For him recognition has been shown by the study to take the form of a differentiation; there are technical aspects of problem-solving *and* there are social aspects of problem-solving.

Meanwhile, other things are going on in the life of the young career person. Family and community statuses are attained, along with memberships in these groups, as well as memberships in social groups in his organization. Together with his concerns about career success, these influences further emphasize the *differentiation* between task and social competences.

The Social Specialists evidenced this same differentiation in their orientations. They were high in preference for Job-Intrinsic Rewards and were high in preference for Belonging Rewards. They tended to be low in need Achievement.

Perhaps their efforts to resolve and integrate the task-social dichotomy diverted their striving energies away from the career achievement theme which characterized the imaginative stories written by the Stars and Technical Specialists. The Social Specialists' behaviors fitted Slater's description (Slater, 1955). They were supportive and tended to avoid controversy. They were rewarded by social identity in that they were perceived as being congenial and adding to the warmth and friendliness of their groups. The identity rewards received by both the Technical and the Social Specialists would tend to reinforce their current orientations and modes of behavior and lead to continuation of the specialist patterns unless somewhere in the process a nonsocially determined self emerged within their personality structures.

R. W. White has the following to say about the stabilization of ego identity:

> . . . As ego identity grows more stably autonomous, the person becomes capable of having a more consistent and lasting effect upon his environment . . . .
>
> One type of event that often contributes to the stabilizing of ego identity is placement in an occupational status or in some other socially recognized position. Social roles provide us with a means of establishing identity. They also provide us with opportunities for action whereby we further define and stablize ourselves . . . .
>
> Consideration of the part played by social roles thus leads us to perceive the types of experience that are most conducive to stabilizing one's ego identity. Stated schematically, any episode has this effect which serves to heighten the efficacy of accumulated personal experience as against new outside judgments, fresh experiences of success or failure, or new objects of possible identification. This heightened efficacy results most readily from a situation of choice in which there are immediate pressures on either side. Decision necessarily turns on becoming more aware of personal preference and of the things for which one really wants one's life to stand . . . (White, 1952, pp. 334–338) .

The kinds and sequences of experiences which the developing person encounters would have much to do with the directions of his development. The structures of formal education and organizational hierarchies would tend to channel role development through the sequence of technical, social, and then integrated role performances. Informal social organization and the biological requirements of social nurturance for the survival and growth of the young human require a reversal of the specializations. The social performance precedes technical specialization. (Parsons and Bales, 1955, pp. 31–131) Being a member of a family group is the first social fact of individual life, and being included in friendship groups on the basis of mutual need satisfactions is the first fact of autonomous group formation. Beyond these initial facts of mutually affectionate relationships, technical competence develops and establishes individuals' statuses in the family or social group. This might be called the prototype of the role development sequence, and can in fact be observed to interact with the more current organizationally imposed sequence which runs in the reverse order.

Before the days when specialized and graduate level education were the prescribed routes to career success, college education was considered by some to be primarily a social experience teaching young persons to get along with each other and to become leaders. Within this pattern, the young graduate would seek employment on the basis of his social skills and would later specialize through on-the-job experience. Certain traditionalistic occupations, such as insurance, security brokerage, banking, etc., may still follow this selection and training philosophy, but the shift from the simple title of "salesman" to the revised title of "sales engineer," or from "customer's man" to "security analyst," are indications that even in those positions where social competence was once considered to be the prime value, the tendency is toward the primacy of specialization. Yet in spite of this tendency, the new member of the organization initially faces the prototypical problem of inclusion or membership in a social group.

As a result of the existence of these two contradictory prescribed sequences, from social to technical in the one instance and from technical to social in the other, individuals may be forced into positions of developing within two or more different out-of-phase sequences. Such a situation was reported in Barnes' study of two engineering groups. (Barnes, 1960, pp. 80–81) In his Department A, members reported transitions from Social to Professional (roughly corresponding to "task") roles in some instances, while his Organizationals (roughly corresponding to Social Specialists or Stars) had all been Technical Specialists (engineers) by training. In this present study the Technical Specialists tended to be younger than the Social Specialists, and this particular variation of the cycle is understandable in terms of the recency and level of education attributable to the two kinds of specialists, the Technical Specialists representing the current trend to higher, more specialized education.

According to a theory of role development, the Stars would have gone through the phases of technical and social specialization, although not necessarily in that order, at earlier times in their lives. This interpretation does not rule out the possibility that the Stars had characteristically integrated roles throughout their history. If they did (and will continue to) resolve successfully dichotomous differentiations by integrating them, the fact that they did, while others who were exposed to similar influences did not, would be evidence that some special personal qualities were required for successful role transition. The relatively low salaries of the Social Specialists and Underchosen participants in relation to their ages, give some indication that their reward and developmental patterns did not proceed according to potential developmental form.

To restate the developmental themes that we shall explore further, the Stars appeared to integrate somewhat disparate role components. They possibly had a developmental history characterized by role integration or possibly their learning experiences resulted in successive moves from social to task specialization to a resolution and integration of expressive and instrumental behavior.

The Technical Specialists engaged in instrumental behavior and either avoided or ignored social-expressive behavior. Given their relatively young age, their existing mode of specialization could perhaps be one phase in their development to be followed by the integration characteristic of the Stars. Or, their histories may reveal specialization as a dominant behavioral trend throughout their several stages of development.

The case of the Social Specialists, with emphasis on social and expressive behavior, suggests a rigid concentration on their existing role repertoire, given their age and relatively low achievement. Presumably, their personal histories should indicate the nature of early learning experience associated with their role patterns.

Finally, the Underchosen represent the closest approximation to a learning problem and developmental failure. Their dominant preoccupation with self and inability to establish suitable work and social contact, at least in the experimental setting, suggests the presence of marked anxiety and constricting mechanisms of defense related to earlier developmental crises.

Role–Taking as an Aspect of Anxiety, Defense, and Early Development

The premise underlying this section of the analysis is that the individual's styles of interpersonal behavior are an integral part of his character structure and system of ego defenses. From the standpoint of development, prior experience in coping with anxiety creates for the individual a characteristic set of defenses with which he continues to combat anxiety. The maintenance of the defensive system requires the expenditure of energy which beyond a certain point could more functionally be expended in work and affective relationships. This view of the defenses has been stated by Freud as follows:

> The purpose of the defensive mechanisms is to avert dangers. It cannot be disputed that they are successful; it is doubtful whether the ego can altogether do without them during its development, but it is also certain that they themselves may become dangerous. Not infrequently it turns out that the ego has paid too high a price for the services which these mechanisms render. The expenditure of energy to maintain them and the ego-restrictions which they almost invariably entail prove a heavy burden on the psychical economy. Moreover, these mechanisms are not relinquished after they have helped the ego through the difficult years of its development. Of course, no individual makes use of all possible mechanisms of defense: each person merely selects certain of them, but these become fixated in his ego, establishing themselves as regular modes of reaction for that particular character, which are repeated throughout life whenever a situation occurs similar to that which originally evoked them. They are, in fact, infantilisms and share the fate of so many institutions which struggle to maintain themselves when they have outlived their usefulness. . . . The adult ego with its greater strength continues to defend itself against dangers which no longer exist in reality and even finds itself impelled to seek out real situations which may serve as a substitute for the original danger, so as to be able to justify its clinging to its habitual modes of reaction. Thus the defensive mechanisms produce an ever-growing alienation from the external world and a permanent enfeeblement of the ego and we can easily understand how they pave the way for and precipitate the outbreak of neurosis. (Freud, 1937, 1959, pp. 340–341)

While there is no evidence on which to consider any of the role types in this study as sharply alienated or as handicapped by severe disturbances, nevertheless the concept of "regular modes of reaction" for particular character types is a useful point of departure for further analysis of the role patterns identified in this study.

The general questions to be explored in the remainder of this chapter include:

1. To what extent do anxiety and defense play a part in the maintenance of the role patterns from the standpoint of the individual? What particular mechanisms of defense appear related to the role types, and what are the qualities of the anxieties against which the individuals in the four role types defend?
2. What particular trends in early development correlate with the role types? Does the fusion or Star type result from uneventful experiences in childhood and the absence of trauma and deprivation? What particular qualities of socialization seem pertinent in distinguishing the role types?
3. To what extent are the patterns of role performance related to the emotional qualities of early development in contrast to discrete socialization events? Can uniformities be discerned showing the different emotional bases of the role patterns? What differences in the experiencing of affection and authority and pressures for independence are associated with the different role types?

Obviously this last set of questions examines the effects on role patterns of two types of experience in early family relationships: (1) The exchange of emotional support, affection, and control; (2) The stress on independence training.

The task of child rearing in our culture is to provide for the legitimate dependency needs of the child and to train the child toward increasing degrees of independence—the ability to take care of himself and ultimately to care for others. Studies reported by McClelland (McClelland, Atkinson, Clark, and Lowell, 1953, Chapter 9) and by Bron-

fenbrenner (Bronfenbrenner, 1961) underscore the interaction of these two processes as a precondition for later life
experience. In McClelland's studies of achievement motivation, he demonstrates the effects of independence training
coupled with emotional support as a condition for strong
achievement motivation in the individual. No small part of
this balance in child rearing practice is attributable to cultural influence. As Bronfenbrenner notes (see also Sears,
Maccoby, and Levin, 1957, Chapter XII) the patterns of
child rearing in middle-class families tend to emphasize *both*
emotional support and independence training, conditions
that would seem favorable for flexibility in role performance.
Analyses of family history of the various role types therefore
will explore social class and mobility phenomena, emotional
experience, and independence training.

Social Class and Mobility

Social class and mobility can affect role patterns in two
ways. First, the social class in which an individual is reared
prepares him to cope easily with certain interpersonal situations, while he experiences other types with some anxiety.
Specifically, the experimental setting in which the subjects
participated was distinctly of a middle class milieu (see
Appendix A) typical of most problem-solving settings in
formal organizations. Those subjects with a middle-class
background would presumably have internalized the modes
of behavior seemingly appropriate for such settings and
would have entered the situation with confidence and relatively low anxiety. The reverse would be expected for those
subjects from class backgrounds distinctly different from that
of the experimental setting.

The second effect of social background relates to the individual's own mobility as a factor inducing anxiety. By and
large, the socially mobile individual, besides facing constantly
new learning situations, must continue to compare himself
with an early object of identification whom he has outdis-

tanced in the so-called success ladder of the American social structure. Of special significance is the outdistancing of one's own father and the potential which this experience provides for provoking feelings of guilt. In extreme cases, the guilt can echo similar feelings associated with the earlier Oedipal conflicts. The mobile individual would potentially face anew conflicts resulting from previous competitive strivings that he would transfer into the experimental setting.

A very simple, but pointed, indication of the validity of the line of analysis presented above is to compare the occupational backgrounds of the subjects' fathers in relation to their own perceived congeniality in the groups. Perceived congeniality choices in the Post Meeting Reaction questionnaire were high for both the Stars and the Social Specialists. Their fathers should have higher occupational status than the fathers of the low congenial types (the Technical Specialists and the Underchosen). The data are presented in Table 7.1 and, while not conclusive, the direction of the table provides some support for the expectation.

Table 7.1

PERCEIVED CONGENIALITY AND FATHER'S OCCUPATIONAL STATUS

FATHER'S OCCUPATIONAL STATUS

		HIGH	LOW	TOTAL
PERCEIVED	High	14	12	26
CONGENIALITY	Low	9	16	25
	Total	23	28	51

$$x^2 = 1.39 \quad .30 > p > .20$$

NOTE: 1. High occupational status consists of professional, executive, and owner categories. Lows consist of worker, salesman, and farmer categories.
2. Data unavailable for 1 subject; the n in the table therefore is reduced to 51.

But looking more intensively at the effects on anxiety of subjects' social class and mobility, one should expect to find the Stars the least mobile, and the Underchosen the most mobile. According to the theory, the Underchosen represent the extreme case of anxiety and defensive behavior in the experimental situation. The two specialists should fall somewhere between the two extremes in social mobility.

Table 7.2 presents a series of social mobility indices. This table shows that the Stars and Underchosen were at the ex-

Table 7.2

INDICES OF SOCIAL MOBILITY

(The higher the number the greater the mobility)

	STARS	TECHNICAL SPECIALISTS	SOCIAL SPECIALISTS	UNDER- CHOSEN
1. S's Educational Attainment vs. Father's	1.7	3.1	1.7	1.7
2. Father's Occupation When S in Grammar School	2.9	3.9	3.3	3.5
3. S's Occupational Mobility	1.0	0.6	0.6	1.6
4. S's vs. Father's Occupation	0.3	0.9	0.6	1.0
5. Wife's Father's Occupation	2.7	2.1	3.6	3.5
6. Sum of Scores 1–5 Inclusive	8.6	10.6	9.8	11.3

NOTE: 1. The construction of the indices above were designed to reflect mobility rates. In the case of Index 2, for example, the lower the occupational status of father the higher the score, to reflect the difference between where the subject is now in the occupational hierarchy compared with his father. All of the subjects were in middle-class, professional-executive positions.

2. Index 4 compares father's occupation when subject became self-supporting with subject's present occupation so that father's mobility is taken into account.

3. Index 5 shows the wife's father's occupational status. The higher the number, the higher the status.

treme in social mobility with the Stars the least mobile and the Underchosen the most. The two specialists fell between the extremes with the Technical Specialists showing higher mobility rates on 3 out of 5 indices than the Social Specialists. The particular forms of mobility revealed by Table 7.2 are interesting. Insofar as changing life style, as reflected in rates of upward mobility, is a cause of uncertainty and anxiety, the fact that the Social Specialists and Underchosen married into higher status families (Index 5) is suggestive. The Technical Specialists' main avenue of mobility seems to have been education, a factor suggested previously as reinforcing a role of idea man.

The sharp contrast between the social status and mobility rates of the Stars and Underchosen provide a useful test of a theory relating these variables to experienced anxiety and defensive behavior. (Zaleznik, Christensen, and Roethlisberger, 1958, pp. 56–74) The Underchosen, whose behavior was characterized by defensive acts, were the most mobile group of the four types. The situation created for them a bind in which on the one hand they probably aspired to perform well, but on the other hand felt most distant from the setting and their coparticipants. Both of these factors are suggestive conditions for generating anxiety and defensive behavior.

The Stars on the other hand were probably well trained for the tasks facing them in the experiment and while desiring to perform well, the setting posed relatively few conditions they could not anticipate with some prior experience at their command. This condition reduces or modifies anxiety aroused by the desire to perform well and therefore is less likely to result in defensive acts. The capacity to be open to new experiences and to other persons, one characteristic of the Stars, is easily mobilized in those situations where the motivation to perform well is high, and generalized anxiety is low.

Emotional Experience in the Family

In the study of the effects of developmental trends on the individual's modes of interpersonal behavior, the early family experience is a central area for analysis. Defensive behavior is usually in relation to anxiety provoking situations whose origin is somewhere in the past experience of the individual. Furthermore, the group as the interpersonal setting resembles the nuclear family and can stimulate transference reactions. We should therefore expect to find the role types differing in their reported early family experience. The extent of experienced close affective relationships, the absence or presence of serious deprivations, the degree of stressful sibling relationships should have a bearing on the preparation of the individual for expressions of warmth as well as aggression, two emotional bases of the role types under consideration in this study.

The data in this section will be grouped into four classes: (1) reported closeness to family; (2) the presence of deprivation events of potential emotional significance; (3) ordinal position within family; (4) independence training.

1. *Closeness to Family:*

As part of the personal history questionnaire, each participant was asked to respond to the following question: "To what extent do you feel you were close to your family as you were growing up?" The three categories of response were: (1) Very Close; (2) Close; (3) Not So Close.

The question, in effect, asked the participants to present an immediate and global reaction to their recollections of the emotional tone of their early family experience. Reference to closeness implies intimacy, the exchange of feeling, support, warmth, and other positive feelings. The assumption underlying the use of this question was an expected positive relationship between the perceived congeniality of the role types and positive emotional experience in the family of origin.

Table 7.3 shows the relationship between the role types and reported closeness to family.

The Stars and Social Specialists, both of whom were ranked high on congeniality, indicated to a greater degree than the other role types "very close" early family relationship. ($x^2 = 2.88$; $.10 > p > .05$) The Social Specialists were the

Table 7.3

ROLE TYPES AND REPORTED CLOSENESS TO FAMILY

(Percent)

	VERY CLOSE	CLOSE	NOT SO CLOSE	TOTAL
EXPECTED PERCENTAGE	40	38	22	100
Stars	47	20	33	100
Technical Specialists	40	50	10	100
Social Specialists	58	42	0	100
Underchosen	20	47	33	100

strongest in this direction while the Underchosen reported the least "close" relationship. ($x^2 = 4.04$; $.05 > p > .02$) The Underchosen who experienced little emotional closeness in their parental family presumably had unsatisfying early experiences in the exchange of feeling with others that carried over into the experimental situation.

It is interesting to note that a somewhat larger proportion of Stars than one would expect reported a "not so close" relationship, suggesting that as a group their patterns of emotional closeness to others were rooted in somewhat more complex development trends than in the case of the Social Specialists who also ranked high on congeniality. The possibility exists that the developmental experience for the Social Specialists resulted in an over-investment in emotional closeness at the expense of the utilization of aggression in the service of work. Some indirect validation of this hypothesis exists in a further analysis of the imaginative stories written in response to a picture that clearly provoked imagery of interpersonal relationships.

This picture showed a young man and an older man in conversation. The picture provokes fantasy of an authority relationship, especially that of father-son. The interesting results of the frequency of father-son stories by role type are reported in Table 7.4.

Table 7.4

FREQUENCY OF FATHER-SON STORIES BY ROLE TYPE

(Percent)

	FATHER-SON	OTHER	TOTAL
EXPECTED PERCENTAGE	54	46	100
Stars	73	27	100
Technical Specialists	50	50	100
Social Specialists	33	67	100
Underchosen	53	47	100

The Stars and the Social Specialists provide the important contrast in the data reported in Table 7.4. The Stars tended strongly to place their stories in the father-son relationship while the reverse was true of the Social Specialists. ($x^2 = 4.48$; $.05 > p > .02$) One can best interpret this finding in the light of anthropological reports on the nature of the affect produced in different types of kinship relationships. (Homans, 1950, Chapters 9–10. See also Homans and Schneider, 1955)

The father-son relationship is one of authority in which distance but respect is generally expected. In contrast, the uncle-nephew relationship, a frequent setting for the stories presented by the Social Specialists, is more egalitarian and marked by warmth and affection. Presumably, the Social Specialists found it less threatening to place their stories in settings where authority is avoided and emotional closeness is fostered. It is also possible that, unlike the Stars, the Social Specialists found exercising authority, with its implied use of aggression and control, anxiety provoking. Instead, their preferred mode of influencing others was through establishing bonds of affection.

An analysis of the stories for the type of affect displayed shows the Social Specialist projecting strong positive feeling while the other role types preferred somewhat negative feeling in a story involving two males. This finding is reported in Table 7.5.

Table 7.5

TYPES OF AFFECT IN THE TWO-PERSON RELATIONSHIP
AND ROLE TYPES

(Percent)

	POSITIVE	NEGATIVE	NEUTRAL	TOTAL
EXPECTED PERCENTAGE	48	37	15	100
Stars	33	47	20	100
Technical Specialists	40	30	30	100
Social Specialists	84	8	8	100
Underchosen	40	53	7	100

The relationship between two males, such as portrayed in the TAT pictures used in this study, is a difficult one in which to express emotional closeness. In fact one is apt to find a tendency to react against feelings of closeness between males and turn the relationship into one of expressed aggression, competition, and a struggle for power and control. With the exception of the Social Specialists, all role types tended to project fantasy involving negative feelings between males, usually in a father-son relationship. ($x^2 = 7.63$; $.01 > p > .001$)

This reaction to closeness in a male, two-person relationship fits in with cultural expectations based on a taboo against homosexuality. It also represents the individual's attempt to assert a dominant masculine identification. In the case of the Social Specialists, their preference for a relationship of equality and their open expression of positive affect is suggestive of a possible maternal orientation and identification. This interpretation is also consistent with their reported closeness to family while growing up. One can suggest that the Social Specialists were involved in a warm and dependent familial bond while growing up, and one that encouraged the avoidance of aggression along with a tendency toward identifying with the role of the mother. This role involves nurture, caring, support and maintenance, behaviors characteristic of the performances of the Social Specialists in the experimental setting. The propensity of the Social Specialists for a caring or maternal role is reflected further in the choice of college major. Of the thirty subjects in this study who reported their college major, ten indicated the social sciences. Six of the ten (60%) were Social Specialists, a proportion well above the expected of 29% based on the proportion of Social Specialists to the total population reporting their college major.

The strong preference of the Stars for the father-son relationship in their imaginative stories suggests a strong masculine identification unlike the Social Specialists. Yet the capacity of the Stars for emotional expressivity suggests, unlike the Technical Specialists and the Underchosen, a nondefensive orientation toward behavior that expresses consideration and caring for others, attributes that resulted in their high congeniality ratings. One could speculate that the Stars, secure in their masculine identification, could be expressive without anxiety and the need to defend.

The performances of the Technical Specialists and Underchosen suggest difficulty with expressive and caring behavior in interpersonal settings, but the interaction between emotional closeness in their early family experience and their resultant identifications do not emerge clearly from the data considered up to now. Other aspects of childhood experience might clarify their emotional development as a precondition for role behavior.

2. *The Presence of Deprivation Events in Childhood:*

The term "deprivation events" as used here refers to potentially traumatic occurrences of an unexpected event such as the death or divorce of parents, serious illness, sharp economic deteriorations in the family's position, and like events. In point of fact, these relatively "objective" events may be the least significant as causes of emotional trauma with consequences for later development. Felt deprivation can exist, quite apart from the occurrence of real events, in the emotional quality of the mother-infant relationship. Since the study did not inquire into felt deprivations, the following examination of the presence or absence of so-called deprivation events as role development influences is limited to "objective" occurrences.

Following the theory of role-taking as a pattern of defense against anxiety, one needs to explore how deprivation events might result in emotional experiences that provoke anxiety and lead to the exaggeration of certain role patterns and the avoidance of other role patterns.

For example, the Stars, who appear to be exaggerating and avoiding least, might have had fewer emotional deprivations that could have interfered with their learning during the formative years. In contrast, the Underchosen, with their aggressive-defensive behavior, might have been the most deprived as a result of traumatic events. They therefore could be exhibiting a lack of trust of others, and an overconcern with attack to destroy the reward providing setting in anticipation of failure on their part to achieve gratifications in interpersonal relationships.

Table 7.6 summarizes the reported occurrence of deprivation events.

The data in Table 7.6 are conclusive in showing that the Stars were anything but free of deprivation events in their early developmental experience. On the average, they reported the most frequent occurrence of events (2.0) while the Social Specialists reported the lowest frequency of deprivation events. Of all the role types, the Social Specialists evidently experienced the greatest stability in their childhood experience as represented by economic stability in their household and infrequent change of home and school. This comparison of the Stars and Social Specialists suggests the possibility that the absence of events for the Social Specialists coupled with strong emotional bonds of closeness in the family resulted in an underemphasis on independence training and a strong orientation toward maintenance of stability and the avoidance of conflict. The fact that the Stars ex-

Table 7.6

REPORTED DEPRIVATION EVENTS IN CHILDHOOD BY ROLE TYPES

REPORTED EVENTS

ROLE TYPE	NUMBER	DEATH OF PARENT	DIVORCE OR SEPARATION	ILLNESS OF PARENTS	JOB LOSS OF PARENT	INCOME REDUCTION	FREQ. CHANGE IN HOME	FREQ. CHANGE IN SCHOOL	ILLNESS OR HANDICAP SELF	AVE. NO. EVENTS
Star	15	5	0	4	3	4	5	6	4	2.0
Technical Specialists	10	1	0	1	1	1	3	2	0	1.0
Social Specialists	12	5	0	0	2	2	0	2	0	0.6
Underchosen	15	3	2	2	1	3	3	2	0	1.1
Total Cases Reported	52	14	4	7	5	10	11	10	4	1.25

perienced relative instability could have enhanced their development toward independence while realizing at the same time emotional support through parents or parent surrogates.

While the incidence of divorce and separation are among the lowest in frequency of the deprivation events shown in Table 7.6, those cases that did occur were reported mainly by the Underchosen. This suggests the possibility that one of the negative developmental experiences impinging upon the Underchosen was marital discord and conflict between their parents. We have no data beyond the reports of separation and divorce and lack of closeness in the early family experience (see Table 7.2) to confirm or refute this supposition, but the presence of conflict between parents, aside from its termination in a family breakup, could have been a major source of anxiety leading to distrust, rage, and other feelings blocking spontaneous interpersonal relationships in the adult life of the Underchosen.

3. Ordinal Position in the Family:

The position of the individual in the sibling configuration creates a third condition governing his socialization and development. Freud pointed out how in sibling relationships feelings of rivalry may develop which then become prototypical of later competitive feelings toward peers in adult interpersonal settings. In addition to competitive feelings, a reaction formation frequently results whereby the individual represses competitive feelings and turns them into the opposite, expressing excessive love and affection toward siblings, resembling the attitudes of the parents. This reaction formation occurs frequently in those cases where the individual has experienced a displacement in his family position by the birth of a younger sibling. Freud stated, "Among other things you will infer from this that a child's position in the sequence of brothers and sisters is of very great significance for the course of his later life." (Freud, 1920, 1938, p. 182)

Biblical references to sibling relationships are many, emphasizing also the feelings of rivalry. The stories of Joseph and his brothers and of Esau and Jacob are two pertinent examples. In both stories the oldest siblings feel maltreated and the youngest benefit. Otto Rank in his *The Myth of the Birth of the Hero* (Rank, 1932, 1959) stresses how frequently in legends the youngest child becomes the "hero" since he is the beneficiary of maternal protection. Freud in *Group Psychology and the Analysis of the Ego* (Freud, 1922, 1960) notes in discussing the legend of the primal horde that it is the youngest who succeeds in displacing the father, again benefiting from maternal protection.

Alfred Adler in distinguishing among the characteristics of the oldest, middle born, and youngest child places the oldest child in the position of advantage. (Adler, 1927, p. 154) He is more powerful than younger siblings and closest to the parents. He easily becomes a parent surrogate and adopts the values of the parents in managing brothers and sisters.

Contemporary researches also indicate interesting differences in personality development stemming from differences in ordinal position in the family. McArthur, in a study of traits of first- and second-born children found the first-born to be adult-oriented, sensitive, serious, and hard working. Second-born children tended to be peer-oriented, easy-going, and friendly. McArthur states, by way of explanation, that the second-born child has "the opportunity to learn from a member of his own age group, instead of having to learn everything from adults." (McArthur, 1956, p. 53) In the absence of older siblings, first-born and only children become adult-oriented, and, in general, managerial types.

In a most intriguing study of affiliative tendencies, Stanley Schachter (Schachter, 1959; see also Sears, Maccoby, and Levin, 1957) provides an excellent review of the literature on ordinal position in the family and integrates the results of experimental work into an explanatory framework. Of particular interest to this study is one of Schachter's explanatory ideas for which he presents solid evidence: first-borns tend to seek interpersonal relationships under conditions of anxiety; later-born children tend to be "loners" under conditions of anxiety. Besides data from experimental studies, conducted by himself and colleagues, Schachter cites evidence to support the view that first-born children have a stronger need to affiliate or to be in contact with other persons. For example, among emotionally disturbed veterans, first-borns tend to enter psychotherapy more frequently and to stay there longer than later-born children. Among alcoholics, in contrast, there is a greater than chance proportion of later-born persons. Under conditions of real danger in which the individual acts alone "later-borns" function more effectively than "first-borns." Schachter cites a study of fighter pilots who became "aces" during the Korean War, an ace being defined as a fighter pilot who was credited with five or more enemy aircraft destroyed. In proportion to their numbers in the fighter group, there were more later-borns and fewer first-borns among the aces.

Basically, Schachter's study shows that first-borns want to be with other persons, especially under conditions of anxiety. Supporting this view are data reported by Capra and Dittes (Capra and Dittes, 1962) who analyzed the responses of a group of students to an invitation to participate in a group experiment. The researchers reported their experiment and its results as follows:

> One hundred Yale freshmen were solicited in their dormitory rooms by a senior student for a small group experiment to be conducted at a later time. The recruiting speech asked freshmen to participate in a small group psychology experiment involving "a group performing a common task cooperatively."

Clearly the stimulus presented to the students was one of participation in an interpersonal setting. The researchers found:

In the hypothetical experiment, had it been conducted, 76% of the subjects would have been first-born. This proportion is substantially greater ($p = .10$) than the 61% first-borns in the Yale freshman population and close to twice as great as the probable percentage of first-borns in the national population, which may be estimated from census data as about 40%.

If first-born persons have stronger tendencies to participate and be with other persons, how would this tendency be related to the types of roles explored in this study? Unlike Schachter's experiment, the conditions surrounding the groups in this study were not designed to induce anxiety. But the situation was clearly interpersonal. Following the concept of the competence-reward cycle discussed earlier, one can reason as follows: that individuals who like interpersonal settings for their activity would anticipate their participation in the experiment with pleasure, and presumably this feeling would enable them to present themselves as interested and highly motivated persons. In other words, the anticipation of a rewarding experience would induce the kind of behavior likely to achieve these rewards. In addition, an individual who anticipates an interpersonal experience with pleasure probably has done well in analogous situations in the past—that is, he has been rewarded in past interpersonal settings. Individuals who have been rewarded in past interpersonal situations are likely to approach a new setting with an absence of strong anxiety and defensive reactions that would tend to distort their performance and yield negative evaluations from others.

Following this line of reasoning, a disproportionately high number of first-born subjects (only and oldest children) should appear among the Stars and a disproportionately high number of later-born subjects among the other role types. The reader will recall that the Stars were highly evaluated on two dimensions: the quality of their ideas in the problem-solving activity and their congeniality. The data are reported in Table 7.7.

Table 7.7

ORDINAL POSITION AND ROLE TYPES

(Percent)

| | SIBLING POSITION | | |
	FIRST BORN	LATER BORN	TOTAL
EXPECTED PERCENTAGE	45	55	100
Stars	73	27	100
Technical Specialists	40	60	100
Social Specialists	25	75	100
Underchosen	36	64	100

The data in Table 7.7 show that the Stars were overrepresented by first-born subjects, confirming the reasoning presented above. ($x^2 = 6.91$; $.01 > p > .001$) In terms of developmental trends, ordinal position in the family represents an aspect of the conditions in which early socialization takes place. First-born children tend to receive more attention from parents during infancy than later-born children for the same period of child-care. This additional nurturance helps induce a sense of trust in others and makes interpersonal activity attractive and potentially rewarding. Another aspect of the socialization of the first-born male is the development of a strong masculine identification. When siblings arrive, the first-born, besides experiencing a displacement, is moving toward a closer relationship to the father, whom he adopts as a role model. He seeks and achieves rewards insofar as he displays competent masculine behavior. The first-born also assumes the role of father surrogate and begins to practice taking the role of father in his relations with brothers and sisters. Out of this mix of experience, the first-born male may develop a managerial orientation with much opportunity for experience in interpersonal relations.

Additional insight into the dynamics of this managerial orientation of the Stars who were predominantly first-born is available in a further analysis of the fantasy evoked in response to the imaginative stories. A point at issue is the exact nature of anxiety experienced by the Stars and the other role types and the effects of particular defense mechanisms.

A skilled reader, unfamiliar with this study, read and scored the stories according to a plan designed to test further the hypotheses presented in this chapter. (A detailed description of the scoring procedure and the results of the analysis are presented in Appendix H.)

The analysis of the fantasy showed that the Stars were not free of anxiety and internal conflict.* Instead, the quality of the anxiety and the methods used to deal with it enhanced the orientation of the Stars as responsible-managerial types. The theme of the stories suggested anxiety over possible failure in work and resulting deprivation to family. The Stars experienced some conflict over gratification to self and to family and if sacrifices had to be made, the deprivation fell on them rather than on the family. The stories suggested that concern for meeting obligations as a responsible man led to internalization of conflict. This internalization placed the responsibility for outcomes squarely on themselves, a characteristic quite favorable to highly motivated and competent activity. The penalty the Stars paid for such internalization of conflict was guilt and intrapunitiveness. Not being readily able to detach themselves from responsibility they experienced feelings of remorse at perceived shortcomings. In a more severe form, not apparent in this group, such internalization may result in moods of depression. The theme of responsibility expressed by the Stars was also suggestive of strong identification with models who, as internalized agents, existed to judge performances and outcomes.†

---

* This finding of presence of anxiety among the Stars is consistent with the theory and findings presented by Schachter. (Schachter, 1959)

† The findings of Sears, Maccoby, and Levin (Sears, Maccoby, and Levin, 1957, pp. 413–418) are consistent with the data on ordinal position, forms of anxiety, and modes of identification of the Stars. They showed that first-born children had more highly developed consciences than later-born children.

Another characteristic of the stories written by the Stars was a fairly rich presentation of fantasy. This fact suggests that the conflict and anxiety experienced by the Stars as "responsible-managerial" types was not deeply repressed and in fact was available to them as a source of richness in associations and ideas utilizable in work.

The quality of fantasy presented in the stories written by the Stars was in sharp contrast to the other role types, notably the Underchosen. The Underchosen generally avoided conflict themes in their stories. They wrote extremely constricted stories suggesting repression as a favored defensive method. Whenever conflict themes appeared, the Underchosen tended to externalize the issues and to project the causes of tension outward on to an impersonal "system" or a malevolent superior. The use of projection is consistent with behavior marked by hostility, suspiciousness, and a lack of trust.

The analysis of ordinal position and role types showed clearly the effects of being first-born on the development of the managerial orientation of the Stars. But it threw little light on how ordinal position relates specifically to other role types except for the tendency for all types other than Stars to be later-born in family position. A more detailed analysis of ordinal position does not clarify this issue. The two specialist and the underchosen groups were about equally represented as middle and youngest children.

4. *Independence Training:*

The final area this study explores in the individual's emotional development in the family as a precondition for selected role behavior is independence training. Researchers in studying the development of achievement motivation (McClelland, Watkinson, Clark, and Lowell, 1953) have found

---

They also indicated that first-born children interact more with their fathers than later-born children and are disciplined more by their fathers, factors conducive to their development of a masculine identification.

that parental emphasis on independence is an important condition for strong achievement drives. This study found that two of the role types, the Star and the Technical Specialist, were high on need Achievement and both were highly evaluated as to quality of ideas. Presumably, there would also be evidence that the childhood environment of the Stars and Technical Specialists emphasized and provided opportunities for establishing independence in contrast to the Social Specialists and Underchosen.

Unfortunately the data permit only limited opportunity to test for the effects of independence training on role performance.

Each of the participants was asked to indicate the age at which he first took various responsibilities that involved decisions or acts fostering independence. The acts were as follows:

1. Selecting and purchasing own clothes.
2. Trips or visits away from parents.
3. Preparing a meal for self.
4. Earning money.
5. Making a personal purchase with money earned outside the family.

Table 7.8 shows the average age reported by the role types at which these events took place.

The data indicate that the Stars experienced the independence acts at a somewhat later age than the other role types which were similar. If these data can be taken as indicators of parental stress on independence, one cannot infer that the Stars and Technical Specialists were reared in home atmospheres that stressed independence to a greater degree than the Social Specialists and Underchosen. The data, however, may be poor indicators of parental attitudes toward independence. Another question on the personal history survey asked the participants to indicate the age at which they became self-supporting. The trend, although small, showed

Table 7.8

INDEPENDENCE EXPERIENCES BY ROLE TYPES

(Average Age)

ROLE TYPE	BUY OWN CLOTHES	TRIPS OR VISITS	PRE- PARE MEAL	EARN MONEY	PERSONAL PUR- CHASES	OVER- ALL AVERAGE
Stars	15	10	12	14	14	13
Technical Specialists	14	10	9	11	13	11.4
Social Specialists	15	10	10	11	13	11.8
Underchosen	15	12	10	10	12	11.8

that the Stars and Technical Specialists (the idea men) became self-supporting at a later age than the Social Specialists. (See Table 7.9.) What these data seem to indicate is that independence in matters of money (both earning and spending) came late for the idea men in the study and evidently was unrelated to the induction of a strong motivation toward achievement. The data are best explained by the fact that the Stars and Technical Specialists spent more years in formal education than the other two types.

Table 7.9

AGE SELF-SUPPORTING BY ROLE TYPES

(Percent)

	20 OR UNDER	21 OR OVER	TOTAL
EXPECTED PERCENTAGE	37	63	100
Stars	20	80	100
Technical Specialists	30	70	100
Social Specialists	50	50	100
Underchosen	47	53	100

SUMMARY

This chapter was devoted mainly to establishing an explanatory framework for the findings on the behavior and motivations of the four role types. The explanation was theoretically oriented around a genetic hypothesis relating here-and-now behavior to the continuities in personal development. An individual's role behavior was viewed as an aspect of character structure and the system of defenses that in turn are established and reinforced in early life experiences.

The conclusions stated in this chapter may be summarized as follows:

1. Role specialization and integration may be phases in adult development paralleling experiences in early childhood. Technical Specialists in particular may have been seen in a stage of development where specialization on task existed as a precursor for integrating emotional with task competencies.

2. High social mobility as an inducer of anxiety and defensiveness seemed related to the condition of the Underchosen. This type was the most upwardly mobile among the participants and, as a result, their social conditioning made the experimental setting least familiar to them. Their defensive behavior may be explained partly by this fact since the Underchosen stood in sharp contrast to the Stars whose social status was initially high and their social mobility therefore low.

3. Emotional closeness in early family life seemed to be related to perceived congeniality in the group. Notably, the Social Specialists were closest to their families, suggesting that early training conditioned them to seek affective bonds with others and to avoid aggressive modes of behavior in work activities. This orientation was suggestive of a maternal identification. The Underchosen reported the least closeness in their parental family, a fact that may explain a related lack of trust in others.

4. The absence of "objective" deprivation events in the family did not characterize the early history of the Stars. The Social Specialists appeared to have the least disrupted childhood, suggesting that in comparing them with the Stars the presence of deprivation events coupled with other

factors such as emotional closeness in the family can induce high motivation to succeed. Success or achievement in problem-solving groups involves communicating ideas as well as establishing bonds with other persons.

The presence of marital conflict between parents seemed a strong possible deprivation affecting the development of the Underchosen. The main effects of such deprivation exist in perpetuating a lack of trust in other persons and distorting the process of identification with parents.

5. Ordinal position in the family is an important aspect of early training. The Stars were predominantly first-born and an analysis of the fantasy produced in response to the ambiguous pictures showed a richness in fantasy marked by a deep sense of responsibility, anxiety over a failure to meet obligations, and a tendency to internalize conflict, attributes consistent with a strong masculine identification and a managerial orientation. This orientation was in sharp contrast to the Underchosen who repressed conflict, as evidenced by constricted stories. They tended also to externalize the causes of conflict and to project hostility on to malevolent authority figures.

6. Independence training as a precondition for high motivation to achieve could not be tested adequately with the data collected in this study. The Stars and Technical Specialists, because of their continued education, became self-supporting at a somewhat later age than the other types. This finding, however, is not necessarily inconsistent with stress on independence in their parental family.

This chapter concludes the presentation of theory and findings and opens the way toward an exploration of the applied aspects of this research. As indicated in Chapter 1, the applications of this study are mainly in the direction of the establishment of development activities where interpersonal competence is a desired objective.

CHAPTER 8

Implications for the Development of Administrators

THIS CONCLUDING CHAPTER shifts attention from description, analysis, and explanation of the research findings to a consideration of the applied contributions of this study. Within the framework of this study the applied problem of personal development for the executive role is selected for special attention.

The executive role, perhaps more so than other occupational entities, places greater demands on the person for competence in interpersonal activity. So much of organized human activity rests on the process of communication that to leave to chance or intuitive development the establishment of competent behavior on the part of leaders is to ignore a crucial area of concern in the preparation of individuals for their chosen life's work. This same comment cannot be said about all occupations. Many types of scientific and academic pursuits, for example, center on individual work so that emphasis on interpersonal competence is less crucial than is the case with administration.

In the nearly two decades since World War II, the recognition of the need for training in interpersonal competence has been dramatic. Most executive development programs feature human relations courses both on and off the job. Professionals, either as full-time staff members or as consultants, devote their energies to planning and conducting development activities that seek to modify the behavior of the executive or supervisor.

The main sense in which this concluding chapter seeks to contribute to the effectiveness of this development work is by focusing upon it the theoretical framework and empirical results of this study. Specifically, what conclusions can be reached about training activities when viewed in the light of the theory of human development? At what levels of personality organization can changes in role behavior be sought within an educational framework? What orientations of the learner appear to be the prerequisites for learning? Is training for interpersonal competence realistic for all executives, or should more attention be given to the problem of selection for the learning experiences? Programs can be compared on the basis of the unit in which change is desired. In some cases, professionals seek to effect change at the level of the group or the organization. For others, the object for change and learning, or the "client," is the person. What differences in these two frameworks become relevant for the participant as well as for the professional change agent? Are these two frameworks of equal validity, and is the choice therefore irrelevant as a practical matter?

These and related questions become the types of issues to which this chapter is addressed. It is written primarily for the professionals within formal organizations as well as the social scientists within professional schools who concern themselves with the use of educational processes for effecting changes in individual behavior. The material in this chapter is organized into four parts: (1) the definition of interpersonal competence; (2) interpersonal competence and continuities in human development; (3) intervention for interpersonal competence; (4) conclusion.

THE DEFINITION OF INTERPERSONAL COMPETENCE

Intelligent discussion addressed to the applied issues indicated above requires a meaningful definition of interpersonal competence. This definition would serve as a point of reference for inferring objectives of development activity as well as for evaluating particular approaches to such educational work.*

In the light of this study, interpersonal competence can be viewed as the capacity of an individual: (1) to work within a broad range of the spectrum of behavior; (2) with a minimum strain on the person's defensive system; and (3) with the optimal use of energy available to the person.

Spectrum of Behaviors

The concept of a spectrum of behavior imagines a definable scale or set of scales to describe all the possible minute behavioral acts open to man. These scales were dealt with in a small way when utilizing the methods described in Chapter 3 for measuring behaviors produced and received in the experimental situations. For the time being, if one examines the differences in mode of activity between task and social-integrative behaviors, a better grasp of the significance of the concept of the behavioral spectrum is possible.

Task behavior involves the individual in an aggressive mode of acting. By thinking and weighing ideas, his own and others, he becomes committed to points of view that he must formulate and assert, both forcefully and confidently, if he is to work with conviction. He seeks to influence other persons, to change and modify their points of view, which involves him in competitive activity. To assert and to compete opens the individual to aggressive behavior from others. If he is functioning in task activity, the individual has to be able to take competitive behavior from others; this includes criticism, evaluation, and attack.

One of the main characteristics of task-oriented behavior is the release of energy and its direction on to a problem-solving situation and at the same time the absorption of energy dis-

---

* For other discussions of interpersonal competence, see Argyris, 1962 and Foote and Cottrell, 1955.

play resulting from the direction of energy by other persons. Developmentally, task-oriented behavior in problem-solving groups closely resembles, in mode of activity, those experiences in childhood and adolescence involving the maximum display of aggressive energy: gross play activity involving muscular exertion and competition. For the individual to function well in task-oriented behavior requires him to make available energy and conversely to use the energy without undue anxiety. Psychologically, the individual must utilize energy that in its derivations may not be too different in kind from the energy used in more primitive-destructive activity. But in effective task behavior, the meaning attached to this use of energy must be detached from any connection with the more primitive behavior (Hartmann, 1958).

Social-integrative behavior involves the individual in a less active mode than task-oriented behavior. Here, the individual is relatively passive and quiescent. He absorbs and incorporates, acknowledges and responds with very little display of energy. Small changes in expression, gesture, posture, and verbalization serve to communicate social-integrative acts.

To act integratively invites others to respond in kind. The individual who engages in social-integrative behavior has to be able to absorb the warm and tender acts of others.

Developmentally, social-integrative behavior most closely resembles the relationships in nurturing and being nurtured. It is maternal in derivation, but to be effective the meaning of social-integrative behavior must be detached from its analog in the earlier, more primitive acts of nurturance. When it is not detached, the behavior tends to become threatening and yields anger and division instead of quiescence and unity.

The descriptions of the two contrasting modes of behavior, both of which seem to be required in effective interpersonal problem-solving activity, suggest the significant shifts required on the part of the individual who attempts to become capable of *both* modes of activity either through fusing them or shifting the modes in response to situational demands.

In normal development, individuals experience and re-experience the two modes in ways appropriate to their stage in the life cycle. But for many persons, if not for most, one or the other of the modes becomes an area of vulnerability. The Technical Specialist, for example, tends to be vulnerable to the integrative mode. Emotional expressivity tends to become an area of avoidance, either because the Technical Specialist experienced undue deprivation in the nurturant relationships, or possibly because his security in aggressive behavior is itself tenuous, requiring some exaggeration of this mode of behavior in the service of supporting an area of uncertainty. The Social Specialist, on the other hand, is vulnerable to aggressive activity.

Earlier discussion referred to Social Specialists as "maternal males," meaning that they seek to play nurturant roles as opposed to aggressive-assertive roles. Presumably, their vulnerability to the use of aggressive behavior relates to excessive emphasis in early stages of development on caring as opposed to doing. The role type called Underchosen may reflect an instability in both modes of action leading to undue or overly rapid oscillation in mood and mode, and the resulting failure to present a sufficiently coherent behavior pattern to others.

The ability to fuse or to alternate modes in cycles meaningful to others may be prevented by the stresses and strains induced on the individual's system of defenses.

Strain on Defensive System

In the process of personal development, individuals develop an organized set of responses to situations which further become defined as sources of anxiety. Anxiety is a generalized state of tension and lack of well being that individuals seek to minimize. The person's characteristic methods of warding off anxiety have been referred to as defense mechanisms. The position taken in this study is that a role pattern in a problem-solving activity can contain strong defensive features. The individual, for example, who finds interpersonal situations basically threatening would orient his behavior toward alleviating the amount of tension and conflict he experiences internally.

In the notion of interpersonal competence under consideration here, competence implies that the individual functions without undue stress on his system of defenses. The interpersonal situation does not provoke so much anxiety as to tax the defensive system to the point where adaptive behavior becomes difficult to maintain. At the same time, competence implies that the defensive system permits a wide range of behavior. Attempting new activity or alternating among a number of modes of activity does not pose a threat, with the result that learning from experience can continue.

The case of the Underchosen probably illustrates the instance where the defensive system dominates the behavior and where experimentation is at a minimum. Here the individual is faced with issues of maintaining self-esteem in interpersonal settings so that risk-taking and experimentation are avoided. Learning, consequently, is at a minimum if not retarded.

But the specialists, also, present interesting possible uses of strong defensive behavior. In the case of the Technical Specialists, their strong orientation toward task implies an avoidance of the ambiguity of feelings. The Social Specialists emphasize emotional expressivity at the expense of aggressive behavior directed toward problem-solving. But in the case of the specialists, their behavior is sufficiently adaptive (i.e., related to functional requirements of problem-solving groups) so that opportunity for reward is open to them. At the same time, learning may be minimized because new behavior directed away from their modes of specialization could burden their structure of defenses. Presumably learning for the specialists would require a selected setting where new explorations in interpersonal behavior would be open to them under relatively controlled and "safe" conditions. To anticipate later discussion, one of the highly pertinent contributions of formal executive development programs is to present the controlled conditions necessary for learning in the sense intimated here.

Optimal Use of Energy

Closely related to the defensive processes is the particular economy an individual experiences in the use of his energy. This aspect of interpersonal competence is significant because the way energy is utilized for given acts, no matter how constructive this appears externally, may involve staggering costs internal to the individual. Excessive energy drain in one activity or sphere of work reduces the reservoir or pool of energy available for the exercise of other competencies in other settings.

The availability of energy is a function of the biological and psychological development of the individual. There is no known way of measuring or describing energy utilization; but despite its apparent vagueness, the concept that individuals have available a finite amount of energy to expend in adaptation to their environment is extremely fruitful in a theory of competence and learning.

The exercise of competence must be examined for its internal reference to the individual's energy utilization. The effectiveness of an action is to be judged in terms of both external outcomes and internal costs. Given outcomes of equal value, the one achieved with the least expenditure of energy is the more efficient and competent.

Learning for interpersonal competence may entail in large measure the realignment of conditions of energy utilization even if it does not involve immediately new kinds of behavior. But in terms of long-range development of individuals, increased efficiency in the use of energy implies a deepening and widening of expressed competence.

INTERPERSONAL COMPETENCE AND
CONTINUITIES IN HUMAN DEVELOPMENT

Any discussion of the process of learning for interpersonal competence implies that one has established a position on the determinants of interpersonal behavior. Two positions, not necessarily dichotomous, are available for consideration.

One position assumes that interpersonal behavior is a function of the forces acting on an individual from within and without. (Lewin, 1951) The time-space dimension relevant to this way of thinking is the here-and-now that defines the field within which forces are elicited. Change or learning requires a change in the forces acting on the individual: a change in the magnitude and direction of forces yields a resultant behavior different from a previous pattern.

A second position, one stressed in this study, centers on genetic or historical trends as relevant for understanding here-and-now behavior. An individual's behavior in the present represents continuity with his past. The meaning of the here-and-now behavior has a referent in the past as well as in the present. To be sure, the more the past dominates the present or determines the here-and-now, as against the requirements of the situation, the less adaptive the behavior will be. But in a real sense, past and present are interlocked —no person escapes his history. In essence an individual maintains a continuity in his personal development.

The findings and interpretations in Chapter 7 demonstrate to some degree how patterns of role-taking in groups can be explained in the light of continuities in personal development. The data showed, for example, how the Underchosen who experienced relative distance and coldness in their early family experience tended to create conditions, through their role behavior, of rejection and underreward. The Underchosen were engaged in a cycle of mistrust-rejection. Because of past experience the Underchosen tended to distrust the immediate situation and persons in it (i.e., a counter-dependent trend). This led to a form of competitive-aggressive behavior characterized by very rapid fluctuations between attack and withdrawal, making it difficult for others to engage them in interpersonal contact. This behavior secured rejection and underreward, reinforcing the initial sense of mistrust. In contrast, the Stars in relation to their developmental history worked on a cycle of reward-competence. Their expectation of a rewarding experience helped to evoke behavior designed to assure their anticipated rewards of achievement and self-esteem, along with esteem from others.

The practical difference these two hypotheses make to those whose professional interest is in the change of behavior are substantial. The change agent's theoretical framework determines whether he considers situational or individual change as strategic; the points of entry for intervention; relative emphasis on cognitive or emotional learning and relearning; the time dimension within which expected learning can occur; and other important considerations. The matter of orientation of the change agent is of no small significance in the process of change he attempts to implement.

To those interested in planned-change programs such as executive development, the concepts and findings of developmental theory will suggest that it is important to examine the places in the cycle of development where learning is rapid and where useful analogs may be sought for the implementation of change. Two learning phases in the life cycle contain some interesting parallels. One occurs during the so-called latency period of development and the second during adolescence.

The latency period falls roughly between the ages of 6 and 10 and is the phase of development marked by rapid learning of basic cognitive skills and content. The capacity to learn during this phase is dependent upon the recession of certain instinctive processes that were dominant in earlier developmental phases. Where the instinctive processes stay in the forefront of fantasy and activity, however disguised, there tends to be a failure in learning. In essence, the learning process of the latency period is predicated upon the existence of a *moratorium* in the instinctual development. (Erikson, 1959, p. 111) When the moratorium is well established internally, the learning process for the individual tends to be rapid and productive.

The second period which serves as a useful analog to the problem under consideration is that of adolescence. This period, too, is marked by rapid change but of another kind. The greatest change is biological and social. The individual matures sexually with the accompaniment of an increase in magnitude of the instinctual drives. Accompanying this change is a period of social experimentation characterized mainly by the emphasis on peer relations and withdrawal from parental control; role experimentation in highly ritualized forms; and highly unstable patterns of behavior, with rapid fluctuation in mood and action.

The behavior of the adolescent is understood best in the light of the social tasks facing him in anticipation of later life tasks. At the conclusion of the period of adolescence, the individual must make a series of significant decisions. He must choose a career and select a mate with whom to share a life of work, family, and community. The learning problem of the adolescent period is the establishment of a sense of identity in which occupational and sex roles take on paramount importance. (Erikson, 1959, p. 110) The experimental behavior of the adolescent in the service of identity formation is sanctioned by society and made possible by the establishment of a second moratorium in development. This moratorium is in the suspension of role responsibilities of the growing person in anticipation of his later full acceptance of the diverse and complex roles of adulthood.

It is significant to note the correlation between the existence of these two types of moratoria and the rapidity of experimentation and learning. It is significant also to note that the moratorium of the adolescent period is the last fully sanctioned period of experimentation. Beyond adolescence any dramatic developmental experience will depend upon an individual's self-declared moratorium.*

In the case of the individual's emotional learning during adult phases of development, the main type of moratorium that has social recognition as such is in the case where the person presents himself for help in the psychotherapeutic relationship. Within this highly specialized relationship rapid learning and experimentation can, potentially at least, occur. But this type of learning moratorium is available mainly for persons who either have experienced severe alienation from their social environment, or for whom the maintenance of their relationships proceeds at severe cost in pain and anxiety.

For individuals such as those who participated in the experimental sessions reported in this study, the moratoria that seem so essential for learning are difficult to establish. The individuals do not define themselves as sick or in the need of significant personal change, yet, for some, their requirements for interpersonal competence seem to call for a significant learning experience supported by their society.

It is in this context that one can profitably explore the learning process implied in programs of executive development, particularly those aimed at helping individuals improve their interpersonal competence.

INTERVENTION FOR INTERPERSONAL COMPETENCE

The third section of this chapter seeks to examine the problem of educational activity as a process of intervention in the course of the developmental history of the individual.

This problem takes on meaning in the light of the previous discussion of individual development and in the context of the moratorium as a prerequisite for learning and behavioral change. The problem, however, is complex. There is evi-

---

* Retirement is a phase in development that has received relatively little attention. This phase may also represent the imposition by society of a psycho-social moratorium on the individual.

dence to suggest that society's establishment of moratoria during latency and adolescence requires little conscious collaboration on the part of the individual. The person does not choose to engage himself with the practices of the moratorium. He does so under the effects of his own instinctual development, the unspoken collaboration of his parents with society, and the norms of his peer group.

An effective moratorium for the adult who is apt to participate in executive development activity does require his conscious collaboration. He has to define himself in a moratorium and not just enter a structure provided for him by authority figures in his work world. Without his conscious intent to enter into the moratorium, little by way of learning can be expected to occur.

In a sense, most executive development activities contain the elements of a moratorium. The executive removes himself from everyday responsibility. He leaves his physical surroundings and enters into a new setting for periods ranging from one or two weeks to several months. His role requirements shift markedly and the usual set of expectancies operating on him is temporarily, at least, halted. Yet he may choose to define himself and his situation in traditional terms —in other words he may refuse to declare the moratorium potentially available for him. The reasons for his refusal to engage in the learning process are many. He may feel little need for change or learning, especially if all his past work behavior has been rewarded. Or, he may find the prospect of change and learning too threatening and he therefore closes out whatever experimental possibilities are available to him.

The effects of an executive development program as an intervention in the individual's developmental process and the use of the experience as one for experimentation depend to a great extent on the individual's conscious intent. So far, little has been said about the types of interventions implied in various kinds of programs. Before returning to the implications of the participant's intent, a few observations about the structure and content of the programs as interventions may be in order.   These observations should also point to issues requiring substantial research in the future.

Following the lead of developmental theory one can see that for a program to have significance as an intervention in the continuity of development, adequate time within the moratorium is necessary.   This means that programs of short duration—say one or two months—can have relatively little effect on those individuals who need the help most.   Conversely, the short-term programs may provide the most help to those who are least in need of developmental help.   It would seem to follow, also, that programs that fail to create the conditions of a moratorium will have less effect than may be desired.   On-the-job experiences would seem to have less developmental efficacy than those settings where the individual is able to detach himself from current expectancies; the longer the time period, the more fruitful the learning possibilities.

Program activities in which the learning design places the individual in a predominantly passive role would seem less likely to provide the opportunity for meaningful experimentation.   The participant would need to engage himself actively in experimentation to optimize learning.   Paired with active experimentation is the necessity for feedback. Through description and interpretation of behavior, the individual can begin to see himself as he is in various interpersonal structures.   In terms of these design criteria, the use of the training groups as a didactic setting holds out much promise.*

Another aspect of the design of developmental experiences has to do with the relative emphasis on the emotional basis of interpersonal behavior as contrasted with cognitive struc-

---

* The work of the National Training Laboratory is significant in the use of the training group (Bradford et al., 1953).   For some of the problems attendant to the use of the laboratory method, see Bennis, 1962.

tures. The emotional basis assumes that much of existing interpersonal behavior of the individual is rooted in emotional attachments and meanings derived from his past experience. Learning therefore requires some re-experiencing of affects and identifying them with particular types of interpersonal structures. The emphasis here is emotional learning and relearning.

The cognitive approach emphasizes observation of events and the flow of interpersonal process external to the individual with the use of suitable cognitive frameworks to help the individual to structure observations. In this approach the individual has to bring sufficient maturity to the learning situation, avoiding especially the tendency to displace emotional meanings and fantasy on to the cognitive material.

Few learning designs are built exclusively on emotional or cognitive foundations. But by and large, training for interpersonal competence requires substantial emotional involvement as a precondition for learning. It avoids over-intellectualization, one of the problems frequently encountered in cognitive approaches.

Much significant thinking and research on the design of developmental programs is necessary to facilitate learning. For the concluding discussion, attention should, however, return to the theme of the individual and his definitions of learning in the continuity of his personal development.

CONCLUSION

Earlier in this chapter, learning for interpersonal competence was presented within the framework of developmental theory stressing as a significant variable how the individual defines himself in a learning context. The most significant learning experience finds the individual utilizing a moratorium granted him and provided for him by society. For the adult executive, the moratorium, while possibly available in the form of a development program that takes him out of his daily routine, cannot exist apart from his conscious intent to declare a halt in his usual behavior patterns and to experiment. The effectiveness of a developmental experience such as is provided executives in "off the job" programs, may well depend on how he thinks about the learning setting even before he enters the new social reality. Does he choose to define himself into a moratorium or does he reassert the reality to which he is accustomed? Does he commit himself to experimentation or to detached observation and minimal personal involvement? Does he make himself available to feedback and new data or will he be inaccessible to new data? How an individual answers these and other questions will have strong import for his learning.

Given the significance of these questions that are answered in large measure in advance of participation in a developmental experience, it is surprising how little attention is given to helping a person prepare to make the most of a learning opportunity. One hears all too frequently of the selection of executives for participation in an educational program with little collaboration on his part. (Chowdhry, 1962) It would seem that attention needs to be given not only to selecting for participation those executives most prepared to use the help available in executive programs, but also to provide the initial help that enables an individual to use the experience to the utmost. This preliminary help can be made available through counseling in which the main emphasis is on exploring why the person is going off to a development program and what range of alternatives are open to him for defining himself in the learning situation. This type of counseling may help individuals to create, on a small scale, the kinds of moratoria most conducive to their personal development.

In conclusion, recognition should again be given to the nature of the discussion in this chapter. The ideas presented here were outside the strict limits of the experimental research and sought to explore implications of this study for development of administrators. The justification for this exploration lies in the basic premises of this research and its findings. The study concentrated on understanding patterns of role-taking in problem-solving groups and tried placing these behavioral patterns within the context of individual development. Insofar as programs in executive development aim at the problem of interpersonal competence, they must take account of what the theory of human development suggests regarding how and why people behave as they do in interpersonal settings, as well as of the natural conditions under which significant change and learning can take place.

APPENDICES

APPENDIX A

Research Operations and Methods

THE EXPERIMENTAL SITUATIONS will be described in the first section of this appendix. The criteria for the selection of the four experimental groups will be described next. The third section will describe the attributes of the individuals who made up the four groups. The final section will describe in general the methods of data collection and processing used by the researchers, while later appendices will expand on methodological problems in greater detail.

DESCRIPTION OF THE EXPERIMENTAL PROGRAMS

Each of the experimental situations was a unit of research activity requiring from four to six hours of work by the participants and the researchers. The six-hour units, involving three of the four groups, included one and a half to two hours for cocktails and dinner. The four-hour unit was administered in two sections, five days apart. These latter experiences took place at the company where the group was employed, during working hours. The first half of their program consisted of completing questionnaires at their workplaces in their departments. During this time they were symbolically and actually isolated by the posting of "guards" to hold off interruptions by persons from outside the department and to intercept incoming telephone calls. The second half of their program took place in a classroom, in the company's training building. At that location, physically isolated from outside disturbance, they viewed the filmed case situation, engaged in their group discussion, and completed some short questionnaires about the discussion experience. In all four programs, from two to four researchers were observers and the discussions were recorded on tapes.

The other three groups were studied at the Harvard Business School. One of the groups had cocktails and dinner with the researchers *before* completing their questionnaires and engaging in their discussion. The other two groups arrived at about 4 o'clock on two Wednesday afternoons, worked on questionnaires for about 45 minutes, saw the film, engaged in their discussion for 40 minutes, spent about 10 minutes completing their questionnaires about the discussion experience, then recessed to have cocktails and dinner with the research team. After dinner they completed another hour of questionnaire work and engaged in a discussion with the researchers about the objectives of the program. Exhibit A.1 is a copy of the memorandum sent to the persons invited to participate in these last two groups, which explained to them the program of activities. These two groups had been invited as individuals and consisted of persons from different organizations. It was intended that they should not be acquainted with each other or the researchers prior to the experimental situations.

Exhibit A.1

Memorandum Mailed to Persons Invited to Participate in Groups 3 and 4

HARVARD UNIVERSITY
GRADUATE SCHOOL OF BUSINESS ADMINISTRATION
GEORGE F. BAKER FOUNDATION

Soldiers Field
Boston 63, Massachusetts

This memorandum outlines briefly the schedule for the experimental group program in which we would like your participation.

The purpose of the experimental group program is twofold: (1) to help us in our current research work on executive roles and group activity, and (2) to provide a way for us to discuss our research plans and findings with interested executives. In attending the session, our hope is that you will find the meeting stimulating and of educational value. In turn, we will be adding to our research data through your participation.

The schedule for the afternoon and evening is as follows:

3:45 P.M.	Meet at the Harvard Business School Alumni Center, Room A. (See enclosed map.)
4:00–5:00 P.M.	Complete first set of tests and questionnaires.
5:00–5:40 P.M.	Group discussion of a filmed case problem. (12 members in the group)
5:40–5:50 P.M.	Complete second set of questionnaires.
5:50–7:30 P.M.	Cocktails and dinner.
7:30–8:00 P.M.	Complete third set of questionnaires.
8:00–9:30 P.M.	Discussion of the research plans, previous findings, and implications.

While the above schedule is not excessively taxing, the session will be long and perhaps tiring after your work day. In addition, some of the questionnaires ask you to provide us with some personal information. Needless to say, this material is confidential, but necessary for our study.

Executives who have worked with us in previous group experiments found them to be of value in part because the work required in completing the questionnaires added to their understanding of the research questions and approaches, and because the experience introduced them to ideas which were related to their personal career concerns.

The sequence of these programs was as follows:

May 14, 1959. Group 2 * consisted of a management-staff team from a
medium-sized manufacturing concern. They met at the
Harvard Faculty Club for dinner with the researchers,
then went to the Audio-Visual department at the Harvard Business School for the remainder of their program.
15 persons participated.

June 25, 1959. Group 1 * completed their questionnaires along with the
rest of the engineers, technicians, and secretaries in their
department, at their company. 39 persons completed
questionnaires.

June 30, 1959. Group 1 met for their discussion in a classroom of their
company's training building. 13 out of the 39 persons in
the department participated in the experimental group.

May 18, 1960. Group 3 met in the lounge of the Alumni Center at the
Harvard Business School. They had cocktails in this
same location but went to a private dining room in
Kresge Hall for dinner. They returned to their original
meeting place for the balance of their program. 11 persons participated.

June 15, 1960. Group 4 met under the same circumstances and followed
the same schedule as did Group 3. 13 persons participated.

Following the showing of the filmed case, but prior to their
discussions, the participants in Groups 3 and 4 were given name
tags to wear and large name cards which they placed in front of
themselves for the duration of the discussion. The participants
in all groups were given dittoed memorandums listing three suggested topics for discussion. All groups were told that the researchers were interested in observing and studying how various
kinds of groups go about solving the same problem. The groups
were given no additional structure by the researchers. No
leaders were appointed, no leadership structure or operating procedures were suggested, and no suggestions about problem-solving
procedures were given. The task was thought by the researchers
to be self-contained, to require no resources from outside the
group, and to be capable of being completed during the 40 minutes allowed. A description of the filmed case situation will be

* Group numbers were assigned according to the typology described in the
next section and hence violate their chronology in the first two instances.

found in the "Introduction for Scorers" in Appendix F. The suggested topics for discussion for Groups 1 and 2 were:

1. What *did* Frank do wrong?
2. Did Frank make the correct choice for promotion?
3. How might Frank have done a better job of talking with Harry?

For Groups 3 and 4 the last question was changed to read:

What, if anything, should Frank do now?

These various behaviors and symbols produced by the research team no doubt had some effects on the predispositions of the participants toward the research programs. In addition, the ways in which they were invited to participate may also have been important, with respect both to their anticipations and to the self-selection aspect of the ultimate population analyzed. Some persons who could have participated in the first two groups and some persons who were invited to participate in the last two groups did not do so. In the known cases where this happened, the nonparticipants were said to have had conflicting engagements.

Most of the members of Groups 1 and 2, the groups drawn from their organizations, had been in prior contact with one of the researchers in connection with his research and training activities. He proposed the participation of these groups in the experiments to their formal leaders and explained the programs to some of the other persons involved. Hence their acceptance and participation were related to both their prior relationships with that researcher and the influence pattern in their own social organizations. Ostensibly, participation was voluntary.

The cooperation of the participants in Groups 3 and 4 was secured in a different manner. The research team received the names of potential participants from persons known by the researchers from prior contacts. These contact persons were known to have expressed interest in the research studies in Organizational Behavior being undertaken by the Harvard Business School. They suggested persons they knew, either from their own organizations or from other organizations, who might be interested in participating in the experiments. Some of the contact persons were willing to do so themselves, although only one of them was invited. Letters were mailed to the prospective participants inviting them to take part in one of the programs. These letters were addressed to the individuals personally at their places of work or at their homes. Exhibit A.2 is a copy of the contents of the letter.

Exhibit A.2
Specimen Copy of Letter of Invitation
Sent to Prospective Participants

HARVARD UNIVERSITY
GRADUATE SCHOOL OF BUSINESS ADMINISTRATION
GEORGE F. BAKER FOUNDATION

Soldiers Field
Boston 63, Massachusetts

Mr. John Smith   June 3, 1960
Jones Company
Lexington, Massachusetts

Dear Mr. Smith:

We learned through Bill Clark that your work and interests are such that you might enjoy joining us for dinner and participating in a one-evening research and educational program which we are conducting on Wednesday, June 15. This program is described in the enclosed announcement.

This program is part of an experiment in combining research activity with a chance for the researchers to explain its purposes to interested executives. If, after reading the announcement, you would like to join this small group of about twelve people, would you please indicate so on the enclosed reply memorandum and return it to us in the addressed envelope provided. If for any reason you are unable to attend, would you indicate this on the reply memorandum, so that we may complete our plans as soon as possible.

A map is also enclosed to help you locate our meeting place. If you have any questions about this program, please call us.

Sincerely yours,
A. Zaleznik
D. Moment

AZ:mvl

Acceptance of the invitations required that the individuals be able to leave their jobs early on the day of the program. Hence those who accepted were in positions of relative autonomy in their jobs and/or had the support of their superiors. In addition, the research program was of sufficient interest for them to give up the evening voluntarily.

These descriptions of the background of the experimental situations help to define some attributes of the experimental population which will be relevant for comparisons of the findings of this study with the findings of others, and which might help explain some of the findings within this population. All the participants were from work situations and had career concerns such that research in small groups was of personal relevance to them. They were all relatively autonomous and/or were encouraged by their superiors in this interest in organizational research. The participants in Groups 3 and 4 were especially likely to be concerned about their future careers and were likely to have already been relatively successful. They all worked in the greater Boston area, and their organizations had evidenced some involvement in the active research of the academic community. Some of their firms were directly involved in research activity, and some of their jobs were involved in research regardless of the main purposes of their organizations. Some of the participants (3 or 4 out of the 52) were graduates of the Harvard Business School. Some were or had been actively engaged in small group training activities in and outside of their own companies. Hence the experimental programs were appropriate to their own professional interests, the discussion experience was in line with their expectations, and the task problem itself, the short human relations case film, was congruent with the concerns of their everyday occupations.

CRITERIA FOR THE SELECTION OF THE EXPERIMENTAL GROUPS

The 1959 experiments involving Groups 1 and 2, while within the ultimate interests of the researchers, were looked upon as explorations in a different form of data gathering. They were in marked contrast to the field study techniques with which the researchers were most familiar. Hence these two groups were chosen primarily on the basis of availability. When these two experiences were reviewed the researchers concluded that the idea of a research package was sound. The participants had been involved with interest in the proceedings and had shown little hesitation at the length and depth of the questionnaire completion task. Further, a preliminary analysis of the data from Group 1, which had previously been studied by one of the researchers using field methods, gave support to the idea that the behaviors in the experimental situations tended to simulate the relationships among the participants in their everyday work settings. For example, the persons who talked the most with other persons in the discussion were likely to be the persons whose behavior on their jobs was observed to involve the most conversation with other persons. This indication of a simulation effect highlighted the likelihood that the behavior in these two groups reflected the social structures of the groups in their home settings.

In reviewing the differences and similarities between these first two groups, two group attributes were thought to be important. The simulation effect would reflect the existence of some degree and quality of social organization among the participants in both groups prior to the experiments. Differences between the emergent group processes of the two groups indicated an important difference between them. For example, Group 1 appointed as moderator the person who had the most ambiguous status in the group, and he behaved like a moderator, doing little more than recognizing people and making a point of apologizing when he did express his own opinion. In contrast, the person appointed as moderator in Group 2 was one of the persons with the clearest, least ambiguous status, and he attempted to influence as well as to moderate, adding his opinions without apology. It was concluded by the researchers that at least part of the differences in the emergent behavior patterns of the two groups could be attributed to the difference in their Status Mixtures. Group 1 consisted of engineers and their supervisor, representing two adjacent statuses at the middle level of the organizational hierarchy. Group 2, on the other hand, was a vertical cross-section of the hierarchy from the middle level to the top, including a technician at one extreme and the company's chief executives at the other. The two group attributes which were finally thought to be important were the Degree of Prior Social Organization, which was similar for both groups, and the Status Mixture, which was very different between the two groups.

By arranging these two group properties as independent attributes of groups, a fourfold typology was suggested:

		STATUS MIXTURE	
		PEER-LIKE	HIERARCHICAL
DEGREE OF PRIOR	High	Group 1	Group 2
SOCIAL ORGANIZATION	Low	Group 3	Group 4

It was decided deliberately to select Groups 3 and 4 to fill out this typology. The Degree of Prior Social Organization would be kept to the minimum by inviting persons who had not known each other prior to the experiment. The spread in Status Mixtures would be approximated by selecting Group 3's participants to be within a relatively narrow age range and selecting Group 4's participants to span a wide range of ages and to include women. With this design in mind, and with some minor modifications to the research package, the experiments with Groups 3 and 4 were planned and executed during the spring of 1960.

The typology represented an attempt to control for various conditions which previous researchers had found to have important effects on the determination of behavior. Prior Social Organization could be expected to exert an influence on individual behavior through norms unique to the history and identity of the particular group (Homans, 1950; Zaleznik, 1956). The Status Mixture could be expected to influence behavior through the effects of cultural prescriptions for behaviors between statuses (opa. cit.). By reverse reasoning, it was expected that unique *individual* predispositions would have the strongest effect, compared to the effects of norms and cultural prescriptions, in situations where there had been no group history and hence no norms to start out with, and in situations where the statuses were either so similar or so ambiguous as to provide few cues on which cultural prescriptions could operate.* The arrangement and selec-

---

* David McClelland developed the use of the Thematic Apperception Test to measure need Achievement and need Affiliation. These measures were used in this study. He proposed that in order to study the effect of individual motivation on behavior the subject should be put into an ambiguous, unstructured situation calling for new behavioral responses. (Atkinson, 1958,

tion of the groups within this typology was intended to establish some baselines for the control of the differential effects of Social Organization, Culture, and Personality as determinants of behavior.

From this design, analysis could have proceeded in two directions. One theme would have sought for comparisons among *four* populations, or samples, in order to determine empirically how Social Structure, Culture, and Personality interact to determine social behavior. For a valid and reliable comparison, this kind of analysis would have required more groups of each type and additional controls for the *quality* as well as degree of Prior Social Organization. Groups would have to be classified as to the *kinds* of norms they featured as well as measured for the relative strengths of those norms. It would further require a careful delineation of the kinds of status cues which are relevant objects of cultural prescriptions. This interesting and promising direction of analysis could have become a major project in itself.

A second direction of analysis could have proceeded from the design of the selection of groups. It would assume that in the aggregated population of 52 persons any effects attributable to the differences between the groups would tend to cancel each other out. For example, if in half the groups (n = 26) there was a positive correlation between the statuses of individuals and their participation rates, while in the other half (n = 26) there was a negative correlation between these two variables, then in the aggregate (n = 52) there would tend to be no correlation between the two variables. In this case it would be appropriate to infer that the relationship, where it was found in the two subpopulations, was attributable to characteristics of the groups rather than

p. 31). The researchers expected that since Group 3 came the closest to meeting these conditions, it would manifest the least social control of behavior. The reverse actually occurred in certain respects. In that group there was the strongest association between status and participation of any of the groups. One explanation is that the *absence* of clearly visible cues for differentiation, such as represented by the relatively narrow age span in Group 3, made it necessary for people to express their statuses in their participation. The acts of eliminating the ambiguities behaviorally established the statuses of the participants. Group 4, featuring the widest status mixture, yielded the least relationship between status and participation. Perhaps the fact that they could see visible age and sex differences eliminated the necessity for behaving out status relationships.

to more general characteristics of individual behavior in social situations. Similarly, when effects were found in the aggregated population (n = 52) they need not be attributed to unique attributes of one group situation, although the common attributes of all four groups would be relevant for interpreting the association.

This second direction of analysis was followed in this study. The effect of the selection of groups was to construct samples from four identifiable types of group situations. These four types are similar to kinds of groups which may be encountered in natural organizational settings but are not intended to be representative of a statistical distribution of such groups. They are intended to represent a mixture of possibilities within a specified range. The compositions of the four groups and the total population are described in the following section.

The size of the groups ranged from 11 to 15 participants. This magnitude, more than 10 but less than 18, was selected because the researchers thought that within this range persons could withdraw more comfortably, if that was their desire, than in smaller groups where low participants tend to be noticed, and could participate more freely than they could in larger groups. Since the groups were intended to start out without formal leadership or procedural structure, it was thought that within this range of sizes there would be reasonable options available for structure. As it turned out, Groups 1 and 2 selected moderators at early stages of their discussions, while in Groups 3 and 4 the question of formal structure was never brought up. The researchers felt that in smaller groups there would be less likelihood for formal structures to be developed while in larger groups there would be more likelihood for formal structures to be adopted. It was anticipated that within the 10 to 18 range the question of formal structure could go either way. The actual numbers who participated in the groups, 13, 15, 11, and 13, resulted from the decisions of the persons invited, which were beyond the control of the researchers.

COMPOSITION OF THE FOUR GROUPS

Group 1 consisted of 11 engineers, a foreman over technicians, and the supervisor of the department from which these men came. In contrast to Group 1, of which 12 out of 13 members shared a common room for their workplaces, Group 2 consisted of management and technical people who did not, as a group, share a common workplace location in the company building, although they interacted with each other intermittently during the work day. Their job statuses ran from President down to Technician, including Sales, Production, Research, and Engineering functions. On their Background Information Questionnaires, these men indicated their current occupations as follows:

OCCUPATION	NUMBER WHO INDICATED THIS OCCUPATION
Salesman-Owner-Engineer	1
Major Executive	2
Minor Executive	1
Physicist	1
Engineer	3
Salesman-Engineer-Chemist	1
Salesman	1
Foreman	3
Accountant	1
Technician	1
Total	15

Although both Groups 1 and 2 were natural groups in a general way, they were strikingly different kinds of groups. Group 1 worked together in time, space, and function, while it would be more correct to say that the participants in Group 2 encountered each other frequently on their jobs than to call them a work group.

It was learned informally from the participants in Groups 3 and 4 that one pair in each group had previously met socially, but in both cases of prior acquaintance there was no work or social relationship other than the brief encounters. One member of Group 4 was acquainted with the researchers prior to the experiment. No other members of Groups 3 and 4 reported any acquaintance with each other or the researchers prior to the experiment. The distribution of the participants in Groups 3 and 4 among job functions is shown in Table A.3.

Table A.3

JOB FUNCTIONS OF INDIVIDUALS IN GROUPS 3 AND 4

	NUMBER OF CASES *		
JOB FUNCTION (FROM BACK- GROUND INFORMATION QUESTIONNAIRE)	GROUP 3	GROUP 4	TOTAL GROUPS 3 & 4
Production	1½	3½	5
Sales, advertising, or promotion	1	2	3
Control, accounting	4	0	4
Finance, credit	0	0	0
Engineering	1	1½	2½
Research	½	2	2½
Personnel, industrial relations, train- ing	2	3	5
Other or not specified	1	1	2
Total	11	13	24

* Cases which indicated two functions were assigned ½ count in each of the two functions.

The design intent was that Groups 1 and 3 should be peer-like, consisting of people of similar status level while Groups 2 and 4 should consist of wide ranges of statuses. Tables A.4 through A.10 summarize the distribution of the measured social attributes of individuals in the four groups. It is evident that Group 1 was peer-like in salary (the measure of job status) and sex only; its members covered a wide range of ages, seniority and experience, and education levels. With respect to age and experience Group 3 had narrower, more peer-like distributions than did the other groups. Although both Groups 1 and 3 were more peer-like than were Groups 2 and 4, they were peer-like in different ways. Differences in the ranges, where thought to be relevant, may be seen by comparing the outlined areas on Tables A.4 through A.10.

Table A.4

SALARY DISTRIBUTIONS *

NUMBER OF PERSONS IN EACH SALARY INTERVAL FOR EACH GROUP

SALARY INTER-VALS, $:	Under 5,500	5,500–6,500	6,500–7,500	7,500–9,000	9,000–11,000	11,000–13,000	13,000–15,000	15,000–20,000	over 20,000	TOTAL
Group 1, NP†	0	3	7	2	1	0	0	0	0	13
Group 2, NH†	1	2	1	4	2	2	1	0	2	15

SALARY INTER-VALS, $:	Under 5,000	5,000–7,500	7,500–10,000	10,000–15,000	15,000–20,000	20,000–30,000	30,000–40,000	over 40,000	TOTAL
Group 3, SP†	0	2	1	7	0	1	0	0	11
Group 4, SH†	0	1	3	3	4	1	1	0	13

* The salary intervals used for Groups 3 and 4 were different from those used for Groups 1 and 2 because different questionnaire forms were used with the two pairs of groups. The groups were rescored on the scale shown in Appendix D for the later analysis.

† N = natural groups having prior social organization

S = strangers, having no prior social organization

P = peer-like status mixture

H = hierarchical status mixture

Table A.5

AGE DISTRIBUTIONS

NUMBER OF PEOPLE IN EACH AGE INTERVAL

AGE:	Under 26	26–30	31–35	36–40	41–45	46–50	51–55	over 55	TOTAL
Group 1, NP*	0	3	2	2	2	1	2	1	13
Group 2, NH*	2	1	4	2	3	2	1	0	15
Group 3, SP*	0	3	6	2	0	0	0	0	11
Group 4, SH*	1	1	3	4	2	2	0	0	13
TOTAL	3	8	15	10	7	5	3	1	52

* See note to Table A.4.

Table A.6

SENIORITY DISTRIBUTIONS †

NUMBER OF PEOPLE IN EACH SENIORITY INTERVAL

SENIORITY:	Under 3 mo.	3 mo.– 6 mo.	6 mo.– 1 yr.	1–3 years	3–5 years	5–10 years	10–15 years	15–20 years	over 20 years	TOTAL
Group 1, NP*	0	0	1	2	0	3	3	1	3	13
Group 2, NH*	0	0	0	3	1	6	4	1	0	15
Group 3 †, SP*	0	0	1	2	4	3	1	0	0	11
Group 4 †, SH*	0	0	1	3	2	3	1	2	1	13
TOTAL	0	0	3	10	7	15	9	4	4	52

* See note to Table A.4.

† Seniority = length of time with present company. For Groups 1 and 2 this may be a rough measure of the groups' historical life, but since members of Groups 3 and 4 came from different companies, seniority has no such relevance to the experiments. For them, however, seniority might be a rough measure of job security and/or stability.

Table A.7

EXPERIENCE † DISTRIBUTIONS

NUMBER OF PEOPLE IN EACH "YEARS OF WORK EXPERIENCE" INTERVAL

YEARS:	0–2	3–4	5–7	8–10	11–13	14–16	17–19	20–24	over 25	TOTAL
Group 1, NP*	0	2	1	1	1	3	1	1	3	13
Group 2, NH*	1	1	0	1	4	2	2	3	1	15
Group 3, SP*	2	1	2	5	1	0	0	0	0	11
Group 4, SH*	2	0	2	0	2	2	3	0	2	13
TOTAL	5	4	5	7	8	7	6	4	6	52

* See note to Table A.4.
† Years of work experience—lower limit of present age interval minus upper limit of "Age at Which First Became Self-Supporting" interval.

Table A.8

EDUCATION LEVEL DISTRIBUTIONS

NUMBER OF PEOPLE IN EACH EDUCATIONAL LEVEL CATEGORY

LEVEL:	Less than High School	Some High School	High School Graduate	Some College	College Graduate	Some Grad. Work	Master's Degree	Doctor's Degree	TOTAL
Group 1, NP *	1	1	1	2	7	0	1	0	13
Group 2, NH *	0	0	0	4	3	3	2	3	15
Group 3, SP *	0	0	0	1	4	2	4	0	11
Group 4, SH *	0	1	0	0	0	7	5	1	13
TOTAL	1	1	1	7	14	12	12	4	52

* See note to Table A.4.

Table A.9

RELIGIOUS PREFERENCE AND NATIONAL ORIGIN DISTRIBUTIONS

NUMBER OF PEOPLE IN EACH CATEGORY

RELIGIOUS PREFERENCE: BIRTHPLACE OF PATERNAL GRANDFATHER:	JEWISH	CATHOLIC	PROTESTANT		TOTAL
			FOREIGN	U. S.	
Group 1, NP *	0	4	2	7	13
Group 2, NH *	1	6	6	2	15
Group 3, SP *	3	1	2	5	11
Group 4, SH *	1	2	4	6	13
Total	5	13	14	20	52

* See note to Table A.4.

Table A.10

MALE-FEMALE DISTRIBUTION

	MALE	FEMALE	TOTAL
Group 1, NP *	13	0	13
Group 2, NH *	15	0	15
Group 3, SP *	11	0	11
Group 4, SH *	11	2	13
Total	50	2	52

* See note to Table A.4.

Although these tables have been arranged to demonstrate similarities and differences between groups, the following statistics descriptive of the entire population of 52 persons may be derived:

ATTRIBUTE	MEDIAN	MODE
Salary	$7,500–$11,000	$5,000–$7,500 *and* $10,000–$15,000
Age	35	31–35
Seniority	5–10 years	5–10 years
Experience	11–13 years	11–13 years
Education	Some graduate work	College graduate
Ethnicity	—	Protestant, Grandfather U. S. born

In addition to these attributes, those derived from the selection process are also relevant. The population was ostensibly interested in career development and in small group research. It was from the Greater Boston area. The organizations in which the participants worked tended to be involved in some way with the academic and research communities and condoned the kinds of interest associated with participation in the experiments. The participants tended to be friendly toward the research program. Many, if not most, of the participants expected to be informed of the findings of this study, and some indicated continuing interest in their later incidental contacts with the researchers.

METHODS OF DATA COLLECTION AND PROCESSING

This section will be presented in two parts:
The Measurement Instruments
The Data Processing Methods
The measurement instruments will be introduced and explained briefly. Appendix C contains specimen copies of the questionnaire forms. Appendix D presents the operational derivations of the various scores. Appendix E presents the backgrounds, the reliability results, and the indicated validities of the motivation measures. Appendix F includes the manuals used by the persons who scored behaviors and discusses the backgrounds of the behavior measures.

THE MEASUREMENT INSTRUMENTS

The Thematic Apperception Test

The Thematic Apperception Test, abbreviated as the TAT, has been administered and scored in many different ways. In this study it was administrated as a pencil and paper test in the form shown in Appendix C. The instructions asked the subject to write imaginative stories about ambiguous pictures. Each picture and its story were treated as a separate unit, both in the writing and in the scoring. A trained scorer, using the system and methods developed by Professor David McClelland and his colleagues (Atkinson, 1958), read and scored each story for achievement and affiliation content. The individual's total score on the achievement content of all four stories was called his need Achievement score, abbreviated as nAch, and the score on affiliation content was called need Affiliation, abbreviated as nAff.

The assumption that these scores are systematically related to the motivational states of individuals has been confirmed by researches done by McClelland and his associates (see Appendix E). It was found that these conditions were highly situational, in that an individual's scores would vary when he was put into different kinds of situations. As far as this study is concerned, the test was completed by the subjects under conditions which were externally, objectively identical for each group.

The Individual Preference Study

This questionnaire was developed by Professor Zaleznik as the Executive Preference Study. It was administered to Group 2 under that title, but the title indicated on the forms was changed to Individual Preference Study for the other three groups. The questionnaire was developed from the needs categories suggested by Maslow (1954) in an attempt to explore empirically some of his theoretical propositions and some alternative theoretical ideas. Maslow's theory, oversimplified for economy of statement, proposes a hierarchy of needs including physiological needs, safety, belonging, esteem, and self-actualization needs, which tend to require satisfaction *in that order,* over an individual's life-time. According to this view, for example, a person could be concerned with satisfying esteem needs only after having satisfied his membership needs. When one level of need is satisfied, the person will tend to seek satisfaction of higher level needs when the opportunities to do so are available. A contradictory idea based on reinforcement theory would hold that a person tends to continue to pursue those rewards which he has found to be attainable in the past. From this viewpoint, a person who has successfully satisfied a need, such as belonging, would be expected to tend to *continue* to pursue activities wherein he could obtain further belonging satisfactions. One general question to which the development of the Individual Preference Study was addressed was: Under what conditions does individual motivation follow hierarchical organization based on sequential satiation of needs and under what conditions does it follow a reinforcement pattern? The Preference Study asked the subjects to indicate their rank ordering of preferences among three statements presented together. Twenty sets of three statements made up the question-naire. Each statement was constructed to represent a rewarding experience obtainable within or around the subject's organizational life. Five kinds of rewards were addressed: Self-Actualization, Job-Intrinsic, Belonging (Membership), Status, and Economic. Each of the three statements presented in each of the twenty sets consisted of different kinds of rewards. Of the sixty statements presented, twelve were in each reward category. The questionnaire form and the breakdown of the statements into reward categories are shown in Appendices C and E.

The subjects' scores on the five categories in the Preference Study consisted of the total of the rank order numbers assigned by the subject to all of the statements in each category, low scores then indicating high preference (or low rejection) and high scores indicating low preference (or high rejection). Each person had a preference profile of five scores, the total of which was 120 points. These scores were processed in the manner indicated in Appendices D and E to yield relative preference or rejection scores for each person compared to each other person, on each of the preference categories.

Comparison of Preference Scores to TAT Needs Scores

The Preference Scores, of which Belonging Preference, Status Preference, and Job-Intrinsic Preference were analyzed in this study, were operationally different from the needs scores, nAch and nAff, in ways which are important for the understanding of the design of this study. The Preference Scores were derived from operations which classified responses according to the conscious, manifest, "face-value" meanings of the statements ranked by the subjects. The stimuli, in the form of predesigned statements, were given to the subjects and they indicated and were scored on their reactions to these various kinds of stimuli. In contrast, the TAT gave them ambiguous pictures as stimuli, and they wrote their stories around whatever pattern of themes was invoked in them by the pictures. The subjects originated their themes and the scorer then analyzed the content of their stories for the occurrence of references to achievement and affiliation themes. Their nAch and nAff scores then reflected the unconscious or preconscious, latent, thematic meanings in the stories written by them. The Preference Scores reflect conscious, manifest concerns while the nAch scores reflect latent concerns. The instruments are therefore assumed to measure not only differentiation in *kinds* of concerns, but also to represent two different *levels* of motivation.

The Behavior Measurement Instruments

Three overlapping behavior measurement systems were developed by the researchers for this study. A fourth system, Interaction Process Analysis (IPA), was used to obtain additional data and as a basis for evaluating the results of the three new systems. Interaction Process Analysis was developed by R. F. Bales and his colleagues (Bales, 1951 and 1955) and was used in a large number of published studies on small groups. His system was relatively established and standardized, but was mainly predicated on a theory about group processes. The newly developed systems borrowed substantially from theories about interpersonal behavior and individual behavior in social situations (especially Schutz, 1958, and Leary, 1957) as these latter theoretical points of view were closer to the objectives of this study than were theories of group process. Since the Interaction Process Analysis system is adequately explained elsewhere (Bales, 1951), the following discussion will be limited to the three new systems.

Interval Event Analysis (IEA)

This system defines the time-space units used as the basis for the other two new systems, which are called Event Content Analysis (ECA) and Interpersonal Behavior Analysis (IBA). Interval Event Analysis involves relatively mechanical operations on the part of the scorer which are thought to be so reliable as to not require special procedures in order to establish empirical standards of reliability. The first step in this system was to subdivide the proceedings of each meeting into equal time intervals. This was done by using a stop watch while listening to the tape recordings and marking the end of each interval on the typescripts on or between the corresponding typed words or sounds. Twelve-second intervals were used. This particular time interval was selected accidentally. At first the counter on the tape recorder was used, the turnover of two numbers seeming to be appropriate in that it could include the comments of only one speaker or, in periods of fast activity, could include as many as five or six speakers. However, it was found that the counter was geared to the spindle rotation rather than tape speed, so that as the tape unwound toward the center of the spool, the counter turned over faster. Two counts took twelve seconds at the beginning of a full 7-inch spool of tape but took only about five seconds near the end. Although the particular choice of the twelve-second time interval was relatively arbitrary, and the use of longer or shorter intervals might conceivably change some of the ultimate measurements, the balance of the operations in this analysis were so mechanical and devoid of judgmental requirements that anyone who wished to investigate the effects of using longer or shorter intervals could easily do so.

Having established the time intervals as the basic quantitative units for analysis, the next step was to identify events within these units. The basic event was the sound of a person's voice. Each person in a group was either heard or not heard during each interval. Work sheets were prepared for each group, listing the identity of the participants at the left end of each row, and including one row for events where the speaker was not identifiable. Columns corresponded to intervals, of which there were approximately 200 for each 40-minute discussion. For each interval a count was entered for each speaker. Comparisons of the total number of counts for each participant gave a relative participation rate, which correlated .95 with the Total Acts scored for each person by the IPA (Interaction Process Analysis) scorer. The number of intervals during which a person spoke *and* others spoke was taken as an index of interaction. Other similar indices were derivable from this system. For example, the number of other persons who shared time intervals with a participant would be an index of his range of interaction. Since the behavior measures were found to be correlated substantially with participation,* the participation score was used in the denominator of

* The correlations (Pearsonian r) between *raw participation score* from IEA (Interval Event Analysis) and the raw behavior scores which were ulti-

certain ratios to indicate the occurrence of certain behavioral events relative to participation. For example, the number of times a person showed agreement would be expected to depend in part on how much he talked and in part on other attributes. Comparing persons on their ratios of agreement to participation would then compare them on the attributes other than participation.

Event Content Analysis (ECA) and Interpersonal Behavior Analysis (IBA)

The scoring manual included in Appendix F gives the instructions for both Event Content Analysis (ECA) and Interpersonal Behavior Analysis (IBA). In content analysis, the events were classified by what the person *said,* while in behavior analysis events were classified by what the person *did.* An example of the former would be Agreement, a kind of event identified by such words as "I agree," "Right," "Sure," etc. An example of the latter would be Interruption, which would be identified by the timing of changes in speakers and the tones of their voices. The time interval was used as a reference unit to avoid the problem of identifying the beginning and end of a particular kind of event, as well as separating compound events into units. For example, the comment "I agree, that's right" might be arbitrarily scored as one or two Agreement events unless there were an established convention. The convention was to score "event-intervals." If the "I agree, that's right" comment(s) occurred entirely within a single interval, one Agreement event count was made for the speaker. If the comment(s) straddled two intervals, two Agreement counts were recorded for the speaker. The identity of the speaker also served to identify an event, so that as many events of

---

mately converted to ratios and used in the study, were as follows, all positive in direction:

Category	Produced by Participant	Received by Participant
Agreement	.63	.61
Disagreement	.45	.68
Personal Recognition	.54	.31
Competitive Questions	.39	.54
Interruption	.75	.63
Shared Intervals	.94	

a particular kind could be scored for an interval as there were *different* speakers during the interval. However, only one event of each kind could be scored for a particular participant during an interval. He could score one each of Agreement, Disagreement, Competitive Questions, etc. during one interval, but could not score more than one count on any one kind of event during that interval.

The effect of these procedures was that the three systems constituted behavior sampling instruments. The scores derived from the systems were probabilistic indices. A Participation score of 100 for a person in a group which lasted 200 intervals would mean that if an observer listened during a random interval the chances were .50 that he would hear the person speaking. An Agreement *ratio* of .40 would mean that if a person were talking during an interval, chances were .40 that he would agree with someone during that interval. For the ultimate analysis, participants were ranked within their groups on each measure, and the rankings were dichotomized into High and Low classes as near to the median as possible. The interscorer reliabilities shown in Appendix F for the ECA and IBA systems were computed using raw scores and ratios. The effect of the dichotomizing classification would be to increase the reliabilities.

Two objectives limited the design of the ECA and IBA scoring systems. First, it was desired that the behavioral cues which were scored as the various kinds of events should be as simple, unambiguous, and devoid of a need for psychological interpretation as possible, and should be easily identified by group observers and participants themselves. It was thought that in order for a variable to be strategic for action, the ultimate user should be able to make the necessary identifications and rough measurements himself.

A second limitation imposed upon the design of the systems concerned the training of scorers. The ultimate goal was that no formal training sessions should be required. In practice, the scorers other than one of the researchers were given the scoring manual, the discussion typescripts, the tape recordings, and some scoring matrix forms, and were asked to go to work with these materials. The researcher answered their questions, and met with two of them together for one hour after they had read the manual and scored one group. No more than one hour of verbal instruction was devoted to each of the other five scorers. The scorers who used both the ECA and IBA systems on all four group discussions estimated that the entire scoring job took about 20 hours per scorer. This did not include adding up the total of the row and column tallies on the scoring matrices, which was done by one of the researchers.

The Post Meeting Reaction Questionnaire (PMR)

This questionnaire was mainly a sociometric instrument, although it included two questions about the subject's satisfaction with the discussion. Most of the questions asked the subject to evaluate the participants in his group, including himself, on several criteria, in the cases of Groups 1 and 2, or to name persons in their groups who stood out on certain criteria in the cases of Groups 3 and 4. The criterion questions were the same for all four groups but the evaluating operations were different between the two sets of groups. Individuals were scored on the number of persons who chose them as standing out on each criterion. To make high evaluations in Groups 1 and 2 comparable with being chosen in Groups 3 and 4, the four or less persons receiving the top evaluations on each of the Group 1 and 2 participants' questionnaires were considered to have been "chosen" by that participant, a procedure which was consistent with the findings of sociometric studies and which was tested for equivalence.*

* From D. T. Campbell, "A Rationale for Weighting First, Second, and Third Sociometric Choices," in the *Sociometry Reader,* J. L. Moreno (Ed.), 1960:

"Good standard procedure is to disregard the order of choice and use the total of all mentions. This procedure will provide a perfect rank correlation with any differential weighting formula if the first, second, and third choices, when analyzed separately, rank the nominees in the same order. With large numbers of judges this will indeed be the case in many situations, or near enough so that differential weighting is meaningless."

In Groups 3 and 4 in this present study, where the PMR form asked the subjects to name persons who stood out on the various criteria, an average of 3.24 names were listed under each of five questions for which comparable figures were desired in the cases of Groups 1 and 2. Since there were many tied ratings at the upper ends of the evaluation scales provided for Groups 1 and 2, it was decided that it would seem reasonable to assume that the top rated four or less persons could be inferred to be "chosen" without violating the meaning of the instrument. If five or more people were tied at the top

The choice criteria were quality of ideas, guidance, congeniality, and leadership for all four groups, and, in addition, attractiveness as a work associate and attractiveness as a social acquaintance for Groups 3 and 4, the persons who had not known each other prior to the experiments. The exact wording of the questions is shown on the PMR forms included in Appendix C.

The PMR was not a standardized instrument as were the TAT and the Preference Study. A vast body of sociometric research, as well as research using sociometric techniques in addition to other methods, has indicated the usefulness of the method, and has contributed to the understanding of the dynamics of the social choice process (e.g., Moreno, 1960, pp. 471–567; Zaleznik et al., 1958; and Bales, 1955). For the purposes of this study it is relevant to point out that the choices made in such questionnaires are functions of both the external attributes of the other persons, their behaviors and physical appearances, and the internal perception-evaluation process of the choosers. The naming of persons as good on ideas, for example, depended both on the behaviors of the persons and on the internal perception mechanisms and implicit criteria for "goodness of ideas" of the persons choosing. The attributes of the choosers, as described, had much to do with what they "saw" other people doing in the groups and with their internal criteria for evaluation. It is likely that these particular 52 persons had been involved in a variety of social situations, both within organizational settings and in other settings, and thus applied standards of performance which had experiental bases of comparison. This characteristic of these groups differentiates them from groups of children, students, institutionalized cases, etc., where the choice mechanisms may be assumed to have been more strongly determined by internal senti-

---

rating, no choices would be counted. If two were tied at the top and three were tied at the next rating, two choices would be inferred, etc. In an equivalence test with the 15 cases in Group 2, where the ranks of the group members on the total evaluation scores received were compared with their ranks on inferred choices received, rank order correlations of .87 and .71 were obtained for the Ideas and Guidance questions. When the scores were dichotomized into High and Low classes on both systems, cross-classifications showed

1	7
6	1

and

1	6
6	2

distribution on the Ideas and Guidance questions respectively.

ment systems than by comparisons against experienced external realities. This proposition does not assume that the 52 persons were more rational or logical in their choices than were the subjects of other studies, but does assume that they had a larger frequency and variety of social experiences upon which to base comparative evaluations.

The Background Information Questionnaire (BIQ)

Three different forms of the Background Information Questionnaire were used with the four groups, the same form being used with both Groups 3 and 4. This form is included in Appendix C along with the other questionnaire forms.

The data from the BIQ which was used in this study included age, salary, seniority, work experience (derived from current age and the age at which the subject first became self-supporting), education level, ethnicity (derived from birthplace of father's father and family religious affiliation), sex, and early experiences in the family of origin.

Other Questionnaires Included in the Research Programs but Not Used in this Study

Although description of the questionnaires not used is irrelevant to the main purposes of this study, mention of them will help indicate the potential of the idea of the research package. These questionnaires were administered in addition to those already discussed.

Group 1 completed questionnaires on Departmental Relationships and Company-wide Relationships, both of which were intended to gather data on social relationships, including work and nonwork interactions, activities, and friendships. Group 2 completed a questionnaire on Group Relationships which had the same purpose, while similar kinds of questions were included in the Background Information Questionnaire given to Groups 3 and 4.

Groups 1 and 2 were given a Job Attitudes questionnaire which was intended to gather information about the individuals' satisfactions with their jobs and their feelings about their supervisors along the dimensions of support, autonomy, and influence.

Groups 3 and 4 completed a questionnaire entitled Career Satisfaction and Development which asked questions about their satisfactions with their jobs and with their personal career development.

The California F-scale was given to Groups 3 and 4 in a form entitled Personal Opinion Survey. This questionnaire was developed in the study published as *The Authoritarian Personality* (Adams et al., 1950; Christie and Jahoda, 1954; Rokeach, 1960). The subjects indicated their agreement and disagreement with items which stated beliefs found to be associated with authoritarianism as defined by that study. Although the results of this questionnaire were used in the early stages of the analysis for this present study, they were not presented in the main text of this book because the associations which were found were weak, the total number of cases involved was small (24), and the theoretical background of the instrument was not closely related to the designed purposes of this study although it is relevant to the purposes of the larger research project of which this study is part. The results by Role Type were as shown in Table A.11.

Table A.11

Role Types and F-Scale Scores

ROLE TYPE	NUMBER	F-SCALE SCORE	
		HIGH	LOW
Total	24	10	14
Stars	6	2	4
Technical Specialists	4	3	1
Social Specialists	8	3	5
Underchosen	6	2	4

TS vs. Others: Fisher's Exact $p = .16$

There were a few reactions by the subjects while taking the F-scale questionnaire which indicated that the manifest content of its items did not seem to be relevant to the interests implied by the other questionnaires. Although some of the subjects indicated that they felt it was "out of field," they and the others completed it and the results would have been usable if it had been completed by all 52 participants.

The Data Processing Methods

Following the collection of data in the four situations described earlier through the use of the measurement instruments also described, it was necessary to organize the data in a manner suitable for subsequent analysis. At that stage of the research project the direction which this present study would take was not yet certain. It was decided to prepare the data for computer processing by recording it in a form suitable for punching onto cards. This involved decisions on which measures should be used, what kinds of indices should be constructed, and how scales should be constructed to convert raw scores and ratios to one- or two-digit numbers. Appendix D, entitled Sources and Derivations of Scores, gives the result of these decisions for the 39 measures and indices used in the analysis for this study. These measures and indices represent a reduction, resulting from preliminary analysis, from a total of approximately 125 such scores which went into the earliest stage of analysis.

The 125 scores for each of the 52 cases were fed into a computer program which yielded 11 different intercorrelation matrices. Each score was correlated with each other score in 11 statistical groupings. Each of the four experimental groups yielded one set of correlations. In addition, Groups 1 and 2, 3 and 4, 1 and 3, 2 and 4, 1 and 4, 2 and 3, and all four groups were aggregated for separate matrices. The resulting matrices were then analyzed informally to find how the various measures were associated with each other, both within the bodies of data and between the bodies of data. In this way it was possible to evaluate the relationships between the various indices and their component measures and thus empirically reduce the number of scores processed by eliminating those which seemed to be highly correlated with others. The objective of this kind of analysis was to select measures and indices which were *independent* of each other. A second kind of analysis at this stage compared the relationships between scores within one body of data, such as the predisposition measures, with scores in other bodies of data, such as the behavior measures, to eliminate those measures which did not discriminate. The objective of this kind of analysis was to select pairs of measures which were *interdependent*. These two kinds of analysis constituted a rough kind of cluster analysis or factor analysis, which, although being methodologically impure, allowed the researcher to become more familiar with the intricacies of the relationships than he would have been had he run the data through a formal, computer-programmed factor analysis. The correlations of the measures used in this study with each other are shown on the Intercorrelation Matrix in Appendix G.

The reduction of scores to manageable proportions went beyond the number used in this study. The final stages of analysis started with a set of only 28 scores for each participant, but as the study progressed other scores were brought back into the analysis. Another reduction, that of dichotomizing all scores into High and Low classes, relative to the groups in which the subjects participated, further simplified the analytical task.

A separate computer analysis was run on the ECA and IBA behavior scores in order to assess the interscorer reliability of these specially developed systems. Five persons had scored the IBA categories and six persons had scored the ECA categories. The arithmetic mean of the several scorers' scores for each participant on each behavior measure was taken as the best estimate of what the scores should have been, and each scorer's scores were then correlated with the mean scores to assess the degree of agreement between each scorer and the mean on each behavioral measure. The results of this interscorer reliability analysis are presented in Appendix F. Of 102 computed reliability figures, distributed among 6 scorers on 19 different scoring categories, the distribution was as follows:

COEFFICIENT OF CONTINGENCY*	NUMBER OF OCCURRENCES
.90 and over	8
.85–.89	51
.80–.84	30
.79 and lower	13
Total computed	102

The highest Coefficient of Contingency was .92, the lowest was .59.

* The Contingency Coefficient was computed as a by-product of a computer program which printed scatter diagrams of the individual scores against the average scores, which could be visually examined to establish cutoff points for collapsing scoring intervals. The Contingency Coefficient is not directly comparable to the usual Pearsonian r Coefficient of Correlation, but shares the feature that 1.00 indicates perfect association and 0 indicates no association. See Siegel, *Nonparametric Statistics*, p. 196 ff.

APPENDIX B

Measurement of Associations Among Variables

STATED IN ANALYTICAL terms, the purpose of this study was to describe a structure of relationships among variables in a system. This appendix will describe how relationships were identified, their directions determined, and their strengths assessed. These assessments will be based upon the prediction activity model and the resulting Lambda statistic explained by Goodman and Kruskal (1954). The workings and meanings of this model will be explained here by using some of the data which appears in the text.

In the process of analyzing PMR data for Chapter 2, the researcher asked the question, "How were the perceived role components (Ideas, Congeniality, and Guidance) related to each other?" This question had to be made more explicit before the question could be answered analytically. Persons had been assigned into High and Low classes on each of the measures (numbers of choices received on each of the three criteria were the measures of perceived roles) depending upon the rank position of their scores in relation to the others *in their own groups*. The top half were called High, the bottom half were called Low. The median score defined the half-way point; hence about 50% of the persons were in each class. If there were no relationship between the measures, then knowing that a person was classified High on Ideas would be of no value in guessing, or predicting, whether he was classed High or Low on the other measures. In the "no effect" model, where measures are assumed to be independent of each other, the distribution of cases among cross-classification cells

Table B.1

No Effect Model, Two Measures, Each Dichotomized into Classes Containing Equal Numbers, Total N = 52

		MEASURE B CLASSES		
		LOW	HIGH	TOTAL
MEASURE A CLASSES	High	13 (Cell HL)	13 (Cell HH)	26 (High on A)
	Low	(Cell LL) 13	(Cell LH) 13	(Low on A) 26
	Total	(Low on B) 26	(High on B) 26	(Total cases) 52

is a function of the numbers in each of the classes. Table B.1 illustrates a no-effect model constructed from a cross classification on measures where each class contained the same number, 26. The no-effect cell expectancy may be computed from the formula:

$$\text{Cell expectancy} = \frac{\text{Cell's Row Total} \times \text{Cell's Column Total}}{\text{Total Number of Cases}}$$

$$\text{Cell HL} = \frac{\text{Total High on A} \times \text{Total Low on B}}{\text{Total Cases}} = \frac{26 \times 26}{52} = 13$$

Using the same marginals (total numbers of cases in each class, 26 in the example shown in Table B.1), the greatest possible degree of association would be represented by tables reading

0	26
26	0

or

26	0
0	26

. In the first of these examples, all persons scoring High on one measure would also have scored High on the other measure (and Lows would have scored Low). This direction of association will be called positive. In the second example, all of the cases scoring High on one measure would have scored Low on the other measure. This direction of association will be called negative.

The activity model used for computing the degree of association between two measures starts with someone wanting to guess or predict the scoring class of a case drawn at random from the population on a particular measure, say measure B on Table B.1. He is assumed to know the number (or proportion) of cases in each of the measure B scoring classes, 26 Highs and 26 Lows. From this information *only,* he would flip a coin for each prediction, and would expect to be in error in his predictions 50% of the time. The next step in this model is to compute the value of having *additional* information about the randomly drawn case before making the prediction. From Table B.1 it can be seen that it would be of no value to know the A class of the case because this knowledge does not change the prediction odds. High A's are just as likely to be Low B's as to be High B's, etc. But if

a measure C yields a

0	26
26	0

cross-classification with B, then

knowledge of the C class of a case completely eliminates the uncertainty as to what its B class will be. All High C's are also High B's, and all Low C's are also Low B's. In this instance, knowledge of the C class of the case has the maximum value that any additional information could have, given the prediction activity model, and the number 1.00 will be assigned to the value of measure C for predicting measure B (or the value of B for predicting C). In the no effect model on Table B.1, the predictive value of these measures in relation to each other is 0.

The degree of association between two measures is, according to this activity model, the value of one of the measures for predicting the other. Since this relationship is not always the same in both directions, as it was in the examples, it is necessary to specify the direction of the prediction activity, and three possibilities are available for doing this:

PV_{AB} = the value of knowing A for predicting B.
PV_{BA} = the value of knowing B for predicting A.
MPV = Mutual Predictive Value, assuming that A will be known when B is predicted and B will be known when A is predicted, and that the activity will involve predicting from A to B half the time and from B to A the other half of the time.

In the examples cited above, $PV_{AB} = PV_{BA} = MPV_{AB} = 0$, and $PV_{AC} = PV_{CA} = MPV_{AC} = 1.00$. Predictive value is defined as the proportional *reduction in the probability of error* resulting from having the additional information, compared to the probability of error in the absence of the additional information. These computations will be illustrated with the PMR example used to introduce the problem. Table B.2 presents the data which will be discussed.

From inspection of the tables shown on Table B.2 it appears that each of the measures is positively related to each other measure (High's on one measure were likely to be High on the other measure), and that it would be of some value to know the scoring class of a randomly drawn case on one measure before predicting its scoring class on another measure. The value of the additional information would lie in the consequent reduction in the probability of predictive error.

Having the class totals only (25 Highs and 27 Lows on *Ideas* and *Guidance,* and 28 Highs and 25 Lows on *Congeniality*), a predicting person would guess that a randomly drawn case from this population would be in the class which numbered 27. He would be in error on $\frac{25}{52}$, or .48 of such draws. If he wanted to guess the Guidance class of a randomly drawn case and was given its Ideas class, the new probability of error would be computed as follows. On $\frac{25}{52}$ of the drawn cases he would be told that the case was High on Ideas, he would predict that the case was High on Guidance, and would be in error on $\frac{7}{25}$ of such cases. On $\frac{27}{52}$ of the draws the case would be Low on Ideas, he would guess Low on Guidance, and would be in error $\frac{7}{27}$ of such cases. His probability of error given the Ideas class is thus $\frac{25}{52} \times \frac{7}{25} + \frac{27}{52} \times \frac{7}{27} = \frac{14}{52} = .27$. His reduction in the probability of error attributable to knowledge of the Ideas class is $.48 - .27 = .21$, which represents a $\frac{.21}{.48} = .44$, or 44% reduction in the probability of error. The value of Ideas for predicting Guidance is then identified as $PV_{IG} = .44$. In this instance $PV_{GI} = .44$ also, and $MPV_{IG} = .44$. By similar computations, $MPV_{IC} = .12$ and $MPV_{CG} = .28$. Of the three relationships, that between Ideas and Guidance was the "strongest" (i.e., of the greatest value) and that between Ideas and Congeniality was the "weakest" (i.e., of the least value). The interpretation of these findings along with others is presented in Chapter 2.

This kind of analysis, computing the predictive value of cross-classified dichotomous measures, was used in the development of the material in Chapter 2. A slightly different kind of analysis

Table B.2

RELATIONSHIPS AMONG PERCEIVED ROLE COMPONENTS:
PMR CHOICES RECEIVED ON IDEAS, GUIDANCE, AND
CONGENIALITY, NUMBER OF CASES IN EACH
CROSS-CLASSIFICATION

	TABLE B.2A	CHOICES RECEIVED ON GUIDANCE		
		LOW	HIGH	TOTAL
CHOICES RECEIVED ON QUALITY OF IDEAS	High	7	18	25
	Low	20	7	27
	Total	27	25	52

	TABLE B.2B	CHOICES RECEIVED ON CONGENIALITY		
		LOW	HIGH	TOTAL
CHOICES RECEIVED ON QUALITY OF IDEAS	High	10	15	25
	Low	15	12	27
	Total	25	27	52

	TABLE B.2C	CHOICES RECEIVED ON CONGENIALITY		
		LOW	HIGH	TOTAL
CHOICES RECEIVED ON GUIDANCE	High	8	17	25
	Low	17	10	27
	Total	25	27	52

NOTE: The unequal numbers in the High and Low classes resulted from having ties at the median scores. In all cases Highs were separated from Lows as close to the median position as possible, with an arbitrary preference for having a smaller number of Highs than Lows in those instances where two possible division points were located equidistant from the median.

based upon the same kind of predictive activity model was used as a basis for the other chapters. This variation involves the four role types identified in Chapter 2. The question upon which the analysis of role types was based was, "Does knowing the Role

Type of a randomly drawn case help (i.e., reduce the probability of error) in predicting the scoring class of the case on various measures?" Table B.3 presents the format of the role analysis tables.

Table B.3

EXAMPLE OF FORMAT OF ROLE ANALYSIS TABLES

ROLE TYPE	NUMBER OF CASES IN ROLE TYPE	PERCENT OF CASES IN EACH ROLE TYPE WHO WERE HIGH ON PARTICIPATION
All Types (Total)	52	48%
Stars	15	80
Technical Specialists	10	30
Social Specialists	12	33
Underchosen	15	40

The predictive activity model used to read Table B.3 would work as follows.

GIVEN:

1. Someone wants to find a case which scored High (or Low) on participation.
2. He has access to the information presented in Table B.3.
3. He has the option of drawing a case from any of the role types.

QUESTIONS:

1. Does the role typology and distribution have any value to him?
2. From which role type will he draw? How does the measure differentiate among the role types? Does one type stand out from the others, do they seem to be similar in pairs, or is there no (or little) apparent differentiation?

ANSWERS (from the example in Table B.3):

If cases were drawn from the undifferentiated population, the predictor would be in error on 48% of his draws. From the above table, his "best bet" on a single draw would be to draw from among the Stars and predict a High Participant. He would then be in error only 20% of such draws. If he wanted to find a Low, he would draw from among the Technical Specialists and be in error 30% of such draws. The Social Specialists were similar to the Technical Specialists in the likelihood of finding a High Participant, but the Underchosen were closer to the population proportion, indicating that the effective interaction between attributes of the role types and Participation is weaker for that type, compared to the others.

It will be unusual to find instances where the proportion of Highs in a role type could exactly equal the proportion of Highs in the population both because of the exact percentage that was scored High on the various measures and because of the relatively small numbers in each role type. For example, if the population proportion High on a measure happened to be 50% and there were no relationship between the measure and a role type numbering 15, the percent High in the role type would still have to be either 47% or 53% merely because of the number of cases involved, with the result that a predictor would do better drawing from the role type than from the undifferentiated population. Since the numbers in the types and the dichotomization processes can have an effect on the outcome of using the predictive model, it is important to consider the numbers involved as well as the percentages in interpreting this kind of table.

From the format of Table B.3 another kind of analysis may be done, reversing one aspect of the prediction activity model. The predictor might want to predict *to the role type* from knowledge of the scoring class of a case on a measure. For example, if a case is known to be a High Participant, what is the best bet as to its role type? This cannot be assessed from the percentages given on Table B.3, but requires that the percentages be converted to numbers, as follows:

ROLE TYPE	NUMBER IN ROLE TYPE	NUMBER HIGH ON PARTICIPATION
Stars	15	12
Technical Specialists	10	3
Social Specialists	12	4
Underchosen	15	6
Total	52	25

On the basis of the numbers in each type (15, 10, 12, 15), Stars and Underchosen are the best bets as to the types of a randomly drawn case. Knowing that a particular case was a High Participant makes Star the best bet, so that the additional information serves to narrow the alternatives rather than to indicate a change of bet from the "no additional information" condition to the condition of knowing the Participation score class of the case.

The differences between the kind of inferences which may be drawn from variations of the predictive activity model identify a potentially important categorization of inferences. A relationship between measures or variables may literally have Predictive Value, in that a consequence may be predicted from a prior measure, or may have Diagnostic or Postdictive Value, in that a prior condition may be diagnosed (i.e., predicted backwards) from a consequence, or it may have value in both directions. Since the major part of this study is analysis of perceived role types (a consequence) according to the activity model where the "prediction" runs backwards, from consequence to prior condition, the main tone of the analysis is diagnostic. The above example of an analysis running from a prior measure (Participation) to a consequence (Perceived Role Type) demonstrated that the role typology could be predictively, as well as diagnostically, useful in relation to some of the measures.

The limitations and qualifications built into the analysis model result in the necessity to qualify the inferences to be drawn from the findings of this study. To specify the qualifications with each statement would result in problems for both the writer and the reader. These complications may be avoided by stating that *all* of the inferential statements are so qualified and limited, whether or not the qualifications are explicitly stated in each instance.

In the tables in the chapters following Chapter 2, the predictive value indices were not computed for each table. From direct inspection of the proportion of Highs in each role type, and a comparison of these proportions with the population's proportion of Highs on the particular variable, it is possible to assess the relative predictive values. This was done in the example of Participation in the discussion above. As an aid to readers who wish to assess the statistical significance of the findings, in which case the population of 52 would have to be thought of as a sample of 52, the probabilities of the results having occurred "by chance" are indicated below the tables and in the text. These probabilities were computed from Chi Square analysis and Fisher's Exact probability formulas (Siegal, 1956).

APPENDIX C

Questionnaire Forms

THE FOLLOWING PAGES contain copies of the questionnaires from which some of the data for this study was obtained. The experimental programs included some questionnaires which were not used in this study. Some of the questionnaires which were used for the study were administered in different forms to different groups. The schedule of questionnaire forms administered to the four groups is shown on Table C.1, which also identifies those forms which are included in this appendix.

EXPLANATION OF DIFFERENCES IN FORMS

1. *Individual Preference Study*

The Individual Preference Study, which is included in this appendix in the form used with Groups 3 and 4, was entitled Executive Preference Study when used with Group 2. (The sequence of the experimental group programs was 2, 1, 3, 4.) The word "Executive" was changed to "Individual" for the other groups because it was known that Group 1 contained individuals (engineers) who might not aspire to executive positions, and it was felt that the word "Executive" might influence responses in the direction of cultural prescriptions for what executives *ought* to prefer. In addition, certain of the statements related to status rewards were revised in order to present more reasonable possibilities to the engineers in Group 1. For example, Group 2 (the management team) and Groups 3 and 4 were confronted with the statement, "To be invited to join a select top executives' luncheon group." On the form used with Group 1, the engineering group, this statement was revised to read, "To be invited to

Table C.1

(Forms included in this appendix are indicated by italicized words.)

DERIVED MEASURES	GROUP 1 JUNE 1959	GROUP 2 MAY 1959	GROUPS 3 AND 4 MAY AND JUNE 1960

Data used in this study:

need Achievement and need Affiliation	*Test of Imagination* (*Thematic Apperception Test*) All groups used the same form.		
Belonging, Status, and Job-Intrinsic Preferences	Individual * Preference Study, Form 6–59	Executive * Preference Study, Form 5–59	*Individual Preference Study*, Form 5–60
Role perceptions, evaluations, and satisfaction	Post Meeting Reaction * Questionnaire, Form 5–59		*Post Meeting Reaction * Questionnaire (PMR)* Form 5–60
Status factors	Background Information * Questionnaire		*Background Information Questionnaire*, Form 5–60
	Form 6–59	Form 5–59	

Data NOT USED in this study:

Role behaviors on the job		Group Member Activity Questionnaire	
Satisfaction and Supervisors' behavior	Job Attitudes		Career Satisfaction and Development
	Form 6–59	Form 5–59	
Work and Non-work activities and interactions	Departmental † Relationships	Group † Relationships	
	Company-wide Relationships		
Authoritarianism			Personal Opinion Survey (F-scale)

* See accompanying text for explanations of the differences between the forms of the questionnaires.

† Friendship choice data from Group 1 and nonwork interaction data from Group 2 were used for one exhibit (Table 2.6) in Chapter 2.

join a luncheon group consisting of key people in the company." Other changes of this nature were as follows:

GROUPS 2, 3, AND 4	GROUP 1 (ENGINEERS)
To receive a letter from the Board of Directors complimenting my work.	"Board of Directors" changed to read "top management."
To be invited to speak to a group of college seniors on the importance of my work and its career opportunities.	"College seniors" changed to read "high school seniors," because it was known that some members of Group 1 were not college graduates.
To get an invitation to join the Board of Directors of an important company.	To get an invitation to join a Committee of Advisors to an important community development project.

In addition to the change in title and in some statements, one other change was made in the Preference Study. The items were rearranged to avoid the bias that listing priority might introduce. This revised form was used with Groups 3 and 4. On this form, the order in which the items within the triads were listed was designed to avoid having any category of item listed in any one position more than in any other position. This would avoid the bias which might be introduced by having Status Reward items, for example, listed in second or third position more often than in first position.

A listing of the preference statements under the *a priori* categories of Self-Actualization, Job-Intrinsic, Belonging, Status, and Economic is included in Appendix E, along with some findings from unpublished research activities involving the Preference Study.

2. *Post Meeting Reaction Questionnaire (PMR)*

This appendix includes the PMR form used with Groups 3 and 4. The form used with Groups 1 and 2 included additional items which were later dropped from the questionnaire. The forms used with Groups 1 and 2 did not include the social attractiveness questions, "Work with" and "Know socially" because these groups existed before the experimental discussions. The questions included in the PMR for Groups 1 and 2 which were excluded for Groups 3 and 4 were as follows:

In many groups there are some people who regardless of how good their ideas are, seem to have strong *influence* on the final group decision. Their ideas and opinions seem to be accepted by the group without much question.

Will you please indicate your impression of the *amount of influence* that each person, including yourself, had in the meeting by circling the appropriate numbers on the scales. 1 indicates "not much influence"; 8 indicates "very influential."

	NOT MUCH INFLUENCE						VERY INFLUENTIAL
(Index)	1 2 3 4 5 6 7 8
(Mark)	1 2 3 4 5 6 7 8
	(etc.)

In many groups there are differences in the extent to which the various members agree or sympathize with the views of other members. Members tend to agree with some people more than with others.

Will you please indicate the extent to which you *agreed* with each of the other people in the discussion by circling the appropriate numbers on the scales. 1 indicates, "I tended to disagree with him"; 8 indicates "I tended to agree with him."

	I TENDED TO DISAGREE WITH HIM						I TENDED TO AGREE WITH HIM
(Index)	1 2 3 4 5 6 7 8
(Mark)	1 2 3 4 5 6 7 8
	(etc.)

There are sometimes differences between the way people act at meetings and the way they usually act outside the meeting.

Will you please indicate your impression of the extent to which each person's actions during the meeting seemed to be similar to his actions in other situations by circling the appropriate numbers on the scales. Please include yourself. 1 indicates that the person was "very much different" from usual at the meeting; 8 indicates that he was "very similar" to what he does outside the meeting.

		VERY MUCH DIFFERENT							VERY SIMILAR
(Index)		1	2	3	4	5	6	7	8
(Mark)		1	2	3	4	5	6	7	8
					(etc.)				

The PMR used with Groups 1 and 2 contained these additional items and called for a different evaluating method than was the case with Groups 3 and 4. Groups 3 and 4 were asked to *list the names* of people in a blank space provided (see the copy of the questionnaire), while the members of Groups 1 and 2 were asked to *evaluate each person* according to the instructions shown with the above items, and according to the following procedure printed on the cover sheet of their PMR forms:

The questions in the following questionnaire refer to the group discussion experience in which you have just participated. We would like your opinions on the participation of yourself and the other members during this meeting. Since this material is for research purposes only, and is completely confidential, please indicate your opinions as honestly as you can.

Eight of the questions refer to all of the people who took part in the discussion, including yourself. In order to help you answer the questions, we have prepared a list of the names of the participants on a card attached to this questionnaire. Following each question, there appears a series of numbered scales. If you line up the index mark on the name card with the index marks to the left of the scales, you will find that a scale will line up following each name. Each question will instruct you on how to use the scales.

We hope that you will find these questions interesting and will answer them as frankly as you can.

The way in which the PMR evaluations from Groups 1 and 2 were processed to make them comparable to the name listing procedure used by Groups 3 and 4 is explained in the subsection on the PMR in Appendix A.

3. *Background Information Questionnaire*

The form of the Background Information Questionnaire used with Groups 3 and 4 is presented in this appendix. Groups 1 and 2 were given different forms. The major differences in the forms were that Groups 1 and 2 were given separate questionnaires about social relations at work and away from work, while these questions were included in the Background Information form for Groups 3 and 4. Also, more questions related to deprivations and other childhood experiences were asked in the form developed for Groups 3 and 4.

The occupational categories used in the questionnaire were derived from the work of W. Lloyd Warner and J. Abegglen (see *Big Business Leaders in America,* New York: Harper & Brothers, 1955; and *Occupational Mobility in American Business and Industry, 1928–1952,* St. Paul, University of Minnesota Press, 1955).

The Test of Imagination (Thematic Apperception Test) form below was used with all four experimental groups.

TEST OF IMAGINATION *

Instructions—*Read carefully before turning the page.*

An important asset in any creative work is imagination—the capacity to think on your feet. This test gives you an opportunity to use your imagination, to show how you can create ideas and situations by yourself. In other words, instead of presenting you with answers already made up, from which you have to pick one, it gives you the chance to show how you can think things up on your own.

On the following pages you are to write out some brief stories that you make up on your own. In order to help you get started there are a series of pictures that you can look at and build your stories around. When you have finished reading these instructions, you should turn the page, look at the first picture briefly, then turn the page again and write a story suggested by the picture. To help you cover all the elements of a story plot in the time allowed, you will find four questions spaced out over the page. They are:

1. What is happening? Who are the people?
2. What has led up to this situation? That is, what has happened in the past?
3. What is being thought? What is wanted? By whom?
4. What will happen? What will be done?

Your over-all time for *each* of the 4 stories is only 5 minutes. So plan to spend only about a minute on each of these questions,

---

* The Test of Imagination is reproduced here with the permission of Professor David C. McClelland of Harvard University.

but remember that the questions are only *guides* for your thinking and need not be answered specifically in so many words. That is, the story should be continuous, not a set of answers to questions. Do not take over 5 minutes per story. You will be allowed only 20 minutes for the whole test, after you get started, although you may finish in less time if you like.

Do not worry about whether there are right and wrong kinds of stories to write because in fact any kind of story is all right. What you have a chance to show here is how you think on your feet, how quickly you can imagine a situation and write out a story about it. What story you write doesn't matter. So don't try to figure out exactly what is going on in the pictures. They are vague and suggestive of many things on purpose. Don't describe them. They are just to help give you an idea to write about.

Make your stories interesting and dramatic. Show that you have an understanding of human nature and can make up interesting stories about people and human relationships.

If you have read these instructions carefully and understood them, turn the page, look at the picture briefly, then turn the page again and write the story suggested to you by the picture. Don't take more than 5 minutes. Then turn the page, look at the next picture briefly, write out the story it suggests, and so on through the booklet.

[The pictures are presented here between pages 330 and 331. They were each followed by a page with the same questions:]

Work rapidly. Don't spend over 5 minutes on this story.
1. What is happening? Who are the people?

2. What has led up to this situation? That is, what has happened in the past?

3. What is being thought? What is wanted? By whom?

4. What will happen? What will be done?

When you have finished your story or your time is up, turn to the next picture. If you haven't quite finished, go on anyway. You may return at the end to complete this story.

The Individual Preference Study form below was used with Groups 3 and 4.

INDIVIDUAL PREFERENCE STUDY

You no doubt prefer some things more than others. Listed below are some things you have experienced or know something about. The list is divided into twenty sections. Each section contains three brief statements describing various experiences.

Which do you prefer? To find out, simply arrange the three statements in each section in the order in which you prefer what they describe.

Use the numbers 1, 2, and 3 to indicate this order. Put down a "1" beside the experience you prefer the most, and a "2" beside the experience you believe is the second most desirable. A "3" beside a statement indicates that you prefer the experience it describes least of all.

Do each section separately. And remember, there are no right or wrong answers. Your first impressions are the best.

1. a. _____ To move to a better community.
   b. _____ To go through an experience that opens up new and exciting possibilities.
   c. _____ To receive help on work problems from a friend.

2. a. _____ To begin a job that is interesting and stimulating.
   b. _____ To get a substantial life insurance policy paid for completely by my company.
   c. _____ To become honorary chairman of an important organization.

3. a. _____ To join a group of close associates for lunch.
   b. _____ To appreciate the meaning in a painting or piece of music.
   c. _____ To work by myself on an interesting work problem.

4. a. _____ To move to a better office.
   b. _____ To participate in group activities at work.
   c. _____ To work on a problem and prepare recommendations.

5. a. _____ To develop in myself new abilities and interests.
   b. _____ To handle easily my job responsibilities.
   c. _____ To receive a letter from the Board of Directors complimenting my work.

6. a. _____ To receive a new job title which involves expanding my department.
   b. _____ To have an opportunity for further personal development.
   c. _____ To receive a special money bonus.

7. a. _____ To spend time with my family.
   b. _____ To sell some personal assets for considerably more than cost.
   c. _____ To receive a strong invitation to present my views before an influential citizens' group.

8. a. _____ To complete a project on time.
   b. _____ To receive a letter from the Board of Directors complimenting my work.
   c. _____ To have an opportunity for further personal development.

9. a. _____ To receive an award from an important professional organization related to my work.
   b. _____ To do a job well, even though no one comments on it.
   c. _____ To receive increased participation in a profit-sharing plan.

10. a. _____ To help a newcomer to the department get settled.
    b. _____ To receive increased annual cash returns on investments.
    c. _____ To find new ways of expressing my capabilities in leisure time activities.

11. a. _____ To receive an option to buy stock at a price below the current market.
    b. _____ To be invited to speak to a group of college seniors on the importance of my work and its career opportunities.
    c. _____ To appreciate the meaning in a painting or piece of music.

12. a. _____ To get a substantial life insurance policy paid for completely by my company.
    b. _____ To become honorary chairman of an important organization.
    c. _____ To assist a person with whom I work closely when he has difficulty with a project.

13. a. _____ To discover suddenly a new approach to a long-standing and baffling question.

b. _____ To have a reunion with friends or family.

c. _____ To have an investment go up sharply in value.

14. a. _____ To receive a special money bonus.

b. _____ To discover suddenly a new approach to a long-standing and baffling question.

c. _____ To work by myself on an interesting work problem.

15. a. _____ To do a job well, even though no one comments on it.

b. _____ To get an increase in salary.

c. _____ To achieve greater sensitivity toward events and people around me.

16. a. _____ To appreciate even more customs and ways of living of persons whose backgrounds differ from my own.

b. _____ To begin a job that has more challenging work.

c. _____ To be a member of a small circle of close friends.

17. a. _____ To move rapidly through a series of complex work problems.

b. _____ To be invited to join a select top executives' luncheon group.

c. _____ To make new friends.

18. a. _____ To develop in myself new abilities and interests.

b. _____ To participate in group activities at work.

c. _____ To get an invitation to join the Board of Directors of an important company.

19. a. _____ To increase my holdings of securities in important companies.

b. _____ To talk about work interests with a close associate.

c. _____ To size up a new work problem rapidly and move toward conclusions.

20. a. _____ To be a member of a small circle of close friends.

b. _____ To find a way of tackling a difficult piece of work.

c. _____ To receive from the company a noncontributory pension plan with greater retirement income.

The Post Meeting Reaction Questionnaire form below was used with Groups 3 and 4.

Post Meeting Reaction Questionnaire

The questions in the following questionnaire refer to the group discussion experience in which you have just participated. We would like your opinions on the participation of yourself and the other members during the meeting. Since this material is for research purposes only, and is completely confidential, please indicate your opinions as honestly as you can.

We hope you will find these questions interesting and will answer them as frankly as you can, taking about 15 minutes.*

In many groups there are some people who, regardless of how effective their opinions are in the group, seem to have exceptionally *good ideas*. They frequently show a very good grasp of the problem and clear reasoning ability.

In the space below, would you please list the names of the people who you think presented the *best ideas* in the discussion?

In many groups there are some people who seem to *guide the discussion* and keep it moving effectively. They try to keep the group on track, suggest procedures to follow, tie together the members' contributions, and act as moderators.

In the space below would you please list the names of the people who you think did the most to guide the discussion?

In many groups there are great differences in the amount of *participation* by members. Some people speak more than others.

In the space below would you please list the names of the people who you think *participated* most in the discussion?

---

* Each question appeared on a separate page on the original questionnaire.

In many groups some people stand out clearly as *leaders,* no matter how one would choose to define leadership.

In the space below would you please list the names of the people who you think stood out as *leaders* during the discussion?

In many groups there are some people who add to the *congeniality and friendliness* of the meeting. They tend to be well liked by the members because they seem to show consideration for others.

In the space below would you please list the names of the people who you think added most to the *congeniality and friendliness* of the discussion?

A. In many groups there are wide differences in how satisfied each member is with the *group decision* or conclusion. Some members will like it, some will not.

> Please indicate how satisfied *you* are with the *decision* or conclusion reached in this meeting by circling the appropriate number on the following scale.
>
> | *Very* | | | | | | | *Very* |
> |---|---|---|---|---|---|---|---|
> | *Dissatisfied* | | | | | | | *Satisfied* |
> | 1 | 2 | 3 | 4 | 5 | 6 | 7 | 8 |

B. In many groups there are wide differences in how satisfied each member is with the way the group *operates.*

> Please indicate how satisfied *you* were with the way this group operated by circling the appropriate number on the following scale.
>
> | *Very* | | | | | | | *Very* |
> |---|---|---|---|---|---|---|---|
> | *Dissatisfied* | | | | | | | *Satisfied* |
> | 1 | 2 | 3 | 4 | 5 | 6 | 7 | 8 |

Which of the people who took part in the discussion do you think you would *enjoy working with* if you have the opportunity in the future?

Which of the people who took part in the discussion do you think you would *like to know better socially* if you have the opportunity in the future?

The Background Information Questionnaire form that follows was used with Groups 3 and 4.

BACKGROUND INFORMATION QUESTIONNAIRE

(17 pages—25 minutes)

In this questionnaire we would like to learn about you, your job, your background, and your family life. Some of the questions are followed by several answers and you are to check the answer or answers that apply to you. Some of the answers provided for you to check may not exactly fit your circumstances; in these cases you may write explanations in the margins or on the backs of the pages if you wish. Other questions have spaces in which you are to write in the answer. In some cases, special instructions appear with the questions. All of this information is for research purposes only and will be held in strict confidence. The questionnaire should take you about 25 minutes to complete.

Your present age:

6

25 or less	(1)
26–30	(2)
31–35	(3)
36–40	(4)
41–45	(5)
46–50	(6)
51–55	(7)
56–60	(8)
over 60	(9)

Sex:

7

male	(1)
female	(2)

Place of Birth:	*Yourself*	*Your Father*	*Your Father's Father*
	11	**12**	**13**
U.S.A.	(1)	(1)	(1)
Other *	(2)	(2)	(2)
* Please specify:			

What was the approximate population of your birthplace at the time of your birth?

14

Over 400,000 (*or a suburb of a city this size*)	(1)
100,000–400,000 (*or a suburb of a city this size*)	(2)
25,000–100,000	(3)
2,500–25,000	(4)
Rural or less than 2,500	(5)

8 Marital status:

single.................................... (1)
married................................... (2)
separated................................. (3)
divorced.................................. (4)
divorced and remarried.................... (5)
widower or widow.......................... (6)

9

10

Extent of schooling of yourself and your father. (Please check only the highest category.)

	Self	*Father*
	15	**16**
Less than high school..............	———(1)	———(1)
Some high school...................	———(2)	———(2)
High school graduate...............	———(3)	———(3)
Some college.......................	———(4)	———(4)
College graduate...................	———(5)	———(5)
Post-graduate study................	———(6)	———(6)

If you are a *college graduate* please answer the following questions. If not, please skip to the questions on page (3).

For college graduates:

Name of college or university awarding undergraduate college degree:

17

Please check:

Earned or borrowed *less than* 50% of total expenses while attending college. . . . . ——(1)
Earned or borrowed *more than* 50% of total expenses while attending college. . . . . ——(2)
G.I. Bill helped finance college expenses. . . . . . . ——(3)

If you have done graduate work:
Name of university awarding highest graduate degree:

Kind of (highest) graduate degree:

19

Master's. . . . . ——(1)
Doctorate. . . . . ——(2)

Please check:

Earned or borrowed *less than* 50% of total expenses while attending graduate school......————(1)
Earned or borrowed *more than* 50% of total expenses while attending graduate school......————(2)
G.I. Bill helped finance graduate school expenses ————(3)

20

Please indicate:

Undergraduate college major field

18

Arts, languages, humanities, etc........	————(1)
Biology, zoology, etc...................	————(2)
Social Sciences.......................	————(3)
Physics or chemistry..................	————(4)
Engineering..........................	————(5)
Business Administration..............	————(6)
Medicine............................	————(7)
Law.................................	————(8)
Other *..............................	————(9)

* Please specify ————

Graduate field

21

	————(1)
	————(2)
	————(3)
	————(4)
	————(5)
	————(6)
	————(7)
	————(8)
	————(9)

22

23

24

After becoming self-supporting, what occupation did you engage in?

(Please check the most appropriate category in each of the
4 columns) ⟶

OCCUPATION	When You First Became Self-supporting	5 Years * Later	10 Years * Later	15 Years * Later
	25	29	33	37
SELF-EMPLOYED:				
Worker—unskilled or semiskilled	(1)	(1)	(1)	(1)
Skilled worker or mechanic	(2)	(2)	(2)	(2)
Farmer: owner without paid help	(3)	(3)	(3)	(3)
Owner or manager with paid help	(4)	(4)	(4)	(4)
Salesman	(5)	(5)	(5)	(5)
Professional: doctor	(6)	(6)	(6)	(6)
lawyer	(7)	(7)	(7)	(7)
engineer	(8)	(8)	(8)	(8)
accountant	(9)	(9)	(9)	(9)
other (Please specify)	(x)	(x)	(x)	(x)
Other (Please specify)	(y)	(y)	(y)	(y)
	26	30	34	38
BUSINESS OWNER:				
Owner of business, sales under $50,000	(1)	(1)	(1)	(1)
sales between $50,000 and $100,000	(2)	(2)	(2)	(2)
sales over $100,000	(3)	(3)	(3)	(3)

EMPLOYED BY AN ORGANIZATION OR OTHER PEOPLE:

	27	31	35	39
Worker—unskilled or semiskilled............	____(4)	____(4)	____(4)	____(4)
Skilled worker or mechanic.................	____(5)	____(5)	____(5)	____(5)
Farmer: farm worker or small tenant........	____(6)	____(6)	____(6)	____(6)
tenant with paid help...........	____(7)	____(7)	____(7)	____(7)
Clerk or retail salesman....................	____(8)	____(8)	____(8)	____(8)
Salesman.................................	____(9)	____(9)	____(9)	____(9)
Foreman or supervisor.....................	____(x)	____(x)	____(x)	____(x)
Minor executive..........................	____(y)	____(y)	____(y)	____(y)
	27	31	35	39
Major executive...........................	____(1)	____(1)	____(1)	____(1)
Professional: doctor.......................	____(2)	____(2)	____(2)	____(2)
lawyer......................	____(3)	____(3)	____(3)	____(3)
minister....................	____(4)	____(4)	____(4)	____(4)
engineer....................	____(5)	____(5)	____(5)	____(5)
accountant..................	____(6)	____(6)	____(6)	____(6)
teacher.....................	____(7)	____(7)	____(7)	____(7)
other (Please specify)........	____(8)	____(8)	____(8)	____(8)
Military service (not as a career)...........	____(9)	____(9)	____(9)	____(9)
Military career...........................	____(x)	____(x)	____(x)	____(x)
Government service	____(y)	____(y)	____(y)	____(y)
	28	32	36	40
Other (Please specify).....................	____(1)	____(1)	____(1)	____(1)
STUDENT	____(2)	____(2)	____(2)	____(2)

* If you have not been self-supporting as long as the column indicates, leave blank.

Principal occupation of your father. (If father deceased, please indicate previous occupation.)

OCCUPATION	When You Were in Grammar School	When You Became Self-supporting
SELF-EMPLOYED:	**41**	**44**
Worker—unskilled or semiskilled	(1)	(1)
Skilled worker or mechanic	(2)	(2)
Farmer: owner without paid help	(3)	(3)
Owner or manager with paid help	(4)	(4)
Salesman	(5)	(5)
Professional: doctor	(6)	(6)
lawyer	(7)	(7)
engineer	(8)	(8)
accountant	(9)	(9)
other (Please specify)	(x)	(x)
Other (Please specify)	(y)	(y)
BUSINESS OWNER:	**42**	**45**
Owner of business, sales under $50,000	(1)	(1)
sales between $50,000 and $100,000	(2)	(2)
sales over $100,000	(3)	(3)
EMPLOYED BY AN ORGANIZATION OR OTHER PEOPLE:		
Worker—unskilled or semiskilled	(4)	(4)
Skilled worker or mechanic	(5)	(5)
Farmer: farm worker or small tenant	(6)	(6)
tenant with paid help	(7)	(7)

Clerk or retail salesman.....................(8) (8)
Salesman..................................(9) (9)
Foreman or supervisor......................(x) (x)
Minor executive............................(y) (y)

43   46

Major executive............................(1) (1)
Professional: doctor........................(2) (2)
lawyer...........................(3) (3)
minister.........................(4) (4)
engineer.........................(5) (5)
accountant.......................(6) (6)
teacher..........................(7) (7)
other (Please specify)............(8) (8)

Military service (not as a career)...........(9) (9)
Military career.............................(x) (x)
Government service.........................(y) (y)
Other (Please specify).......................(z) (z)

47

Principal occupation of your *father's* father. If you are married, the principal occupation of your *wife's* father, also.

OCCUPATION	Your Father's Father **48**	Your Wife's Father **52**
SELF-EMPLOYED:		
Worker—unskilled or semiskilled...........	(1)	(1)
Skilled worker or mechanic...............	(2)	(2)
Farmer: owner without paid help..........	(3)	(3)
Owner or manager with paid help....	(4)	(4)
Salesman................................	(5)	(5)
Professional: doctor.....................	(6)	(6)
lawyer.....................	(7)	(7)
engineer...................	(8)	(8)
accountant.................	(9)	(9)
other (Please specify)......	(x)	(x)
Other (Please specify)...................	(y)	(y)
BUSINESS OWNER:	**49**	**53**
Owner of business, sales under $50,000....	(1)	(1)
sales between $50,000 and $100,000....	(2)	(2)
sales over $100,000....	(3)	(3)
EMPLOYED BY AN ORGANIZATION OR OTHER PEOPLE:		
Worker—unskilled or semiskilled...........	(4)	(4)
Skilled worker or mechanic...............	(5)	(5)
Farmer: farm worker or small tenant.......	(6)	(6)
tenant with paid help..........	(7)	(7)

	50	54
Clerk or retail salesman	(8)	(8)
Salesman	(9)	(9)
Foreman or supervisor	(x)	(x)
Minor executive	(y)	(y)

	51	55
Major executive	(1)	(1)
Professional: doctor	(2)	(2)
lawyer	(3)	(3)
minister	(4)	(4)
engineer	(5)	(5)
accountant	(6)	(6)
teacher	(7)	(7)
other (Please specify)	(8)	(8)
Military service (not as a career)	(9)	(9)
Military career	(x)	(x)
Government service	(y)	(y)
Other (Please specify)	(z)	(z)

56 How long have you been with your present company?

- less than 3 months (1)
- 3 months, but less than 6 months (2)
- 6 months, but less than 1 year (3)
- 1 year, but less than 3 years (4)
- 3 years, but less than 5 years (5)
- 5 years, but less than 10 years (6)
- 10 years, but less than 15 years (7)
- 15 years, but less than 20 years (8)
- 20 years and over (9)

57 How long have you been at your present level of job responsibility?

- less than 3 months (1)
- 3 to 6 months (2)
- 6 months to 1 year (3)
- 1 to 2 years (4)
- 2 to 3 years (5)
- 3 to 4 years (6)
- 4 to 5 years (7)
- 5 to 10 years (8)
- over 10 years (9)

60 Your income from your occupation (salary plus bonus) estimated for the year 1960:

- less than $5,000 (1)
- $5,000–$7,499 (2)
- $7,500–$9,999 (3)
- $10,000–$14,999 (4)
- $15,000–$19,999 (5)
- $20,000–$29,999 (6)
- $30,000–$39,999 (7)
- $40,000–$49,999 (8)
- $50,000 and over (9)

61 Approximately what is the income (salary plus bonus) received by the highest ranking executive in your organization?

- not sure (0)
- less than $25,000 (1)
- $25,000–$34,999 (2)
- $35,000–$44,999 (3)
- $45,000–$54,999 (4)
- $55,000–$64,999 (5)
- $65,000–$74,999 (6)
- $75,000–$99,999 (7)
- $100,000–$200,000 (8)
- over $200,000 (9)

How many people do you supervise, directly or through subordinates?   **58**

none, other than myself.	(1)
one or two.	(2)
three, four, or five.	(3)
six to ten.	(4)
ten to twenty.	(5)
twenty to forty.	(6)
over forty.	(7)

Which one of the following categories most nearly describes the kind of work done by you or the people under you?   **59**

production.	(1)
sales, advertising, or promotion.	(2)
control, accounting.	(3)
finance, credit.	(4)
engineering.	(5)
research.	(6)
personnel, industrial relations, training.	(7)
other (Please specify)	(8)

How long ago did you receive your last increase in salary?   **62**

less than 3 months ago.	(1)
3 to 6 months ago.	(2)
6 months to 1 year ago.	(3)
1 to 2 years ago.	(4)
2 to 3 years ago.	(5)
3 to 4 years ago.	(6)
4 to 5 years ago.	(7)
5 to 10 years ago.	(8)
over 10 years ago.	(9)

63   **64**   **65**

On your job, about what percentage of the time do you spend *working alone?* **66**

less than 10% .... (1)
10% to 25% .... (2)
25% to 50% .... (3)
50% to 75% .... (4)
75% to 90% .... (5)
over 90% .... (6)

How many trade associations or professional societies do you belong to, if any? **67**

_____
(number)

In how many of the above number of associations or societies, are you, or have you been, an officer? **68**

_____
(number)

How many company committees or task groups have you participated in in the past year, if any? **69**

_____
(number)

If you take coffee or coke breaks at work, with whom do you take them? **74**

Do not take breaks. .... (1)
Take break alone (usually). .... (2)
Usually join someone, but rarely the same people. .... (3)
Usually take break with the same person or group. .... (4)
Other arrangements * .... (5)

* Please specify_____

How do you usually spend your lunch time during the work week? **75**

Usually eat at home. .... (1)
Usually eat alone at work or alone at restaurant .... (2)
Usually eat with work associates:
   With different ones at different times ...... (3)
   With a regular partner or group. .... (4)
Usually eat with customers, suppliers, consultants, or friends in other companies:
   With different ones at different times ...... (5)
   Frequently with the same people. .... (6)
Other lunch arrangements * .... (7)

* Please specify:

In how many of the above committees or groups did you, or do you, have a leadership position, if any?

70

_____
(number)

71

72

73

With whom do you usually travel to and from work?

76

Usually commute alone. . . . . _____(1)
Usually commute with work associates:
  With different ones at different times. . . . . . _____(2)
  With a regular partner or group . . . . _____(3)
Usually commute with people who do not work
  in my organization:
  With different ones at different times. . . . . . _____(4)
  With a regular partner or group. . . . . _____(5)
Combinations of the above or other arrange-
  ments * . . . . _____(6)

* Please describe_____

77   **78**   **79**   **80**

Which, if any, of the following statements apply
to your early family experiences? **6**

You were an adopted child. . . . . (1)

You lived part or all of your childhood with
foster parents. . . . . (2)

You were raised by people other than natural,
adoptive, or foster parents—such as older
brothers or sisters, aunts or uncles, etc. . . . . (3)

You spent at least part of your early childhood
in an institutional setting, such as a large foster home or boarding school. . . . . (4)

You lived with and were raised by several different people in different homes. . . . . (5)

Other unusual arrangements *. . . . . (6)

* Please specify:

How many brothers did you have? **8**

none. . . . . (1)
one . . . . (2)
two . . . . (3)
three . . . . (4)
four or more . . . . (5)

How many brothers and/or sisters were younger
than you? **9**

none. . . . . (1)
one . . . . (2)
two . . . . (3)
three . . . . (4)
four or more . . . . (5)

How many children were in your family (besides yourself)?   **7**

none. . . . . ———— (1)
one. . . . . ———— (2)
two. . . . . ———— (3)
three. . . . . ———— (4)
four or more. . . . . ———— (5)

If you checked "none," please omit the next three questions and go on to page [248].

If you checked "none," please omit the next question and go on to page 9.

How old were you when another child first entered the family?   **10**

(Please check only the highest category)

less than a year old. . . . . ———— (1)
less than two years old. . . . . ———— (2)
less than three years old. . . . . ———— (3)
less than four years old. . . . . ———— (4)
less than five years old. . . . . ———— (5)
less than six years old. . . . . ———— (6)
less than seven years old. . . . . ———— (7)
less than eight years old. . . . . ———— (8)
nine years or older. . . . . ———— (9)

11   **12**   **13**

Thinking back over your childhood and early youth, which of the following events, if any, can you recall as having happened to you?   **14**

the death of one or both of your parents .... (1)
the divorce of your parents .... (2)
a lengthy separation between your parents .... (3)
being separated from your parents (other than vacations, holiday trips, etc.) .... (4)
a prolonged illness of one or both your parents .... (5)
loss of job for a long time by your father .... (6)
a sharp reduction in family income for a long time .... (7)
a frequent change in home location .... (8)
a frequent change in schooling .... (9)
a long illness or severe physical handicap (self) .... (x)
other hardship * .... (y)

* Please specify: _____

Thinking back over your childhood and early youth, at about what age did your parents or guardians first allow you to select and buy your own clothes?   **15**

under 8 years old .... (1)
eight years, but less than 10 years old .... (2)
ten years, but less than 12 years old .... (3)
twelve years, but less than 14 years old .... (4)
fourteen years, but less than 15 years old .... (5)
fifteen years, but less than 16 years old .... (6)
sixteen years, but less than 17 years old .... (7)
seventeen years, but less than 18 years old .... (8)
eighteen years of age or older .... (9)

At what age did your parents or guardians first allow you to take trips or go on visits away from them for at least one night?

16

under 8 years old .... ____ (1)
eight years, but less than 10 years old .... ____ (2)
ten years, but less than 12 years old .... ____ (3)
twelve years, but less than 14 years old .... ____ (4)
fourteen years, but less than 15 years old .... ____ (5)
fifteen years, but less than 16 years old .... ____ (6)
sixteen years, but less than 17 years old .... ____ (7)
seventeen years, but less than 18 years old .... ____ (8)
eighteen years of age or older .... ____ (9)

At what age did you first prepare a meal for yourself?

17

under 8 years of age .... ____ (1)
eight years, but less than 10 years old .... ____ (2)
ten years, but less than 12 years old .... ____ (3)
twelve years, but less than 14 years old .... ____ (4)
fourteen years, but less than 15 years old .... ____ (5)
fifteen years, but less than 16 years old .... ____ (6)
sixteen years, but less than 17 years old .... ____ (7)
seventeen years, but less than 18 years old .... ____ (8)
eighteen years of age or older .... ____ (9)

At what age did you first earn money for yourself in jobs outside your home (for example, working in a garage, delivering newspapers, working at a soda fountain, etc.)?

18

under 8 years old...	(1)
eight years, but less than 10 years old..................	(2)
ten years, but less than 12 years old...................	(3)
twelve years, but less than 14 years old................	(4)
fourteen years, but less than 15 years old..............	(5)
fifteen years, but less than 16 years old...............	(6)
sixteen years, but less than 17 years old...............	(7)
seventeen years, but less than 18 years old.............	(8)
eighteen years of age or older..........................	(9)

At what age did you first buy something important to you, like a bicycle, a camera, etc., with money you had really earned outside your family?

19

under 8 years old . . . . (1)

eight years, but less than 10 years old . . . . (2)

ten years, but less than 12 years old . . . . (3)

twelve years, but less than 14 years old . . . . (4)

fourteen years, but less than 15 years old . . . . (5)

fifteen years, but less than 16 years old . . . . (6)

sixteen years, but less than 17 years old . . . . (7)

seventeen years, but less than 18 years old . . . . (8)

eighteen years of age or older . . . . (9)

20   21   22   23

While you were growing up and in school, *at about what age* did you first have your *own* friends, outside of your immediate family, relatives, or children of your parents' friends?   **24**

less than 6 years old	(1)
7 or 8 years old	(2)
9 or 10 years old	(3)
11, 12, or 13 years old	(4)
14, 15, or 16 years old	(5)
17, 18, or 19 years old	(6)
20 years or older	(7)

If you lived away from your parents while attending school, at what age did this first take place?   **25**

less than 6 years old	(1)
7 or 8 years old	(2)
9 or 10 years old	(3)
11, 12, or 13 years old	(4)
14, 15, or 16 years old	(5)
17, 18, or 19 years old	(6)
20 years or older	(7)

If you have had military service, where did you live at the time you entered?   **28**

with parents	(1)
away from home, at school	(2)
in own apartment or home	(3)
other (Please specify)	(4)

At what age did you start to live away from your parents *permanently?*   **29**

18 or younger	(1)
19 years old	(2)
20 years old	(3)
21 years old	(4)
22 years old	(5)
23 years old	(6)
24 years old	(7)
25 or older	(8)
still live with parents, or they live with you	(9)

Was your family in a nationality or religious minority group in the community(s) in which you grew up?   **26**

Yes..................................(1)
No...................................(2)
Yes at some time,
No at others......................(3)
Don't know........................(4)

If you have had military service which took you away from home, at what age did you enter service?   **27**

17 years or younger...........(1)
18 years old.......................(2)
19 years old.......................(3)
20 years old.......................(4)
21 years old.......................(5)
22 years old.......................(6)
23 years old.......................(7)
24 years old.......................(8)
25 years or older................(9)

At what age did you first become self-supporting (do *not* include temporary military service or benefits of G.I. bill)?   **30**

16 or younger....................(1)
17–18...............................(2)
19–20...............................(3)
21–22...............................(4)
23–24...............................(5)
25–26...............................(6)
27 and over.......................(7)

To what extent do you feel you were close to your family as you were growing up?   **31**

very close...........................(1)
close.................................(2)
not so close.......................(3)

32   **33**   **34**

35

In your current marriage or family situation, which of the following, if any, apply to you, your wife, or your children?

Have wanted to have children, but haven't yet had any. . . . . _____ (1)

Have had children, but none currently living. . . . . _____ (2)

One or more children now living, but have lost one or more children in the past. . . . . _____ (3)

Have children now living, but one or more have a serious permanent handicap. . . . . . _____ (4)

Your wife (or husband) has a serious prolonged illness or permanent handicap. . . . . . _____ (5)

An *unexpected* accident or serious handicap has affected your wife (or husband), child, or yourself. . . . . . _____ (6)

Health problems (yourself) such as ulcers, colitis, diabetes, high blood pressure, etc.. . _____ (7)

A permanent handicap (yourself). . . . . _____ (8)

Other recent or present family disturbance, such as marital difficulties, serious problems with children, etc. . _____ (9)

The loss of your wife (or husband) or a child recently. . . . . _____ (x)

In your current relations with relatives and close friends outside of your immediate family, which of the following, if any, apply to you?

36

A close relative or friend has a serious prolonged illness or permanent handicap . . . . _____ (1)

Now caring for an elderly or invalid relative or friend, or have done so in recent past . . . . _____ (2)

An *unexpected* accident or serious handicap has affected a close relative or friend . . . . _____ (3)

The *unexpected* sudden loss of a close relative or friend recently . . . . _____ (4)

Other recent or present disturbances or problems in your relations with close relatives or friends, such as marital problems in their families, emotional disturbances, etc. . . . . _____ (5)

Please indicate the religious affiliation of:

	Your Father	Your Mother	Your self	Your Wife	Wife's Mother	Wife's Father
	37	38	39	40	41	42
Catholic, active	___ (1)	___ (1)	___ (1)	___ (1)	___ (1)	___ (1)
Catholic, inactive	___ (2)	___ (2)	___ (2)	___ (2)	___ (2)	___ (2)
Protestant, active	___ (3)	___ (3)	___ (3)	___ (3)	___ (3)	___ (3)
Protestant, inactive	___ (4)	___ (4)	___ (4)	___ (4)	___ (4)	___ (4)
Jewish, active	___ (5)	___ (5)	___ (5)	___ (5)	___ (5)	___ (5)
Jewish, inactive	___ (6)	___ (6)	___ (6)	___ (6)	___ (6)	___ (6)
Other, active *	___ (7)	___ (7)	___ (7)	___ (7)	___ (7)	___ (7)
Other, inactive *	___ (8)	___ (8)	___ (8)	___ (8)	___ (8)	___ (8)
	___	___	___	___	___	___
	43	44	45		46	

* If "other," please specify

Number of Relatives and How Often You See Them

		Your Children	Your Grand-children	Your Parents	Your Grand-parents	Your Brothers	Your Sisters	Your Nieces & Nephews	Your Aunts & Uncles
Please indicate the NUMBER now living ⟶									
	Please enter in the appropriate spaces the NUMBER of each kind of relative whom you see as often as indicated below. ↘								
At least once a day									
Not once a day, but at least once a week									
Not once a week, but at least once a month									
Not once a month, but at least twice in the past year									
Not twice, but at least once in the past year									
Not in the past year, but at least once in the past two years									
Not in the past two years but at least once in the past five years									
Haven't seen for over five years									

47   48   49   50

How long have you lived in your present community?

(Please check highest category)

51

less than 6 months................	(1)
6 months to 1 year...............	(2)
1 year to 3 years................	(3)
3 to 5 years.....................	(4)
5 to 10 years....................	(5)
10 to 20 years...................	(6)
over 20 years, but not entire life..	(7)
your entire life.................	(8)

Do you live in an apartment?.......... (1)

     or a house?..................... (2)

52

Do you rent?.......................... (1)

     or own?........................ (2)

53

Community activities:

	Check here if you are active	Check here if you are, or were, an officer
Parents' activities:		
P.T.A., Boy Scouts, Girl Scouts, Little League, etc.	____	____
Service Organizations:		
Lions, Kiwanis, C. of C., etc.	____	____
Church or synagogue	____	____
Charity drives— (United Fund Collector, etc.)	____	____
Local government	____	____
Local political organization	____	____
Others (please specify):	____	____
_____	____	____
_____	____	____

How does your rent or the value of your home compare to others in your neighborhood?

57

Higher than most................	(1)
About the same as most..........	(2)
Lower than most.................	(3)

Does your immediate family share your residence with others? **54**

No. . . . . (1)
Live with your parents. . . . . (2)
Live with wife's (or husband's) parents. . . . . (3)
Live with brothers or sisters, or spouse's brothers or sisters. . . . . (4)
Other arrangements. . . . . (5)

Are you a member of a church or synagogue? **55**

Yes. . . . . (1)
No. . . . . (2)

If yes, does your church or synagogue identify you with a minority group in your community? **56**

Yes. . . . . (1)
No. . . . . (2)
Don't know. . . . . (3)

How do rents or home values in your neighborhood compare with other neighborhoods in your community? **58**

Higher than most. . . . . (1)
About the same as most. . . . . (2)
Lower than most. . . . . (3)

How do rents or home values in your community compare with those of nearby communities? **59**

Higher than most. . . . . (1)
About the same as most. . . . . (2)
Lower than most. . . . . (3)

60   61   62   63

The next questions refer to the number and kinds of friends you have. In order to help you answer them easily, would you first list, on a separate sheet of paper which is *not* to be handed in with this questionnaire, the names of individuals or families whom you would consider to be friends? Include only people whose homes you visit socially, or who visit your home, on a continuing basis, or with whom you keep up a continuing correspondence and visit periodically. After you have made up this list, turn this page and work on the four questions referring to your list. Do *not* turn in the list with this questionnaire—keep it or destroy it. And please do not add to the list after starting on the questions. Thank you.

The following four questions refer to the list you prepared according to the instructions on the previous page.

1. How many names (individuals or families) are on the list you just completed?

_____
(number)

2. How many people or families (count a family as 1 friend) on the list you just completed fall into each of the following descriptive categories? If a name falls into more than one category, count it in as many categories as are appropriate.

64

Indicate
number

Neighbors and former neighbors .... _____
Friends from church or synagogue .... _____
Old family or childhood friends .... _____
Schoolmates (yours or spouse's) .... _____
Service buddies .... _____
Relatives .... _____
Work associates (same company) .... _____
Business associates .... _____
Former work or professional associates .... _____
Other * .... _____

* Please specify:

3. In the above list of categories, indicate by an (X) after your number those categories in which your very best friends are counted.

65

4. Of the people on your list, how many are more than 5 years *younger* than you?

66

_____
(number)

How many are more than 5 years *older* than you?

67

_____
(number)

INTEREST, HOBBIES, AND LEISURE ACTIVITIES

Please list in the spaces below your *interests*, *hobbies*, and *leisure activities*:

With whom, if anyone, do you share these interests, hobbies, and leisure activities? (Please check where applicable. "Work associates" refers to *people in your company*.)

| | *Talk* about them with: | | | Actively participate in them with: | | |
	No one outside of family	Work associates	Other friends	No one outside of family	Work associates	Other friends
	68					
	69	70	71	72	73	74
	75	76	77	78	79	80

[Note: 9 spaces provided on original questionnaire]

APPENDIX D

Sources and Derivations of Scores

THIS APPENDIX describes the flow of data from their sources to the forms in which they were ultimately analyzed. The main part of the analysis consisted of constructing contingency tables using dichotomous High and Low classes. Individual cases were assigned to High or Low classes on each measure on the basis of the ranking of their score on the measure compared with the scores of the other participants in their groups. The study made reference to correlations between measures in some instances. These correlations were among derived scores and thus did not reflect the relationships of individuals to the others in their groups. The derived scores were scaled in relation to the entire 52 participants.

The scores were constructed to yield one or two digit numbers which would be suitable for machine processing using an existing computer program. In general, scales from 0 through 9 or 00 through 99 were superimposed upon the range of raw scores so that the highest raw score would be converted to 9 or 99 and the lowest score to 0 (or 1 in some cases). In some cases the natural, untransformed scores met this condition. For example, choices received on the PMR ran from 0 to 9 for the most part. In other cases, notably the ratios (e.g., the ratio of agreement events to the originator's participation), numbers such as .016 characterized the raw scores. Although the scaling processes had no effect on the dichotomous classifications ultimately used, they were very relevant to the correlation results. Different scaling methods would have resulted in different correlations. Hence, the contents of this appendix are relevant for anyone who wishes to evaluate the few correlations quoted in the body of the study and/or who wishes to pursue some ad hoc hypotheses by consulting the intercorrelation matrix in Appendix G.

The following presentation will follow the order in which the measures were introduced in the body of the study, starting with Role Perception scores and concluding with Satisfaction scores. The data used in Chapter 7, Developmental Trends, were analyzed by discrete categories not requiring scaling. The following abbreviations will be used for the sources:

ABBREVIATION	SOURCE	DESCRIPTIVE REFERENCES
PMR	Post Meeting Reaction Questionnaire	Appendix C and Appendix A
IEA	Interval Event Analysis	Appendix F and Appendix A
ECA	Event Content Analysis	Appendix F and Appendix A
IBA	Interpersonal Behavior Analysis	Appendix F and Appendix A
IPA	Interaction Process Analysis (Bales' System)	Appendix F and Appendix A
TAT	Test of Imagination (Thematic Apperception Test)	Appendix C, Appendix E, and Appendix A
IPS	Individual Preference Study	Appendix C, Appendix E, and Appendix A
BIQ	Background Information Questionnaire	Appendix C and Appendix A

In the following descriptions some of the scoring operations involve multiplying by constants or adding constants. These operations converted raw scores to one or two digit whole number scores. These arithmetic conversions were designed to stretch or compress the range of raw scores into a 0 to 9 or 00 to 99 scale for punching onto IBM cards. The symbol (2) appearing before the descriptions of scoring operations indicates that the measure was expressed as a two-digit number. All other scores were expressed as single digits. In almost all cases any decimal fraction remaining after the conversion operation was dropped rather than rounded off to the nearest whole number.

VARIABLE: ROLE PERCEPTIONS

Measure: 1. Quality of Ideas   Source: PMR, p. 1

Scoring Operations: In Groups 3 and 4, each individual was assigned the total number of PMR's on which his name was listed on page 1. Totals higher than 9 were scored as 9.

VARIABLE: ROLE PERCEPTIONS
                   For Groups 1 and 2 choices were inferred according
                   to the scheme discussed in Appendix A.

Measure: 2. Guidance   Source: PMR, p. 2
Scoring Operations: As above

Measure: 3. Leadership   Source: PMR, p. 4
Scoring Operations: As above

Measure: 4. Congeniality   Source: PMR, p. 5
Scoring Operations: As above

VARIABLE: SOCIAL ATTRACTIVENESS
Measure: 5. "Work With"   Source: PMR, p. 7
Scoring Operations: As above

Measure: 6. "Know socially"   Source: PMR, p. 8
Scoring Operations: As above

VARIABLE: GROUP PROCESS BEHAVIORS PRODUCED
Measure: 7. Participation   Source: IEA
Scoring Operations: (2) Number of intervals during which subject talked.

Measure: 8. Interaction   Source: IEA
Scoring Operations: (2) Ratio: $\dfrac{\text{Number of intervals shared}}{\text{Participation}} \times 100$

Measure: 9. Social Emotional Acts Source: IPA
Scoring Operations:

(2) Ratio: $\dfrac{\text{Acts in IPA Categories 1, 2, 3, 10, 11, 12}}{\text{Total IPA Acts}} \times 100$

Measure: 10. Ask Acts   Source: IPA
Scoring Operations: Ratio: $\dfrac{\text{Acts in IPA Categories 7, 8, 9}}{\text{Acts in IPA Categories 4 through 9}} \times 33\frac{1}{3}$

Measure: 11. Tension Release   Source: IPA
Scoring Operations: Ratio: $\dfrac{\text{Acts in IPA Category 2}}{\text{Total IPA Acts}} \times 40$

VARIABLE: INTERPERSONAL BEHAVIORS PRODUCED
Measure: 12. Interruption   Source: IBA and IEA
Scoring Operations: Ratio: $\dfrac{\text{No. of Successful Interruptions (IBA)}}{\text{Participation (IEA)}} \times 30$

VARIABLE: INTERPERSONAL BEHAVIORS PRODUCED

Measure: 13. Competitive Questions   Source: ECA and IEA

Scoring Operations: Ratio: $\dfrac{\text{No. of Competitive Questions (ECA)}}{\text{Participation (IEA)}} \times 80$

Measure: 14. Personalness   Source: ECA and IEA

Scoring Operations: Ratio: $\dfrac{\text{No. of Personal References (ECA)}}{\text{Participation (IEA)}} \times 20$

Measure: 15. Agreement   Source: ECA and IEA

Scoring Operations: Ratio: $\dfrac{\text{No. of Supportive Actions (ECA)}}{\text{Participation (IEA)}} \times 40$

Measure: 16. Disagreement   Source: ECA and IEA

Scoring Operations: Ratio: $\dfrac{\text{No. of Negative Actions (ECA)}}{\text{Participation (IEA)}} \times 40$

VARIABLE: INTERPERSONAL BEHAVIORS RECEIVED

Measure: 17. Interruption Attempts   Source: IBA and IEA
Scoring Operations:

Ratio: $\dfrac{\text{No. of Interruption Attempts Rec'd. (IBA)}}{\text{Participation (IEA)}} \times 40$

Measure: 18. Competitive Questions   Source: ECA and IEA
Scoring Operations:

Ratio: $\dfrac{\text{No. of Competitive Questions Rec'd. (ECA)}}{\text{Participation (IEA)}} \times 50$

Measure: 19. Personal Recognition   Source: ECA and IEA
Scoring Operations:

Ratio: $\dfrac{\text{No. of Personal References Rec'd. (ECA)}}{\text{Participation (IEA)}} \times 20$

Measure: 20. Agreement   Source: ECA and IEA

Scoring Operations: Ratio: $\dfrac{\text{No. of Supportive Actions Rec'd. (ECA)}}{\text{Participation (IEA)}} \times 20$

Measure: 21. Disagreement   Source: ECA and IEA

Scoring Operations: Ratio: $\dfrac{\text{No. of Negative Actions Rec'd. (ECA)}}{\text{Participation (IEA)}} \times 50$

VARIABLE: MOTIVATION

Measure: 22. Need Achievement   Source: TAT
Scoring Operations: Refined nAch score $\times$ .50 (See Appendix E)

Measure: 23. Need Affiliation   Source: TAT
Scoring Operations: Refined nAff score $\times$ 1.00 (See Appendix E)

Measure: 24. Belonging Preference   Source: IPS

Scoring Operations: *Rejection-Preference Score*   *Derived*
                          (See Appendix E)   *Score*
                          $-7, -6, -5$ 0
                          -4 to $+4$ add 5
                          $+5, +6$ 9

Measure: 25. Status Preference   Source: IPS
Scoring Operations: *Rejection-Preference Score*   *Derived*
                          (See Appendix E)   *Score*
                          $-12, -11$ 0
                          $-10, -9$ 1
                          $-8, -7$ 2
                          $-6, -5$ 3
                          $-4, -3$ 4
                          $-2, -1$ 5
                          $0, +1$ 6
                          $+2, +3$ 7
                          $+4, +5$ 8
                          $+6, +7, +8$ 9

Measure: 26. Job-Intrinsic Preference   Source: IPS
Scoring Operations: This measure was not included in the intercorrelation
                          program. The Rejection-Preference scores (See Ap-
                          pendix E) were ranked within groups and dichoto-
                          mized into High and Low classes.

VARIABLE: STATUS AND DEVELOPMENT

Measure: 27. Salary   Source: BIQ, Question 60, p. 6
Scoring Operations: Since the salary ranges for Groups 1 and 2 were not
                          the same as those provided for Groups 3 and 4, the
                          answers on the various forms were all transformed ac-
                          cording to the following scale:

VARIABLE: STATUS AND DEVELOPMENT

Groups 1 and 2 Indicated Salary Interval	Groups 3 and 4 Score Checked	Transformed Score
$ 5,499 or less	1	1
5,500– 6,499	2	2
6,500– 7,499	–	3
7,500– 8,999	3	4
9,000–10,999	–	5
11,000–12,999	4	6
13,000–14,999	–	7
15,000–19,999	5	8
over $20,000	6 and 7	9

Measure: 28. Age   Source: BIQ, Question 6, p. 1

Scoring Operations:

Age Interval Checked on BIQ	Score
25 or less	1
26–30	2
31–35	3
36–40	4
41–45	5
46–50	6
51–55	7
56–60	8
over 60	9

Measure: 29. Seniority   Source: BIQ, Question 56, p. 6

Scoring Operations:

Category Checked on BIQ	Score
less than 3 months	1
3 mos., but less than 6 months	2
6 mos., but less than 1 year	3
1 year, but less than 3 years	4
3 years, but less than 5 years	5
5 years, but less than 10 years	6
10 years, but less than 15 years	7
15 years, but less than 20 years	8
20 years and over	9

Measure: 30. Experience   Source: BIQ, Question 6, p. 1
                                and Question 30, p. 11

Scoring Operations: To obtain years of experience, the *upper* limit of the category checked in answer to Question 30, page [11] (age at which person became self-supporting) was

VARIABLE: STATUS AND DEVELOPMENT

subtracted from the *lower* limit of the category checked in answer to Question 6, page [1] (your present age). The resulting number of years was assigned a score according to the following scale:

Years	*Score*
0, 1, 2	1
3, 4	2
5, 6, 7	3
8, 9, 10	4
11, 12, 13	5
14, 15, 16	6
17, 18, 19	7
20 through 24	8
25 and over	9

Measure: 31. Education Level Source: BIQ, Question 15, p. 1 and 19, p. 2

Scoring Operations: The answers to these questions were scored on the following scale:

Category	*Score*
Less than high school	1
Some high school	2
High school graduate	3
Some college	4
College graduate	5
Some graduate work, no master's degree	6
Master's degree	7
Doctor's degree	8

Measure: 32. Ethnicity Source: BIQ, Questions 11, 12, 13, p. 1 and 37, 38, 39, p. 12

Scoring Operations: The *pattern* of answers to these questions was scored on the following scale:

Patterns	*Score*
Subject's religious affiliation as Jewish *or* either parent's affiliation checked as Jewish and subject's affiliation checked as *other*.	2
Subject or either parent or spouse Catholic.	4
Subject Protestant, but father's father *not* born in U.S.	6

VARIABLE: STATUS AND DEVELOPMENT
                   Subject Protestant and father's   8
                   father born in U.S.

Measure: 33. Sex   Source: BIQ, Question 7, p. 1
Scoring Operations: Females were scored 2, Males scored 8

Measure: 34. Social Status   Source: Measures 28 through
                       Index   33
Scoring Operations: A raw score on Social Status was computed by adding
                   the following scores:

                   28, Age + 29, Seniority (Groups 1 and 2 only) + 30,
                   Experience (Groups 3 and 4 only) + 31, Education
                   Level + 32, Ethnicity + 33, Sex.

                   Seniority *or* Experience were included in the total, not
                   both.

                   A scale was constructed assigning a Social Status
                   score as follows:

Raw Score	*Derived Score*
20 or less	1
21, 22	2
23, 24	3
25, 26	4
27, 28	5
29, 30	6
31, 32	7
33, 34	8
35 and over	9

Measure: 35. Total Status   Source: Measures 27 and 34
                       Index
Scoring Operations: Five times the score on 27, Salary, was added to the
                   raw score on Total Status. The raw scores were as-
                   signed a derived score as follows:

Total Status, Raw Score	*Derived Score*
34 or less	1
35–39	2
40–44	3
45–49	4
50–54	5
55–59	6
60–64	7
65–69	8
70 and over	9

VARIABLE: STATUS AND DEVELOPMENT

Measure: 36. Reward-Investment   Source: Measures 27 and
(R–I) Index   34

Scoring Operations: Reward-Investment raw score = 5 × salary score
— Social Status raw score

R–I Raw Score	Derived Score
−25 or lower	1
−19 through −24	2
−13 " −18	3
− 7 " −12	4
− 6 " − 1	5
0 " + 5	6
+ 6 " +11	7
+12 " +17	8
+18 and over	9

Measure: 37. Congruity-Ambiguity   Source: Measures 28
(C–A) Index   through 33

Scoring Operations: A raw C–A score was computed by taking the sum of
the differences between each of the scores going into
the figuring of the Social Status raw score and each
of the other scores, disregarding sign. This procedure was illustrated in Zaleznik, Christensen, and
Roethlisberger (1958), pp. 70–71.

Raw C–A Score	Derived Score
over 35	1
32–34	2
29–31	3
26–28	4
23–25	5
20–22	6
17–19	7
14–16	8
13 or less	9

VARIABLE: SATISFACTION

Measure: 38. Satisfaction with   Source: PMR, p. 6, item A
Group Decision

Scoring Operations: Assigned scores corresponded to the numbers (1
through 8) circled on the PMR.

Measure: 39. Satisfaction with   Source: PMR, p. 6, item B
Group Operation

Scoring Operations: As above.

APPENDIX E

Backgrounds of the Motivation Measures

THIS APPENDIX will present some comments about the theoretical and empirical backgrounds of the Individual Preference Study and the Test of Imagination (Thematic Apperception Test) scored for need Achievement and need Affiliation. Copies of both of these instruments are included in Appendix C. Discussion of their relationships to the design of this study is presented in Chapter 2, Chapter 5, and Appendix A. Several books and journal articles have been published about McClelland's need Achievement studies. The TAT will therefore receive a minimal treatment here, but references will be cited. Nothing has been published to date about the Individual (or Executive) Preference Study, although Professor Zaleznik has been working with it in his teaching activities at Harvard Business School since 1958, and has used it in several as yet unpublished research activities. The major part of this appendix will be concerned with the Preference Study.

INDIVIDUAL OR (EXECUTIVE) PREFERENCE STUDY

Some of the purposes behind the development of the Preference Study were explained in Appendix A. Professor Zaleznik began work on this instrument as an outgrowth of the conclusions reached in the final chapter of Zaleznik, Christensen, and Roethlisberger, *The Motivation, Productivity, and Satisfaction of Workers*. At the time, the idea of the hierarchy of needs developed by Maslow (Maslow, *Motivation and Personality*) seemed to explain plausibly many research findings about the effects of environmental constraints on the motivation, productivity, satisfaction, and development of workers. This trend of explanation was followed by J. V. Clark in his article entitled "Motivation in Work Groups: A Tentative View" (Lawrence et al., 1961, p. 229).

Zaleznik and others, while not denying the utility of the Maslow theory for explaining developmental trends over time, raised the question, *"Under what conditions* does needs satisfaction proceed according to an hierarchical pattern and under what conditions does needs satisfaction follow a pattern of reinforcement?"* The issue resolves around two extreme possibilities. Satiation of a need may lead to the pursuit of *other* needs, leading to a sequence of new adventures and risks. On the other hand, successful satisfaction of a need may result in pursuit of the *same* goals, a sequence of "betting on sure things." The Preference Study was developed to accumulate empirical data which might clarify this question. Maslow's needs categories were used as the basis for constructing statements which simulated the kinds of experiences which the satisfaction of each kind of need would involve. Zaleznik conceived of these experiences as rewards. The statements presented in the form of the Preference Study used in this present research study were as follows, classified by reward categories and identified by their location on the questionnaire form:

SELF–ACTUALIZATION REWARDS

1b. To go through an experience that opens up new and exciting possibilities.

3b. To appreciate the meaning in a painting or piece of music.

5a. To develop in myself new abilities and interests.

6b. To have an opportunity for further personal development.

8c. To have an opportunity for further personal development.

10c. To find new ways of expressing my capabilities in leisure time activities.

11c. To appreciate the meaning in a painting or piece of music.

13a. To discover suddenly a new approach to a long-standing and baffling question.

14b. To discover suddenly a new approach to a long-standing and baffling question.

15c. To achieve greater sensitivity toward events and people around me.

16a. To appreciate even more customs and ways of living of persons whose backgrounds differ from my own.
18a. To develop in myself new abilities and interests.

JOB–INTRINSIC REWARDS

2a. To begin a job that is interesting and stimulating.
3c. To work by myself on an interesting work problem.
4c. To work on a problem and prepare recommendations.
5b. To handle easily my job responsibilities.
8a. To complete a project on time.
9b. To do a job well, even though no one comments on it.
14c. To work by myself on an interesting work problem.
15a. To do a job well, even though no one comments on it.
16b. To begin a job that has more challenging work.
17a. To move rapidly through a series of complex work problems.
19c. To size up a new work problem rapidly and move toward conclusions.
20b. To find a way of tackling a difficult piece of work.

BELONGING REWARDS

1c. To receive help on work problems from a friend.
3a. To join a group of close associates for lunch.
4b. To participate in group activities at work.
7a. To spend time with my family.
10a. To help a newcomer to the department get settled.
12c. To assist a person with whom I work closely when he has difficulty with a project.
13b. To have a reunion with friends or family.
16c. To be a member of a small circle of close friends.
17c. To make new friends.
18b. To participate in group activities at work.
19b. To talk about work interests with a close associate.
20a. To be a member of a small circle of close friends.

STATUS REWARDS

1a. To move to a better community.
2c. To become honorary chairman of an important organization.
4a. To move to a better office.
5c. To receive a letter from the Board of Directors complimenting my work.
6a. To receive a new job title which involves expanding my department.

7c. To receive a strong invitation to present my views before an influential citizen's group.

8b. To receive a letter from the Board of Directors complimenting my work.

9a. To receive an award from an important professional organization related to my work.

11b. To be invited to speak to a group of college seniors on the importance of my work and its career opportunities.

12b. To become honorary chairman of an important organization.

17b. To be invited to join a select top executives' luncheon group.

18c. To get an invitation to join the Board of Directors of an important company.

ECONOMIC REWARDS

2b. To get a substantial life insurance policy paid for completely by my company.

6c. To receive a special money bonus.

7b. To sell some personal assets for considerably more than cost.

9c. To receive increased participation in a profit-sharing plan.

10b. To receive increased annual cash returns on investments.

11a. To receive an option to buy stock at a price below the current market.

12a. To get a substantial life insurance policy paid for completely by my company.

13c. To have an investment go up sharply in value.

14a. To receive a special money bonus.

15b. To get an increase in salary.

19a. To increase my holdings of securities in important companies.

20c. To receive from the company a noncontributory pension plan with greater retirement income.

The raw scores for each of the five categories of rewards was obtained by totaling the rank order numbers assigned to the 12 statements in each category. A correctly completed questionnaire would contain 20 items ranked "one," 20 ranked "two," and 20 ranked "three," giving a total of 120 points to be allocated to five categories of rewards. Low scores would indicate high preference and high scores would indicate low preference. Each individual then would have a profile of preferences consisting of five scores.

These scores measured the *relative* preference of the individual for each kind of reward compared to *his* preference for the other kinds of rewards. The scores did *not* measure a strength on a standard scale by which different individuals' scores could be compared with each other. For example, if person A scored 20 on preference for Status rewards and 28 on preference for Belonging rewards, while person B scored 18 on preference for Status rewards and 26 on preference for Belonging rewards (lower scores indicated higher preferences), it could not be inferred that A preferred Status and Belonging rewards more than did B, but it may be inferred that in both cases, the individuals indicated more preference for Status rewards than for Belonging rewards.

This study was interested in analyzing the relationships between individuals' expressed preferences for Status, Belonging, and Job-Intrinsic rewards, and the other variables measured. To do this required a method of analyzing each person's 5-score preference pattern and expressing the "position" of Status, Belonging and Job-Intrinsic reward preferences in relation to each other and to the other categories in a way that would allow person-to-person comparisons. The following theory and method intended to accomplish this purpose.

1. A subject who was perfectly indifferent in his preferences would complete the questionnaire by a process similar to dice-throwing or coin-tossing, and would be expected to score near 24 on each of the 5 categories.
2. Three different kinds of dynamic processes may be at work when the individual ranks each set of 3 statements according to his preferences:
   A. "Real" preference; the subject feels positive preference for one item over the others, or two items over the third.
   B. Rejection; the subject can easily assign a "3" rank to an item because it appears undesirable to him in relation to the other items.
   C. Indifference; the subject has no patterned preferences among the 3 items, but will arbitrarily rank the item or items according to some temporary, nonconsistent process similar to dice-throwing.

These three different choice dynamics could yield 9 possible "types" of patterns, as follows:

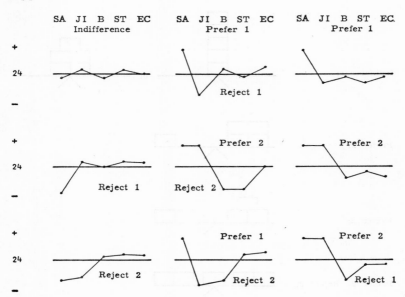

Active preference or rejection of 4 or 3 categories would, due to the nature of the scoring process, yield patterns identical to rejection or preference for 1 or 2 categories. The process is similar to a balancing game where the subject would be given 5 *equal* weights, each labeled (say colored, for example) differently, and would be asked to arrange them in a scaled order of preference on a balancing beam, but with the limitations that the beam must finally balance (the sum of the distances left and right of balance point to each weight must be equal) and the distances to the weights must not exceed 12 units either side of the balance point (lowest possible score is 12, highest possible is 36, indifference point is 24). Thus, the pattern types would have mechanical analogs:

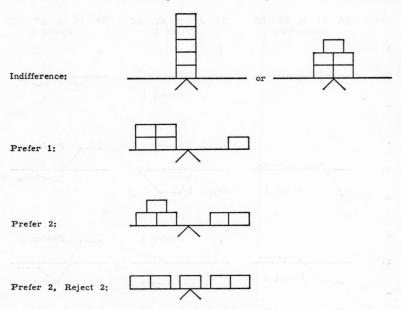

Indifference:

Prefer 1:

Prefer 2:

Prefer 2, Reject 2:

The three dynamics and this analog demonstrate that the position of any of the "weights" or category scores may be attributed to:

   A. Active Preference
   B. Active Rejection
   C. Indifference. In the presence of active preference and/or rejection for *other* categories, any particular category's position may be the residual result of the necessary balancing operation. For example, a subject actively prefers A and B and actively rejects C:

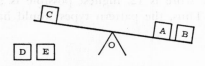

The placement of D and E will then follow in such a manner as to balance the pattern: they both have to be between C and A, right (+) or left (−) of the O point depending on the relationship between distances CO and AO and BO. As a result of this residual effect, it can be seen from inspection of the 9 types of patterns that *the median score will always be a "residual"* and thus may be described as indicating a point in a "zone of indifference."

3. To arrive at derived preference scales for each person, the following operations are performed on each person's 5-score preference pattern:

a. Transform Median score to zero. $(0 \pm i$ defines a "zone of indifference." From inspection of the data it appears that $i = 2$ might be a reasonable value.)

b. Scale other scores in relation to Median by subtracting each of them from original Median score. Plus $(+)$ values indicate categories which are preferred more than the Median category, minus $(-)$ values indicate categories which are preferred less than Median category. Numerical values *roughly* indicate *how much* more or less preference was expressed for the other categories in relation to the Median. Values within $O \pm i$ may be described as "indifferent." Values greater than i may be described as expressing active preference, while values below $-i$ may be described as expressing active rejection.

c. Subtract 24 from the Median Score. (This figure equals $\frac{1}{5}$ the sum of the differences between each category score and the median score.) The resulting number may be called a "pattern index"; a plus value indicates a pattern characterized by strong preferences of one or two categories, a minus figure indicates a pattern characterized by strong rejection of one or two categories. Zero (0) indicates a balanced pattern, which may contain either balanced extremes or balanced indifferent scores.

d. Subtract lowest score from highest score to determine the range of the pattern.

4. From the above theoretical discussion and method of transforming scores, 7 indices may be derived for each person from his performance on the Preference Study questionnaire:

a. Range of scores. A high range would indicate sharp discrimination, a low range would indicate a relative lack of discrimination.

b. Pattern index. A plus value indicates the predominant expression of relative preferences, a negative value indicates the predominant expression of relative rejections, while a zero value indicates a balanced pattern.

c. (d, e, f, and g) Indices of preference (+ values), rejection (− values), or indifference (0 ± i) may be computed for each subject for each of the 5 reward categories.

For this study, each participant was scored on his relative preference for (or rejection of, or indifference to) Belonging, Status, and Job-Intrinsic rewards. Persons were then ranked within their experimental groups on each of the three scores and they were classified High or Low in preference or rejection of each of the three categories of rewards. Although this procedure did not allow the inference that persons scoring High on Status preference, for example, preferred Status rewards more than did the persons scoring Low, it did allow the inference that persons scoring High on Status preference had stronger preferences (or weaker rejections) for Status rewards *in relation to the other kinds of rewards* than did persons scoring Low on Status preference. The other derivable indices were not analyzed for this study, hence their utility is yet to be determined.

While this procedure seems theoretically more correct than ranking persons on their raw preference scores, it was found from a limited analysis that the results of the two methods were close enough to allow interchangeability within the limits of accuracy acceptable for the kind of research which this study represents. The members of Group 1 (n = 13) were ranked by both their raw scores on Status preference and their scores derived by the above method. The two kinds of scores yielded a rank order correlation of .934. When both rankings were dichotomized, the following distribution resulted:

		RANKING ON DERIVED SCORE ON STATUS PREFERENCE		
		LOW	HIGH	TOTAL
RANKING ON RAW SCORE ON STATUS PREFERENCE	High	0	7	7
	Low	6	0	6
	Total	6	7	13

Zaleznik's work with groups of management people and managerial aspirants using the Preference Study compared individuals on their raw preference scores. His preliminary analyses used dichotomous High and Low classes. The facts that he found some associations which were meaningful and that his scoring method was nearly equivalent to the procedures proposed above indicate the practical validity of comparing individuals on their raw scores.

RELIABILITY OF THE PREFERENCE STUDY

To compute reliability figures on the Preference Study, Zaleznik used the results from two groups of Harvard Business School Advanced Management Program members, numbering 98 and 138. He had two sets of scores computed for each of the 236 questionnaires. One set consisted of scores on the five categories derived from the answers to the even numbered questions only, the other set consisted of scores derived from the odd numbered questions only. The two sets of scores were then correlated with each other. These odd-even correlations were in effect similar to the method of computing split-half reliability. The resulting corrections for the two groups were as follows, including both the raw correlations and the correlations corrected for discontinuity using the Brown-Spearman formula, corrected correlation $= \dfrac{2r}{1+r}$ (McNemar, 1955, pp. 156–157).

	Group n = 98		Group n = 138	
REWARD CATEGORY	r	B–S r	r	B–S r
Self-actualization	.66	.80	.46	.63
Job-Intrinsic	.11	.20	.57	.73
Status	.37	.54	.67	.80
Belonging	.54	.70	.52	.68
Economic	.77	.87	.75	.85

FINDINGS RELATED TO THE PREFERENCE STUDY

Zaleznik found that groups of upper management persons and business aspirants tended to rank the rewards in the order Self-actualization, Job-Intrinsic, Belonging, Status, and Economic. This was also true in the four groups in this present study. This would indicate the possibility that some dynamic related to social desirability was at work, resulting in relatively uniform rejection of status and economic rewards. This would not affect analyses which compare the degree to which different individuals prefer or reject particular reward categories.

The relationships between reward preferences and age in Tables E.1 through E.3 were found in Zaleznik's studies of the upper management groups:

Table E.1

BELONGING PREFERENCE AND AGE

N = 138

BELONGING	40 OR LESS	41–45	46–50	51 AND OVER
High	35%	49%	51%	69%
Low	65%	51%	49%	31%
Total	100%	100%	100%	100%

Table E.2

STATUS PREFERENCE AND AGE

N = 138

STATUS	40 OR LESS	41–45	46–50	51 AND OVER
High	69%	45%	49%	38%
Low	31%	55%	51%	62%
Total	100%	100%	100%	100%

Table E.3

ECONOMIC REWARD PREFERENCE AND AGE

N = 138

ECONOMIC	40 OR LESS	41–45	46–50	51 AND MORE
High	58%	59%	26%	44%
Low	42%	41%	74%	56%
Total	100%	100%	100%	100%

The interpretation of these data is limited by the given lower level cutoff age (40 or less). The patterns of these findings from the given lowest age category up to age 50 and over suggest at least three kinds of explanation:

1. *Legitimacy of goals.* The degree to which an individual expresses purposes which do not conform with the current social values increases with the attainment of stabilized social position. The young businessman is expected to value status and economic rewards and devalue belonging rewards within the subculture of the business community. As his age increases, his job responsibilities and salary increase, his social identity becomes more solidly established, and he becomes more free to deviate in his expressed goals. He has less to lose by such deviation than does the younger person whose social identity is not yet as well established.

2. The pattern of *attainment and deprivation of rewards* determines the concerns which the individual expresses. The younger persons in the groups tested were likely to be more closely engaged in their family groups including growing children, but to be of lower status and salary than the older persons. They were attaining belonging rewards but were deprived of status and economic rewards relative to the older persons. The older persons' children were more likely to have grown up and be in the process of leaving the home, thus depriving their parents of belonging rewards. The older persons had attained high status and economic rewards relative to the younger persons. The persons in the extreme age classes tended to express the highest concern, or preference, for those rewards that they were currently being deprived of, relative to persons at the opposite extreme of age.

3. The individuals' preferences reflected the *developmental impact of the historical epoch* surrounding their impressionable years. A person aged 42 in 1959 was born in 1917 and was growing through the ages 12 to 22 during the depression years 1929 to 1939. Economic deprivation, along with status anxiety for middle class families, characterized that period. A need to remedy these conditions was etched into the developing personalities of persons experiencing these conditions during

the years of their life in which career plans and personal goals were developing. Older persons in the tested groups, by virtue of being older during the depression epoch, had already attained some social identity and personal goals and thus had a more stable identity with which to counter a situational stress.

These three explanations, and other unspecified explanations, are all consistent with the manifest, intended meanings of the reward categories around which the Preference Study was constructed. In this present study there was behavioral confirmation of the meaning of High Belonging Preference (see Chapter 5), an inferred confirmation of the meaning of High Job Intrinsic Preference, but little data on the meaning of High Status Preference, possibly because the groups were all of a similar range of statuses compared with the population of employed persons in the surrounding culture.

To further investigate and elaborate upon explanations derived from the associations of the reward preferences with age, reward preferences were compared to the individuals' perceptions of the social climate in the families in which they grew up. The subjects were asked to indicate how close to their parental families they were while growing up by checking "Very close," "Close," or "Not so close." The findings are shown in Tables E.4 through E.6.

These findings indicate that felt deprivation of early familial belonging rewards ("Not so close" to family) were associated with High preferences for Status and Economic rewards and Low preference for Belonging rewards. These findings indicate that:

Table E.4

BELONGING PREFERENCE AND CLOSENESS

N = 138

	CLOSENESS		
BELONGING	VERY CLOSE	CLOSE	NOT SO CLOSE
High	59%	46%	41%
Low	41%	54%	59%
Total	100%	100%	100%

Table E.5

STATUS PREFERENCE AND CLOSENESS

N = 138

STATUS PREF.	CLOSENESS		
	VERY CLOSE	CLOSE	NOT SO CLOSE
High	42%	50%	63%
Low	58%	50%	37%
Total	100%	100%	100%

Table E.6

ECONOMIC REWARD PREFERENCE AND CLOSENESS

ECONOMIC PREF.	CLOSENESS		
	VERY CLOSE	CLOSE	NOT SO CLOSE
High	45%	41%	59%
Low	55%	59%	41%
Total	100%	100%	100%

1. Current concern with Status and Economic rewards may have a compensatory relationship to early deprivation of belonging rewards. Unsuccessful attainment of one kind of reward led to the pursuit of other kinds of rewards.
2. Successful attainment of belonging rewards in the early years was associated with a continuing maintenance of the value of belonging rewards at a high level. This would indicate a tendency for reinforcement with respect to belonging rewards at the conscious level.

Another aspect of reward preferences with which Zaleznik was concerned related to satisfaction. He proposed the relationship

$$\text{Satisfaction} = f\left(\frac{\text{Attained rewards}}{\text{Expected rewards}}\right).$$

This relationship would lead to the hypotheses:

1. At a given level of attained reward, persons who expected the most would be the least satisfied.
2. At a given level of reward expectation, persons who attained the most would be the most satisfied.

Table E.7
Economic Preferences, Rewards, and Satisfaction

PREFERENCE FOR ECONOMIC REWARDS, AS MEASURED BY EXECUTIVE PREFERENCE STUDY QUESTIONNAIRE		ANNUAL SALARY PLUS BONUS						TOTAL NUMBER
		LESS THAN $20,000		$20,000–$30,000		OVER $30,000		
		HIGH SAT.*	LOW SAT.	HIGH SAT.	LOW SAT.	HIGH SAT.	LOW SAT.	
High		4 25%	12	10 43%	13	5 56%	4	48
Low		7 30%	16	7 50%	7	9 69%	4	50
Total Number		11 $\overline{39}$	$\overline{28}$	17 $\overline{37}$	$\overline{20}$	14 $\overline{22}$	$\overline{8}$	$\overline{98}$

* Underlined figures show percent high satisfied with monetary reward, as measured by an executive satisfaction questionnaire.

Assuming that Preference for Economic Rewards reflected an expectation and that salary (plus bonus) level measured attainment of the related reward, the hypotheses were confirmed by the finding in Table E.7.

The first hypothesis is confirmed by reading down each salary range column. In all three columns (i.e., given economic reward levels), the lower the expressed preference for economic rewards, the higher the expressed satisfaction. The second hypothesis is confirmed by reading across each of the two Economic Reward preference rows. In both rows (i.e., given levels of preference), the higher the attained reward, the higher the expressed satisfaction.

These findings from the use of the Preference Study with managerial persons give limited confirmation to the theoretical validity and the relational fertility of the Preference Study as an instrument for measuring concerns which were relevant to the experience and goals of the individuals. The behavioral and perceptual data from this present study confirm the value of the Preference Study as an instrument which may be related to the behavior of individuals in social situations.

Test of Imagination (Thematic Apperception Test, TAT)

A comprehensive discussion of the TAT as used in this present study will be found in *Motives in Fantasy, Action, and Society,* edited by John W. Atkinson (1958). Scoring manuals for need Achievement and need Affiliation are presented on pages 179 to 204 and 205 to 218, respectively, of that reference. The person scoring the TAT stories looks for certain specific cues, signals, or conditions in each story, and scores one count for each of the conditions that is met. The subject is then given a score corresponding to the total number of such counts entered for him for all four stories. Separate scoring schedules are kept for the two kinds of motives, achievement and affiliation.

The conditions which were scored for need Achievement were as follows:

CODE	CONDITION
UI, TI, AI	There is achievement imagery in the story, reflected in competition with a standard, unique accomplishment, and/or long term involvement.

CODE	CONDITION
N	The need is experienced in the story. Someone *wants* to achieve, accomplish, or be successful at something.
I	Someone in the story is engaged in instrumental activity toward a goal.
I+	The instrumental activity attains the goal.
I−	The instrumental activity does not attain the goal.
Ga+	Successful goal attainment is anticipated.
Ga−	Failure is anticipated.
G+	Positive emotions are experienced in goal attainment.
G−	Negative emotions are experienced in goal attainment.
Nup	Nurtural press. Someone is trying to help or sympathize.
Bp	There is a block in the subject, preventing him from attainment.
Bw	There is a block in the world.
Th	Achievement becomes the main theme, or plot, of the story.

Similar conditions were used to score need Affiliation. Affiliation is identified as friendly relationships between two or more persons. The above conditions are used but limited by special definitions and rules to instances where affiliation is the goal, object, or concern.

The TAT's for the 52 participants in the groups used for this study were scored at three different points in time by a single scorer. The protocols from Groups 1 and 2 were scored in October 1959. Those from Groups 3 and 4 were initially scored in June 1960. In order to assess the scorer's reliability over time, 36 randomly selected protocols from both batches, with their identities masked, were re-scored by the same person in July 1960. The correlations (Spearman Rank Order Correlation) between the scoring done at the different times were as follows:

1. nAch rs
    a. October 1959 vs. July 1960   .925
    b. June 1960 vs. July 1960   .757

2. nAff
    a. October 1959 vs. July 1960   .817
    b. June 1960 vs. July 1960   .59

Since the correlations between June 1960 and July 1960 scores were much lower than the correlations between October 1959 and

July 1960 scores, it was inferred that the scorer's special problems around the completion of his Ph.D. work in June had influenced his scoring at that time. Therefore, the 6 (out of 24) TAT's from Groups 3 and 4 which had not been included with the 36 which were rescored for the reliability check in July were separately submitted for rescoring later in the month. The July 1960 scores for Groups 3 and 4 were used in the study along with the October 1959 scores for Groups 1 and 2.

Underlying the development of the TAT were repeated findings that situationally imposed conditions, such as hunger, achievement, affiliation, power, sex, fear, and aggression came out in the stories written by persons during or immediately following exposure to the stimuli conditions. Behavioral studies confirmed and/or elaborated the relationship between TAT themes and measurable behaviors. McClelland has done cross-cultural studies, including content analysis of public documents (such as readers used by Soviet and American elementary school children), which find associations between cultural conditions and individuals' TAT scores. Zaleznik analyzed nAch and nAff scores in relation to the data obtained from the upper management people previously referred to. Some of his findings are given in Tables E.8 and E.9.

The association between nAch and Closeness was in the same direction as were the associations between Status and Economic Reward Preferences and Closeness. This would indicate that two levels of motivation, conscious and unconscious, tended to be congruent with respect to achievement and its culturally recognized measures. Need Affiliation shows a direction of association with Closeness which is the inverse of that which was found with Belonging Preference and Closeness. Persons who checked "Not so Close" tended to score *High* on nAff. The indication here is that the deprivation of early needs for affectionate relationships with other persons is associated with a high currently active need for affiliation, which is a relatively unconscious condition compared to Belonging Preference. When the two measures related to rewards from interpersonal relationships are compared, the repression or denial dynamic discussed in Chapter 5 is suggested.

When need Achievement was analyzed in relation to satisfaction, the general finding was that the higher the nAch score, the

Table E.8

NEED ACHIEVEMENT AND CLOSENESS TO FAMILY

N = 138

	CLOSENESS		
NACH	VERY CLOSE	CLOSE	NOT SO CLOSE
High	43%	41%	63%
Low	57%	59%	37%
Total	100%	100%	100%

Table E.9

NEED AFFILIATION AND CLOSENESS TO FAMILY

N = 138

	CLOSENESS		
NAFF	VERY CLOSE	CLOSE	NOT SO CLOSE
High	45%	55%	70%
Low	55%	45%	30%
Total	100%	100%	100%

lower the proportion of persons who were High in satisfaction with their career, their company, their superiors, and their opportunities for advancement. It was also found that nAch was associated with the individuals' job functions, as shown in Table E.10.

Table E.10

NEED ACHIEVEMENT AND JOB FUNCTIONS

NEED ACHIEVEMENT	PRODUCTION AND ENGINEERING N = 25	CONTROL AND FINANCE N = 29	MARKETING N = 24	TOTAL N = 78
High	36%	41%	75%	50%
Low	64%	59%	25%	50%
Total	100%	100%	100%	100%

Persons in marketing tended to score higher on nAch than did persons in control and finance, who, in turn, tended to score higher than did persons in production and engineering. These associations could be related to the selection of the occupational function by persons, given certain levels of need for achievement; or to the criteria for promotion within a function, given that the persons were selected by their organizations; or to the influence of the environment on persons, given that the demands of the functions are different and that persons' needs are to some extent fashioned by interaction with their environments. The problem of interpretation is contingent upon the difference between situationally aroused motives, which the TAT purports to measure, and long-term conscious plans and goals, which are in some way related to the more fleeting and spontaneous situational concerns. Zaleznik's data indicate that relative TAT scores were related to long-range, nonsituational life trends. This would indicate that although specific motives may be stimulated by unique situational factors, the *intensity* of the aroused motive is a function of the more general life-processes involving goal orientation and identity.

APPENDIX F

The Measurement of Behavior

THIS APPENDIX presents the backgrounds of the systems which
were used to measure behavior for this research study. These
systems were discussed briefly in Appendix A. They are Bales'
Interaction Process Analysis (IPA) (1951) and three interrelated
systems developed by Moment for this study. The three newly
devised systems are called Interval Event Analysis (IEA), Event
Content Analysis (ECA), and Interpersonal Behavior Analysis
(IBA).

IPA SYSTEM

Bales' IPA system consists of twelve mutually exclusive and
collectively exhaustive categories within which all identifiable
behavioral acts that occur in small groups may be placed. Most
of the categories are defined in terms of the content of the participants' verbal communications, but some of them, notably the ones
concerned with tension management, include nonverbal behaviors. The twelve categories are conceptually related to each
other through a theory of group process which conceives of the
two broader kinds of problems and activities identifiable as
Social-Emotional and Instrumental-Adaptive. Social-Emotional
problems and activities are concerned with the maintenance of
the group as an entity and the concomitant satisfaction of the
individual needs which serve to relate individuals to the group.
Instrumental-Adaptive problems and activities relate to *external*
problem-solving, the influencing of the environment by the group
and the adaptation by the group to influences from the environment. These latter kinds of activities constitute work, produc-
tiveness, and problem-solving in the usual senses of the words.

Chart F.1

INTERACTION PROCESS ANALYSIS SYSTEM OF CATEGORIES *

SOCIAL-
EMOTIONAL   A
AREA:
POSITIVE

1 *Shows solidarity*, raises others' status, gives help, reward:

2 *Shows tension release*, jokes, laughs, shows satisfaction:

3 *Agrees*, shows passive acceptance, understands, concurs, complies:

TASK
AREA:
NEUTRAL

B

4 *Gives suggestion*, direction, implying autonomy for other:

5 *Gives opinion*, evaluation, analysis, expresses feeling, wish:

6 *Gives orientation*, information, repeats, clarifies, confirms:

C

7 *Asks for orientation*, information, repetition, confirmation:

8 *Asks for opinion*, evaluation, analysis, expression of feeling:

9 *Asks for suggestion*, direction, possible ways of action:

SOCIAL-
EMOTIONAL   D
AREA:
NEGATIVE

10 *Disagrees*, shows passive rejection, formality, withholds help:

11 *Shows tension*, asks for help, withdraws out of field:

12 *Shows antagonism*, deflates others' status, defends or asserts self:

a   b   c   d   e   f

KEY:

a Problems of Communication
b Problems of Evaluation
c Problems of Control
d Problems of Decision
e Problems of Tension Reduction
f Problems of Reintegration

A Positive Reactions
B Attempted Answers
C Questions
D Negative Reactions

* Taken from Bales, *Interaction Process Analysis*, p. 59

Detailed discussions of the IPA system may be found in Bales, *Interaction Process Analysis* (1951) and Bales, "The Equilibrium Problem in Small Groups" (1955). Chart F.1 presents a diagram taken from *Interaction Process Analysis* which shows the twelve IPA categories and their schematic relationships to each other. Further definitions of the scoring categories may be found in the same reference.

For this study a trained IPA scorer from the Harvard University Department of Social Relations worked from the tape recordings and the typescripts of the four group discussions to score each participant and the unidentifiable speakers on their production of IPA acts. He did not score the "to whom" aspect of the acts, only the "from whom" initiators. The general interscorer reliability of the IPA system is documented in Bales' and others' works. The specific person who did the IPA scoring for this study reported that his own scoring performance had been correlated against that of one of his colleagues in a project involving an eleven-member training group which met in 26 one-hour meetings. These meetings were scored "live" by the two researchers while observing the group in action. They were working on developing revisions to the original IPA system so that not all of their scoring categories were directly comparable. For those categories which were directly comparable they found the following correlations between the two scorers' counts of the number of acts produced by each participant in each category:

IPA CATEGORY	r
1	+.35
2	+.81
3	+.71
7 + 8 + 9	+.60 (approx.)
10	+.56
11	+.30
12	+.21

It is generally found that interscorer reliability is higher when the scorers work from tape recordings and/or typescripts than when they work directly from live group performances.

Correlations which were found between IPA scores and scores for comparable (but not identical) categories in the new systems

were as follows, for those pairs from which one member was
used in this study:

	COMPARABLE (BUT NOT IDENTICAL) MEASURES	
MEASURES FROM NEW SYSTEMS	FROM IPA SYSTEM	r
X Participation (IEA)	Total Acts	+.95
Tension Reduction (ECA)	XR Shows Tension Release (Category 2)	+.25
XR Support (Agreement, ECA)	Agrees (Category 3)	+.54
XR Negative (Disagreement, ECA)	Disagrees (Category 10)	+.43

X identifies measures used in this study.
XR identifies measures converted to ratios for use in this study (see Appendix D).

IEA, ECA, AND IBA SYSTEMS

The general operations of these systems and the reasons for
their development are explained in Appendix A. On the following pages are copies of the "Introduction for Scorers" and the
"Manual for Scoring the Behavior of Individuals in the Experimental Group Situation." These documents were used by the
six persons, including one of the writers, who scored behavior under the new systems. The "Introduction" describes the purpose
of the scoring operations and gives a summary of the content of
the film which the participants were shown immediately prior to
their group discussions. The scoring manual describes the rules
followed by the typist in preparing the typescripts from the tape
recordings and then describes the operations for scoring under the
three systems, including the definitions of the scoring categories.
The three systems (IEA, ECA, and IBA) were not identified by
name in the manual. Following these documents, Table F.2 presents the interscorer reliability statistics for the six scorers using
the ECA and IBA systems. The behavior scores ultimately used
in the study were the averages of the several scorers' scores for
each participant on each measure. Not all of the categories
scored were used in the study. The correlations presented are
the coefficients of contingency of each scorer's score with the
average score for each participant on each of the categories.

The three new systems are different from the IPA system in that they use categories which are neither mutually exclusive nor collectively exhaustive. They do not represent a single, integrated theory of either individual or group behavior. Their several theoretical backgrounds are described in Chapters 2 and 4. The writers are convinced that future development of individual and group behavior theories will require the use of several independent scoring systems. This will resolve the dilemma of the closed scoring system which imposed artificial distinctions between instrumental and emotional behaviors. For example, the "competitive question" used as a scoring category in the ECA system identifies an event that is *both* instrumental and emotional; it is related to "external" work *and* it is related to interpersonal aggression and competition. Perhaps separate schemes will be developed to measure work activity, using the logics of communication and data-processing theory; to measure social activity from the points of view of *social* integration and differentiation; to measure interpersonal behavior in terms of aggression, submission, affection, hostility, dependency, counter-dependency, autonomy, and similar dimensions; and to measure manifestations of differentiation and integration within the personality systems of the individuals. Under these conditions associations between measures made using different systems could lead to integrated findings relating the effects of culture, social organization, and personality to individual behavior in social situations.

INTRODUCTION FOR SCORERS

We are asking your assistance to help us develop a reliable method for the description of individual behavior in group situations. The materials with which you will work will consist of a scoring manual giving instructions for scoring the behaviors, typescripts of the group situation where from eleven to fifteen people are involved in a case discussion, and the tape recording from which the typescript was prepared.

The four different groups with which we are working were voluntary subjects for our research project. Besides taking part in the group discussion, each of the participants completed several questionnaires and psychological tests. The research analysis will consist of investigating the relationships between the questionnaire and test data and the behavior of individuals in the group situations. Groups 1 and 2 consisted of people who usually worked together on the job in their respective companies, while the people in Groups 3 and 4 came from different organizations and had not worked with each other before. Members of Groups 1 and 3 were of similar job status or age, while Groups 2 and 4 included wider ranges of ages and job statuses.

The descriptions of behavior on which you will be working will constitute the dependent variables in our analysis. The goal of scoring the behaviors is to present behavioral descriptions of individuals in quantitative form. As you will see in the manual, the behavior description for each person will consist of scores on each of several kinds of behavior. The scores will be "counts" of the number of times each person did certain things or was involved in certain kinds of "events."

The groups were told that we were interested in studying how different groups go about solving the same problem. They were shown a filmed case situation lasting about seven or eight minutes which presented a problem. Then they were given a dittoed memo on which were listed three suggested topics for discussion, and were finally left alone for forty minutes of discussion. The researchers observed the discussion and noted the identity and sequence of speakers while the discussion was being recorded on tape.

The filmed case was entitled "Promotion By-Pass." In the film, Frank Robbins, office manager, was asked on the telephone by a Mr. Radford to pick one of Robbins' office men to head up a similar office at the company's Lake City Plant. Robbins had two men from which to choose. One was an old-timer, Harry Stevens, who was described by Robbins as a highly competent worker who tended to be gruff with people and careless in his appearance. Bob Randolph, the younger man, was described as neat, a "university graduate," and "got people to do things his way." The film showed scenes of both men in action. Robbins decided to give Randolph the promotion. The main part of the film showed Robbins talking with Stevens in Robbins' office. He complimented Harry on his work, explained that a promotion opportunity had arisen, and told Harry he had two alternatives, Harry and **Bob**. At this stage, Harry seemed pleased, but when Frank told him that he was giving the promotion to Bob, Harry showed surprised shock. At the end of the talk, Harry said he had one thing to say. Frank said, "Out with it, Harry." Harry said, "I quit," and walked out of the office. Frank turned to the film audience and asked, "What did I do wrong?", after which the film ended.

The suggested topics for discussion for Groups 1 and 2 were:

1. What *did* Frank do wrong?
2. Did Frank make the correct choice for promotion?
3. How might Frank have done a better job of talking with Harry?

For Groups 3 and 4, the first two questions were the same, but the third was changed to read:

3. What, if anything, should Frank do now?

The scoring manual is divided into four parts. The first part consists of instructions for the person who worked from the tape recording and the observer's notes to make up the typescript, and explains conventions followed on the typescript. The second part explains a kind of analysis which, we feel, has "built-in" reliability and thus does not have to be scored by several people. The third and fourth parts are the instructions from which we would like you to work. The first two parts should be studied, however, as background for your work with parts 3 and 4.

MANUAL FOR SCORING THE BEHAVIOR OF INDIVIDUALS
IN THE EXPERIMENTAL GROUP SITUATION

I. *Preparation*

The basic materials upon which these scoring procedures are based are a tape recording of the group discussion and the observers' notes indicating the identity and sequence of the speakers. From these two sources, a typescript of the meeting is constructed. On the typescript, the following conventions are followed:

1. The identity of each speaker is indicated by a number in the lefthand margin. Each time a speaker changes, a new line is started. When a speaker refers to another person in the group by name, the number of the other person is entered in brackets in the typescript in place of the name (for example, [1]).

2. When a speaker stops talking before finishing a complete

sentence, a dash (—) is typed after his last word. When a speaker's words are unintelligible, this is indicated by ellipses in place of the indistinguishable words, as follows: (. . .)

3. When two or more people are talking at the same time, and their identities are established, the notation (together) is made in the left margin between the identifying numbers of the speakers. When a second speaker starts to talk before the preceding speaker has finished talking, and continues to talk after the preceding speaker stops, the notation (overlap) is used in the left margin adjacent to the last line spoken by the preceding speaker and above the number preceding the second speaker's initial words.

4. Periods when several people are talking at once are indicated by the symbol (babble) on a separate line, with the identity of the participants, if known, indicated in the left margin, or by the notation (together) between the names of the participants if the words spoken are distinguishable.

5. The actual sequence of sounds made by the speaker are typed as accurately as possible, including "uh," "er," "ah," etc., but pronunciation is corrected. For example, "gonna" and "wanna" sounds are typed "going to" and "want to."

6. Periods of conspicuous nonactivity are indicated by the symbol (silence) on a separate line, whether or not the preceding speaker continues after the silent period.

7. Outbreaks of laughter are indicated by the symbol (laughter) on a separate line. If no further notation is made, this indicates "group-wide" laughter. Notations are made describing less than group-wide laughter, such as:

(light laughter) or
(a few chuckles) .

8. Nonverbal agreement and disagreement, symbolized by nodding or shaking heads and/or appropriate grunts, is indicated in the same manner as if spoken, that is, by an entry on a new line, when such behavior has been noted by the observer and was judged to be of sufficient strength to be noticeable to others in the group. However, running agreement, in the form of repeated "uh huh's" throughout another person's talking, is indicated in the margin, along with the identity of the agreer, if known, in parenthetical form.

9. During the original typing, the tape recorder counter number is indicated at the top and bottom of each page, with the corresponding entries in the observer's notes also being so coded, to enable locating questionable passages, etc.

Following the completion of the typescript, which covers about 25 double-spaced pages for a 40-minute discussion, the entire recording is rerun. On the rerun, a stop watch calibrated in tenths and hundredths of a minute is used to indicate on or between the appropriate words or sounds on the typescript, the beginning and end of 12-second intervals, which are indicated on the stop watch as .2 minutes. These intervals are consecutively numbered on the typescript.

These 12-second intervals constitute the scoring unit for the analysis of behavior, the entire 40-minute session covering about 200-interval units.

II. *Scoring Quantity and Direction of Interaction*

A scoring sheet is made up listing the identity symbols of the participants in such a manner as to identify each horizontal row with one particular participant, and indicating the interval numbers across the top of the form at the head of approximately 200 narrow columns. The identity of each person who spoke during each interval is noticed on the typescript and a check mark entered in each speaker's cell in the appropriate interval column. Thus, a horizontal total of check marks for each person indicates *the number of intervals during which he participated.* A row is also provided for unidentified participants.

A secondary analysis from the same scoring sheet is entered on a matrix where the participants are listed in the same order in both column and row headings. Each row is scored separately for the number of intervals shared by the row person with each of the column persons. This is done by moving horizontally across the interaction scoring sheet for one person at a time, entering a tally on the appropriate matrix cell for each time each other person talked during the same interval as the row person.

From the interaction scoring sheet and the shared intervals matrix, the following behavioral measures and indices are computed for individuals:

1. Participation amount: the number of intervals during which each individual participated.
2. Interaction amount: the number of intervals during which an individual participated which were *shared,* i.e., during which others also participated.
3. Monological participation: the number of intervals during which an individual participated which were not shared with others.

Participation amount = Interaction amount + Monological participation.

An "exclusiveness" index is derived from the pattern indicated on the interaction matrix. This index measures the degree to which each person's interactions with each of the other persons varies from the amount of interaction that would be expected with each other person if interaction were proportional to the other's participation. The *lower* the "exclusiveness" index, the closer the person's interaction pattern to the proportional expectancy. The higher a person's "exclusiveness" index, the greater his tendency to be selective in his interaction in terms of speaking more or less with some people than with others, to a degree which exceeds the variation which would be expected based on differences in the others' participation rates.

III. *Scoring Manifest Interpersonal Behaviors from Analysis of Content of Typescript*

Four kinds of behavior are scored from the *content* of the group discussion. The units here are events within intervals. The events are the occurrence or nonoccurrence of certain kinds of verbal expressions. For each event there are three aspects: an actor, an action, and an object. The object, in this section of the scoring manual, is always a *specific* other person in the group. The actor is usually the speaker who is at the center of the group's attention at the moment, but may be a speaker who is speaking "behind," "under," or along with the main, "feature" speaker. Four kinds of *action* will be scored: supportive behaviors, negative behaviors, personal references, and questions to specific others eliciting defense. A separate scoring matrix form is kept for each of these four kinds of action.

In most cases, the scorer need not pay attention to the interval during which a scored event takes place. However, the interval-event combination as the scoring unit is relevant for repeated behaviors, where the same actor takes the same action toward the same object repeatedly. In these cases, only one scoring count is recorded for each interval under the appropriate actor and object cell on the scoring form applying to the action involved. For example, when actor A says, "I agree with that," "right," "yes," etc., to object B, the behavior "A supports B" is scored only once for each interval in which these words occur. However, each change in actor, action, or object is scored as a separate count, even though one or two of the aspects may remain the same during an interval. For example, the behaviors "A supports B," "A supports C," "A is negative to B," "A makes personal reference to B," would all be counted, whether or not they occurred during the same interval, because in none of these events is the triad "actor, action, and object" constant.

Definition of Actions

1. *Supportive actions* are those events where the actor agrees with or tries to help the object. The words, "Yes," "Right," "I agree," "Uh huh," are the cues which we score as "agreement" *unless* they are followed by "but." In a supportive situation, as defined here, the supportive person does not attempt to discredit the other person, as would be indicated by a "Yes, but—" comment. Additional content of the supporter's comments, if any, will be further elaboration of the supported person's ideas. A helping action, as defined here under supportive action, consists of the actor "finding words" for the other, when the other is stumbling or looking for words, or restating the other's ideas in different words. In this sense, the supportive person does not attempt to discredit the other person nor does he use this kind of "help" as a handle with which to pull himself into the attention of the group and express his own new and different ideas. The helping comment will be followed by either an acknowledgment, such as "that's right," from the other, or further supportive elaboration by the actor. On the scoring form, a supportive event will be counted by indicating the interval number during which the event occurred in the cell at the intersection of the actor's row with the object's column on the scoring matrix. "A supports B

during interval 11" will be scored by writing in a small "11" in the cell located by row A and column B on the matrix form used for scoring supportive behavior.

As with the other kinds of behaviors which will be defined, if the scorer is in doubt about an event's meeting the given definitions, he should *not* score it. "U" rows and columns are provided for unidentified actors and objects.

2. *Negative actions* are those events where the actor expresses disagreement with the other person's statement. The words "No," "I disagree," "That's not right," "Uh uh," are the major cues which we score as disagreement. Responses to *statements* prefaced by "but," or "on the other hand" are scored as negative. This kind of response in answer to a *question* is *not* scored as negative.

3. *Personal references* are those events where the actor refers to specific other people in the group by saying the other's name, or referring to him as "you," "he," or "she." Personal references may be in supportive or negative events, in which case the event is scored on both the supportive (or negative) behavior form and on the personal reference form. In some cases, a personal reference may be made with no supportive or negative connotation, for example, "When you said that the guy in the film was upset, it reminded me of a situation— . . . ," would be scored as a personal reference but not as supportive or negative. On the other hand, such comments as, "I disagree with that, John," would be scored both as a personal reference and as negative.

4. Questions to specific others which elicit defense are those events where the actor addresses a question to a specific other person about the content of the other's previous remarks, and which evoke from the other defensive or justifying explanations. The simplest form of this behavior is the question, "Why?". A more complex form is a restatement of the other's ideas in a form which causes the other to elaborate further, rather than accept the restatement. The "helping" kind of restatement described under 1, above, is usually acknowledged as help by the object, other person, in the form of the words, "right," "yes," etc., after which the other continues his comments. However, the "question eliciting defense" may be identified by the act of defense by the other.

The qualification that the question be addressed to a specific person rules out questions addressed to the group in general, such as, "Anyone want to start?", "What should we do about question 3?", etc.

Examples for the use of all four scoring matrices:

1. John: (Statement)
   George: That's right.   } Score: George supports John.

2. John: (Statement)   } Score: George supports John and
   George: That's right, John.   }   George makes personal
                                            reference to John.

3. Sam: (Statement)
   Pete: I disagree, because as John and George said a few minutes
            ago—. . .
                        Score: Pete negative to Sam.
                               Pete supports George.
                               Pete supports John.
                               Pete makes personal reference to
                               John.
                               Pete makes personal reference to
                               George.

4. Dave: (Statement)
   Bill: I disagree with that, because you aren't taking into ac-
            count—. . .
   Jim: Right.
                        Score: Bill negative to Dave.
                               Bill makes personal reference to
                               Dave. ("you")
                               Jim supports Bill.

5. Ray: (Statement) } Score: Mel negative to Ray.
   Mel: I disagree. }   Tony supports Mel.
   Tony: Me, too.   }   (Notice: Tony's comment is *not*
                                   scored as negative to Ray.)

6. Art: (Statement)
   Harry: In my opinion, there's not much you can do in a situation like
            this.
                        Score: No score. The "you" in this case is
                               a "generalized" other which may
                               refer to people in general, the other
                               members of the group, etc. "You"
                               is a cue for a personal reference *only*
                               when it refers to a *specific* other person
                               in the group, as in example 4 above.

7. Doug: . . . I think he should have at least given him a raise.
   Charlie: Why?
   Doug: Because he deserved it, if he was really just as good as . . .
   > Score: Charlie asks Doug a question elicit-
   > ing defense.

8. Harold: . . . Maybe they wanted him to quit.
   Bob: You mean, Harold, that they wanted to get rid of him?
   Harold: No, not that, but just that maybe they wouldn't mind if he did.
   > Score: Bob asks Harold a question eliciting
   > defense. Bob makes personal refer-
   > ence to Harold.
   > (Notice: Harold's reply, which starting out
   > "no," is *not* scored as disagreement
   > with Bob.)

IV. *Scoring Aspects of Interaction Other Than Verbal From Typescript and Tape Recording*

Four kinds of events are scored in this analysis: competitive interruption, "babble," group laughter, and silence. Descriptions and definitions of these events do *not* make reference to the content of the interaction, the words people use. The event-interval unit is to be used in the same manner as described for scoring support, negative, and personal reference behavior from content in Section III of this manual.

1. Competitive interruption is scored on a matrix form, with the specific cells identifying both the interrupter and the interrupted person. Unlike the matrices used to score content categories, each row of the Competitive Interruption Matrix consists of two lines: a top line for successful interruptions and a bottom line for attempted interruptions which failed. Interruption is defined as a second person taking over the group's attention before the first person completes his comments. In a successful interruption, the second person "takes over" from the first. In a failed attempt, the first person continues without allowing the second person to take over, after the second person tries to interrupt.

If a speaker's voice trails off into silence or mumbles, indicating that he does not want to continue talking, but perhaps doesn't know how to stop, the next speaker is *not* interrupting, according to this scoring procedure. Short statements of agreement and short supportive comments by a second speaker are not counted as interruptions, when the second speaker does not continue to talk beyond the supportive comments.

Interruptions by unidentified persons are counted in the row marked "U" under the column of the person being interrupted.

The following kinds of events are scored on tabular forms, rather than matrices, the aspects being "actor" and "action" only, with no "object" identification.

 2. "Babble" is the shorthand word used to describe situations where two or more persons are talking at the same time. For each "babble" event, we want to count three different relationships of people to the event:

  1. Who is involved in the "babble"?

  2. Whose comment or statement induced the "babble"?

  3. Who "came out on top"?; who emerged from the "babble" as sole participant?

Since we are counting these relationships as indicators of tension and competition, we do *not* count those babble situations where consensus is being expressed, where, for example, a speaker's comment is followed by a chorus of people saying "no" or "yes."

For some babble events we will not be able to answer all of the three questions above. When we cannot determine who induced the babble, no count is made. Similarly, there are some babble events which do not terminate with the emergence of a single participant. Examples of this kind include situations when the babble terminates in group laughter or silence.

When the typist was not able to distinguish the words of different people talking at the same time, the notation "babble" was used. However, some events defined here as babble were not so identified by the typist. Whenever the symbols (babble) or (together) appear in the typescript, a babble situation or an interruption event will be recorded. Babble would *not* be recorded if the event could be clearly identified as interruption.

When two people start talking together at approximately the same instant following a third person's completed comment, the two are involved in babble. However, if they start talking at approximately the same instant while the third person is still talking, they are both considered to be interrupting.

 3. Group laughter refers to situations where two or more

Table F.2
INTERSCORER RELIABILITIES, ECA AND IBA
COEFFICIENTS OF CONTINGENCY, EACH SCORER AGAINST THE
AVERAGE OF ALL SCORERS, FOR EACH BEHAVIOR MEASURE

			SCORER			
	1	2	3	4	5	6
CATEGORY:						
Support Produced	.92	.86	.89	.83	.86	.90
Support Received	.90	.88	.88	.89	.89	.87
Negative Produced	.86	.87	.81	.85	.85	.86
Negative Received	.88	.86	.84	.87	.86	.88
Personal Produced	.87	.89	.86	.87	.87	.86
Personal Received	.91	.90	.89	.91	.89	.90
Comp. Ques., Prod.*	.80	.73	.73	.70	.68	.71
Comp. Ques., Recd.	.79	.82		.85	.85	.77
Inter. Att. Prod.†	.87	.87	.85	.88	.87	
Inter. Succ. Prod.‡	.89	.87	.84	.86	.87	
Int. Att. Recd.	.90	.83	.87	.87	.87	
Int. Att. Recd., Failed	.84	.59	.85	.86	.84	
Babble Involvement	.83	.80	.83	.84	.83	
Induced Babble	.59	.82	.81	.67	.84	
Babble Break	.87	.87	.85	.80	.86	
Induce Laughter	.83	.88	.89	.87	.84	
Stopped Laughter	.64	.86	.87	.81	.80	
Induce Silence	.83	.83	.82	.81	.82	
Break Silence	.79	.82	.79	.81	.81	

SUMMARY

COEFFICIENTS OF CONTINGENCY	NUMBER OF INSTANCES	
Over .90	3 }	8
.90	5 }	
.89	8 }	
.88	6 }	
.87	18 }	51
.86	12 }	
.85	7 }	
.84	7 }	
.83	8 }	
.82	5 }	30
.81	6 }	
.80	4 }	
Under .80	13	13
Total	102	

* Competitive Questions Produced.
† Interruption Attempts Produced.
‡ Successful Interruptions Produced.

persons other than the initial speaker join in laughter, and during which no one person is talking. For these events, we want to know:

    1. Whose comment, statement, or behavior induced the laughter?

    2. Whose comment stopped the laughter?

Again, there may be laughter incidents in which one or both of these questions cannot be answered. For example, the laughter may emerge from babble, and/or the laughter may terminate in silence. Where we can determine who induced the laughter and who stopped the laughter, we score these actions for the identified persons, otherwise we do not have anything to count.

    4. Silence refers to a noticeable gap in the discussion during which the members seem to be either "stopped cold" by the previous comment, and/or are waiting for someone to "break the ice." For these events, we want to know:

    1. Whose behavior induced the silence?

    2. Whose comments broke the silence?

As with babble and laughter, these questions may be unanswerable in some cases, or may require counts for more than one person. For example, at the beginning of the discussion we score a count for the person who breaks the silence, but have no one to credit with inducing the silence. If the silence is broken by babble, we have more than one person to credit with breaking the silence. If the silence follows babble, we do not credit anyone with inducing silence.

APPENDIX G

Intercorrelation Matrix

AN INTERCORRELATION matrix on which the correlation of each of 38 measures with each of the other 37 * is shown in three parts in the following pages. These correlations were computed on IBM equipment at the Littauer Statistical Laboratory of Harvard University using a computer program devised by Arthur Couch of the Harvard Department of Social Relations in connection with his factor analysis work. The correlations on these tables are for the aggregated four groups, n = 52, except for the "Work with" and "Know socially" measures, which were applied to Groups 3 and 4 only, where n = 24. Appendix D explains the scales and scoring operations used to derive the scores on the various measures.

The three parts are sections of a single matrix, 38 measures by 38 measures square. They are arranged as follows in relation to the matrix and to each other:

---

* 39 variables are shown on the matrix, but correlations were computed among only 38 of them.

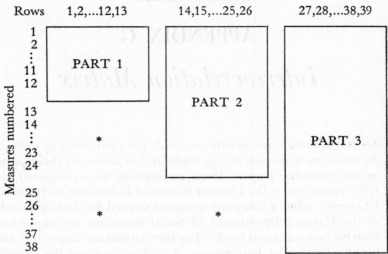

Enumeration of Measures on Intercorrelation Matrix

Perceptions and Evaluations:
1. Quality of Ideas
2. Guidance
3. Leadership
4. Congeniality
5. "Work with"
6. "Know socially" $\Big\}$ n = 24

Produced Behaviors:
7. Participation
8. Interaction
9. Social-Emotional Acts
10. Ask Acts
11. Tension Release

12. Interruption
13. Competitive Questions
14. Personalness
15. Agreement
16. Disagreement

Received Behaviors:
17. Interruption Attempts Received
18. Competitive Questions Received
19. Personal Recognition Received
20. Agreement Received
21. Disagreement Received

* Since the matrix is symmetrical around the diagonal running from the upper left-hand to lower right-hand corners, only the upper right-hand half is shown on the tables in this appendix.

Predispositions:
22. Need Achievement Score
23. Need Affiliation Score
24. Belonging Preference
25. Status Preference
26. Job-Intrinsic Preference *

Social Determinants:
27. Salary
28. Age
29. Seniority
30. Experience

31. Education Level
32. Ethnicity
33. Sex
34. Social Status Index
35. Total Status Index
36. Reward-Investment Index
37. Congruity-Ambiguity Index

Satisfaction:
38. Satisfaction with Decision
39. Satisfaction with Operation

In order to interpret the correlations shown in the tables, some statistical significance criteria may be used. The assumption underlying the use of these significance figures is that the 52 (or 24) cases were a *sample* drawn from a population in a way which made the sample representative of that population. This assumption was *not* made for the analysis in the body of this study, where it was assumed that the 52 cases were in themselves a population. However, if the sampling assumption is made, the following statistical significance statement would apply to the correlations found in the sample:

If there were really *no association* between two measures in the population, then the likelihood of finding correlations between the same two measures in the *sample* would be as follows:

n	LIKELIHOOD	r
50	.05	.231
50	.01	.322
24	.05	.330
24	.01	.453

These figures were taken from Walker and Lev, *Statistical Inference* (1953), pp. 249–254 and p. 470. They should be read as follows, for example:

> If a sample of 50 cases were to be drawn from a population in which it is known that the correlation between two measures is 0.00, the likelihood of finding a correlation as large as .231 between the two measures in the sample is .05.

* Job-Intrinsic Preference scores were not used in the initial stages of analysis, hence that measure is not included on the matrix. The numbering of measures corresponds to the presentation in Appendix D.

	1	2	3	4
		GUID-		CON-
	IDEAS	ANCE	LEAD.	GEN.
1. Ideas		.64	.75	.50
2. Guidance			.72	.48
3. Leadership				.60
4. Congeniality				
5. Work with *				
6. Know Socially *				
7. Participation				
8. Interaction				
9. Social-Emotional				
10. Ask Acts				
11. Tension Release				
12. Interruption				

* n = 24

5 WORK* WITH	6 KNOW* SOC.	7 PAR- TICIP.	8 INTER- ACT.	9 SOC.- EMOT.	10 ASK ACTS	11 TENS. REL.	12 INTER- RUPT.	13 COMP. QUES.
.70	.50	.53	−.26	−.06	−.05	−.02	−.00	−.11
.36	.27	.69	−.25	−.05	.02	.15	.06	−.08
.60	.71	.72	−.13	−.14	.10	.04	.06	.04
.31	.38	.52	−.11	.10	.14	.08	−.10	−.18
	.74	.36	.03	.51	−.21	−.05	.33	−.08
		.40	.23	.31	−.05	.04	.46	.08
			−.08	−.03	.23	−.04	.16	.04
				.08	.38	−.17	.29	.34
					−.15	−.01	.14	−.27
						−.09	.11	.40
							.09	−.20
								.16

	14 PER-SONAL	15 AGREE-MENT	16 DIS-AGREE.	17 INT. RECD.
1. Ideas	.10	−.10	−.05	.09
2. Guidance	.28	−.07	−.00	−.03
3. Leadership	.28	−.07	−.06	−.10
4. Congeniality	.33	.11	−.07	−.16
5. Work with *	.33	.38	.40	.26
6. Know Socially '	.38	.34	.56	.11
7. Participation	.26	−.06	−.02	.01
8. Interaction	−.04	.31	.11	.23
9. Social-Emotional	.06	.31	.25	−.06
10. Ask Acts	.01	−.08	−.16	.31
11. Tension Release	−.13	−.11	.00	.05
12. Interruption	−.01	−.16	.33	.34
13. Comp. Questions	−.13	−.21	.24	.25
14. Personalness		.21	−.07	−.15
15. Agreement			.02	−.15
16. Disagreement				.07

17. Interruption Recd.
18. Comp. Ques. Recd.
19. Pers. Rec. Recd.
20. Agreement Recd.
21. Disagreement Recd.
22. nAch
23. nAff
24. Bel. Pref.

   * n = 24

18	19	20	21	22	23	24	25	26
COM.Q. RECD.	PERS. RECD.	AGREE. RECD.	DIS. RECD.	NACH	NAFF	BEL. PREF.	STA. PREF.	J–I† PREF.
.02	−.17	−.15	−.07	.20	−.25	.05	.04	
.02	−.06	−.34	.09	−.12	.02	−.13	−.05	
.04	−.17	−.19	.04	.13	−.26	−.05	−.02	
−.13	−.13	−.17	−.05	.03	−.08	.15	−.10	
−.00	.32	−.21	.18	.18	.20	.17	−.29	
−.02	.10	.07	.25	.28	−.10	.18	−.08	
.12	−.32	−.38	.17	.07	−.06	−.10	−.16	
.16	−.13	.32	.19	−.02	.06	−.02	−.00	
.11	.25	−.01	.31	.09	.20	−.02	−.22	
.11	−.30	−.26	−.13	−.07	.08	−.15	.05	
.32	.22	−.25	−.09	−.07	−.04	−.01	−.01	
.16	.12	.02	.33	−.01	.04	.05	−.12	
.12	.17	−.02	.07	.03	−.08	.05	.13	
−.25	.27	−.04	−.04	.06	.08	.02	−.24	
−.17	.19	.25	−.05	−.02	.10	.13	−.02	
.04	.29	−.09	.55	−.05	.06	−.02	.09	
.29	−.08	−.13	−.01	.13	−.04	.03	−.20	
	−.14	−.05	.15	−.01	−.06	.05	−.08	
		.11	.14	−.13	−.06	.01	−.08	
			−.10	.06	−.26	.31	.01	
				−.08	.25	.03	−.07	
					−.36	−.02	.15	
						.05	−.07	
							−.41	

† Correlations not available for Job-Intrinsic Preference.

	27 SAL-ARY	28 AGE	29 SENIOR-ITY	30 EXPE-RIENCE
1. Ideas	.42	−.06	−.19	−.08
2. Guidance	.35	.02	−.00	−.02
3. Leadership	.48	.00	−.11	.02
4. Congeniality	.22	.26	.13	.23
5. Work with *	.39	−.03	−.06	−.01
6. Know Socially	.28	−.17	−.21	−.04
7. Participation	.46	.03	−.06	.03
8. Interaction	.07	−.08	.01	−.05
9. Social-Emotional	−.07	.41	.28	.35
10. Ask Acts	.11	−.11	−.09	−.01
11. Tension Release	.19	.24	.10	.20
12. Interruption	.15	.05	.18	.10
13. Comp. Questions	.04	−.28	−.12	−.20
14. Personalness	−.10	.22	.16	.27
15. Agreement	−.20	.06	−.04	−.08
16. Disagreement	−.22	.02	.22	−.00
17. Interruption Recd.	−.07	−.16	−.10	−.05
18. Comp. Ques. Recd.	.35	.09	.06	.18
19. Pers. Rec. Recd.	−.37	.27	.26	.30
20. Agreement Recd.	−.04	−.15	−.13	−.09
21. Disagreement Recd.	.06	.17	.24	.17
22. nAch	.10	−.23	−.20	−.20
23. nAff	.05	.20	.30	.24
24. Bel. Pref.	.07	.10	.16	.15
25. Status Pref.	.03	−.39	−.26	−.43
26. J–I Pref. †				
27. Salary		.06	.02	.06
28. Age			.69	.91
29. Seniority				.67
30. Experience				
31. Educ. Level				
32. Ethnicity				
33. Sex				
34. Social Status				
35. Total Status				
36. Reward-Investment Index				
37. Congruity-Ambiguity Index				
38. Satisfaction with Decision				

   * n = 24

   † Correlations not available for Job-Intrinsic Preference.

31 EDUC. LEVEL	32 ETH-NICITY	33 SEX	34 SOC. STAT.	35 TOT. STAT.	36 R-I INDEX	37 C-A INDEX	38 SAT. DEC.	39 SAT. OPER.
.16	.08	.03	.02	.38	.45	.07	.19	−.05
−.11	−.18	.15	−.13	.25	.42	−.03	.09	−.01
.01	.00	.09	.02	.42	.50	.15	.13	.01
−.13	.04	−.24	.08	.22	.22	.05	.27	.04
−.25	.22	.29	.16	.42	.39	.08	.10	−.27
−.30	.24	.28	.12	.27	.29	.09	.06	.15
−.05	−.25	−.03	−.18	.36	.54	−.02	−.04	−.06
.13	.17	−.13	.07	.11	−.02	−.09	−.19	−.17
−.29	.12	.05	.30	.08	−.20	.07	.12	−.00
.36	−.22	−.06	−.05	.11	.11	−.03	−.21	−.26
.05	−.07	.06	.15	.21	.09	.30	.13	.07
−.11	−.11	.25	.14	.18	.06	.20	−.05	−.01
.27	.07	−.02	.00	.03	.02	−.16	−.48	−.21
−.44	.12	.03	.13	−.07	−.10	−.04	.22	.14
−.27	.21	.10	−.01	−.11	−.18	−.28	.17	.08
−.25	−.12	.13	−.03	−.20	−.24	−.09	−.06	−.02
.11	−.14	.17	−.03	−.01	−.07	.02	−.17	−.20
.25	−.03	.04	.23	.42	.24	.25	−.05	−.09
−.28	.07	.21	.31	−.24	−.49	.12	.30	.27
−.07	.26	.03	.05	−.00	−.09	−.04	.20	.19
−.25	−.11	.22	.05	.08	.01	.08	−.03	.05
.12	.11	.11	−.03	.08	.12	−.11	.11	.12
−.15	−.14	−.03	.04	.08	.04	.01	−.13	−.06
−.15	.19	.17	.28	.17	−.02	.16	.10	.07
.38	−.09	−.01	−.24	−.10	.09	−.34	.09	.05
.45	−.02	−.01	.19	.94	.93	.34	.05	−.19
−.33	.21	−.14	.72	.28	−.17	.65	.31	.29
−.38	.14	−.27	.55	.19	−.18	.34	.10	.20
−.32	.17	−.15	.73	.29	−.18	.68	.29	.32
	−.14	−.12	−.03	.36	.43	.03	−.17	−.33
		−.11	.60	.15	−.19	.15	.28	.32
			.05	.00	−.01	.03	.31	.04
				.45	−.14	.65	.38	.31
					.78	.49	.13	−.09
						.12	−.04	−.30
							.22	.21
								.44

APPENDIX H

Scoring Procedure, Analysis, and Interpretation of Fantasy in TAT's

THE FOLLOWING ANALYSIS of the Thematic Apperception Tests used in the study is intended as corroborative data, related to the analyses presented in Chapters 5, 6, and 7 of the text. The conclusions and interpretations represent clinical inferences based on the distribution of various content themes among the four role types. The TAT pictures are between pages 330 and 331 and are discussed in Appendix C under the "Test of Imagination."

The coded stories were given in an undifferentiated group to a reader who had had no previous connection with the study, had not read the main work, and was unfamiliar with the typology. The analysis given below was, in effect, blind, and the fact that it agrees substantially with the main body of this study is its primary claim to validity.

The reader read the stories on four separate occasions. The original hope was that they would provide information with which to build a picture of the participant's perception of his relationship to his family, his work situation, and feelings within himself. The first reading consisted of scoring the first story for the presence or absence of specific themes. This scoring was designed to take from the stories a possible form that might provide guidelines of further analysis of thematic content.

The categories used for the first reading were:

CONFLICT AND NONCONFLICT: This characteristic was scored on the presence or absence of alternatives of behavior, ambivalence about the possible rewards and sanctions of alternatives as might be indicated by a pre-choice reflection situation, and/or the expressed or implied necessity of choice.

DEPRIVATION, GRATIFICATION, SACRIFICE: This category was scored "yes" or "no" in answer to the questions: were the hero and/or family receiving something that was felt to be wanted and desirable (gratification) ; if they were not receiving this desirable entity, was this expressed with anger, resentment, and hostility (deprivation) or acceptance, willingness, and implied previous choice (sacrifice) ? The desirable entity was also described as related to the work situation or to outside pleasure and enjoyment.

CLOSURE: If the story had an ending, was the closure favorable to the hero, was he rewarded (scored positively), or did his story end with the hero unrewarded, punished, and unhappy (scored negatively) ?

FANTASY: The richness of the stories was scored from 1 to 5 depending on how many of the following qualities were present. Stories lacking all five were rated 0 or (−). (−) rated stories were one line answers to the trigger questions: 1) how much did the story involve people—naming the characters, endowing them with expression, emotion, and personality; 2) how involved was the author in his story—how alive was it, was the phrasing emotion-laden or emotion-free, were descriptions indicative of any personal feeling; 3) was there a plot, a problem with a beginning and end; 4) how rich were the associations and how much did the stories go beyond the actual situational possibilities; and, 5) how much of the structure and content seemed a response to trigger questions and how much seemed to flow from the author's own stimulus?

DEPERSONALIZATION: Stories which were scored low on fantasy were separately scored for little or no mention of people, little author involvement, a dependence on trigger questions, and a feeling of detachment, and terseness.

The second reading of all stories was aimed at discovering what kinds of problems seemed to be involving the characters in the stories and the writers of the stories. What pleased them? What did they feel they should do? What happened when "oughts" were not followed? In what situations did they feel angry or guilty? Following the guidelines of the original categories, the reader sought to discover the poles of conflict, the reasons for deprivation and gratification, and positive and negative endings for stories. These were listed and a third reading noted their presence or absence of each of the stories. These thematic traits were: (1) failure in task situation; (2) failure in interpersonal relations; (3) concern with chaos, confusion, and conflict; (4) fears and anxieties which were unfocused on a large "they" which could be a company or the total system; (5) fears arising in and concerned with the individual and his capacity and doubts, or problematic situations between two people; (6) concern with death, loss, and embarrassment; (7) concern with values, worth, and worthlessness; and (8) a general inconclusiveness, tentativeness, uneven terseness, and lack of imagination.

The original categories provided outlines and these new categories provided shading, filling in the descriptions of concerns more completely. The fourth reading attempted to tie them into the three aspects of the individual's life—work, family, and self.

WORK

A concern for work was important to all of the respondents and was expressed in almost all stories including those relating to pictures which might have elicited a different response.* This concern centered around both the external reward and punishment system and an internal feeling of satisfaction. One of the primary imperatives in most stories was the need to succeed in order to provide for one's family and to fulfill oneself. Yet while there was an over-all feeling that rewards and successes were forthcoming, there was an underlying feeling that the work situation was uncertain, made great demands, and was slightly hostile to the individual.

Deprivations and Gratifications from Work

It was expected that one of the primary considerations for the participants would be the satisfaction or dissatisfaction which they gained from their work, and that this would be expressed through their stories' heroes receiving gratifications or deprivations of rewards and successes. Seventeen of the participants ex-

---

* The research program was presented within the context of business (see Appendix A). The same pictures presented in different contexts may have evoked different themes. The references cited under the description of the TAT in Appendix E contain some evidence on the effects of the immediate situation on thematic content.

plicitly dealt with deprivations and gratification by actually rewarding or punishing the heroes in their stories. Table H.1 shows the breakdown of these 17 cases by role types. Proportionally more Stars and Technical Specialists indicated explicit concern with rewards and punishments than was the case with either of the other two types. The Underchosen were least likely to express these themes in their stories. Deprivation themes were most common among the Stars and did not appear at all among the Social Specialists and Underchosen.

Table H.1

DEPRIVATIONS AND GRATIFICATIONS FROM WORK: NUMBER OF CASES WHERE THEMES WERE PRESENT AND ABSENT

ROLE TYPE	THEMES PRESENT		TOTAL, THEMES PRESENT	THEMES ABSENT	TOTAL CASES
	DEPRIVA-TION	GRATIFICA-TION			
Stars	4	2	6 (40%)	9	15
Technical Specialists	1	3	4 (40%)	6	10
Social Specialists	0	4	4 (25%)	8	12
Underchosen	0	3	3 (20%)	12	15
Total	5	12	17 (33%)	35	52

Work Hard for Success

Coincident with the theme that rewards would be forthcoming in a vague future was the theme that they would be attained only by hard work and the sacrifice of pleasure. Nineteen of the respondents mentioned this necessity explicitly. Eight of these 19 were Stars. The remaining 11 were distributed among the other role types in rough proportion to their total numbers. These results are shown in Table H.2.

Conflict: External Demands versus Personal Satisfaction

Six of the 52 sets of stories contained the theme of conflict between what would personally satisfy the central figure and what would satisfy the external system. Four of these instances were in Stars' stories; the other two writers were Technical Specialists.

Table H.2

WORK HARD FOR SUCCESS:
NUMBER OF CASES WHERE THEME WAS PRESENT AND ABSENT

ROLE TYPE	THEME PRESENT	THEME ABSENT	TOTAL CASES
Stars	8 (53%)	7	15
Technical Specialists	3 (30%)	7	10
Social Specialists	4 (33%)	8	12
Underchosen	4 (27%)	11	15
Total	19 (37%)	33	52

Impersonality of Work System

While fewer of the Underchosen were concerned with the necessity of working hard for success (Tables H.1 and H.2), they did show a greater inclination to feel that the business world was impersonal than did the other types. The theme of a noncaring, confusing corporation runs through many of the stories, but proportionally fewer of the other types appeared to be concerned about this aspect of the system. These results are shown in Table H.3.

Table H.3

IMPERSONALITY OF WORK SYSTEM:
NUMBER OF CASES WHERE THEME WAS PRESENT AND ABSENT

ROLE TYPE	THEME PRESENT	THEME ABSENT	TOTAL CASES
Underchosen	7 (47%)	8	15
All Others	10 (27%)	27	37
Total	17 (33%)	35	52

The themes analyzed so far were related to emotional responses to work situations. These emotional responses centered around the necessity of making sacrifices to one's work, worry about possible reward or failure, the impersonality of the system, and the potential conflict between individual satisfaction and external requirements. Viewed together, these feelings present an underlying theme that the business system is inimical to the individual and his growth. Twenty-one respondents expressed this generally latent concern quite clearly, stressing the hostility and potential destructive force of the corporation system. The results of this analysis are presented in Table H.4.

Table H.4

ADVERSITY OF SYSTEM:
NUMBER OF CASES WHERE THEME WAS PRESENT AND ABSENT

ROLE TYPE	THEME PRESENT	THEME ABSENT	TOTAL CASES
Stars	7 (47%)	8	15
Technical Specialists	5 (50%)	5	10
Social Specialists	5 (42%)	7	12
Underchosen	4 (27%)	11	15
Total	21 (40%)	31	52

The relatively consistent incidence of concern among three of the four types in describing an adverse system appears inconsistent with the previous analysis. The Stars showed a consistent pattern of greater anxiety in the work situation than was the case with the other types. The Underchosen were relatively consistent in stating little explicit concern with rewards and the necessity for working hard, and were more likely to describe the business system as a cold and impersonal force than were the other types.

Summary of Emotional Themes Related to Work

The imaginative stories were analyzed for four emotional themes related to work. The themes, and the role types most likely to express the themes, were as follows:

(1) Table H.1: Work as a source of rewards and punishments—Stars and Technical Specialists.
    (a) Work as a source of deprivations—Stars.
(2) Table H.2: The need to work hard for success—Stars.
(3) Table H.3: The impersonalness of the work system—Underchosen.
(4) Table H.4: The adversity of the work system—proportionally fewer Underchosen participants' stories expressed concern with this theme.

These results may be interpreted as indicating that the Stars and Specialists experienced relatively high emotional involvement with work while the Underchosen felt emotionally distant and removed from work. A higher level of felt conflict and anxiety around work, conditions which represent strong feelings of personal responsibility, distinguished the Stars, and to a lesser degree the Technical Specialists, from the Social Specialists.

FAMILY

Forty-one out of 52 sets of stories expressed a necessity for providing for families at present and in the future. These stories expressed the desire that families should have a higher standard of living, opportunities for a college education, and a certain social status. However, this large number was spread unevenly, with Stars and Technical Specialists showing a greater concern than Social Specialists and the Underchosen, as indicated on Table H.5.

Table H.5

PROVIDE FOR FAMILY:
NUMBER OF CASES WHERE THEME WAS PRESENT AND ABSENT

ROLE TYPE	THEME PRESENT	THEME ABSENT	TOTAL CASES
Stars and Technical Specialists	24 (96%)	1	25
Social Specialists and Underchosen	17 (63%)	10	27
Total	41 (79%)	11	52

Many of the stories reflected a belief that the necessary provision comes through business success. For many the necessity of providing for the family was the seed of conflict, since business activity often demands separation from the family in traveling and extra work. This separation might lead to a "growth away from the family" and an inability to provide them with love, companionship, and personal care. A variety of emotional attitudes which might represent an individual's emotional resolution of this dilemma provided a basis for further analysis of the content of the imaginative stories.

Family: Feelings of Guilt

The themes of growth away from family, temporary separation, and permanent loss of family through death or divorce could indicate punishment for having wronged the family and could express a feeling of not deserving their love or care. Three stories explicitly stated that because the hero had neglected his family, he must lose them. Table H.6 shows the distribution of this kind of content among the role types. Stars showed a greater tendency toward this view than did the other types.

Table H.6

GUILT ABOUT FAMILY:
NUMBER OF CASES WHERE THEME WAS PRESENT AND ABSENT

ROLE TYPE	THEME PRESENT	THEME ABSENT	TOTAL CASES
Stars	9 (60%)	6	15
Technical Specialists	3 (30%)	7	10
Social Specialists	5 (42%)	7	12
Underchosen	5 (33%)	10	15
Total	22 (42%)	30	52

Family: Support and Anchor

Nineteen participants did not recognize a potential conflict between work and family and conceived of their families as a source of escape and relaxation from the outside world. The Underchosen showed the greatest tendency to express dependency on families in their stories, a reaction which may be related to their greater tendency to describe work situations as cold and impersonal. The findings of this analysis are shown in Table H.7.

Table H.7

FAMILY AS SUPPORT, ANCHOR:
NUMBER OF CASES WHERE THEME WAS PRESENT AND ABSENT

ROLE TYPE	THEME PRESENT	THEME ABSENT	TOTAL CASES
Stars	4 (27%)	11	15
Technical Specialists	3 (30%)	7	10
Social Specialists	4 (33%)	8	12
Underchosen	8 (53%)	7	15
Total	19 (37%)	33	52

Repudiation of Family

It would appear that the themes of the Underchosen participants' stories which centered around relationships with families were more complex than the previous findings indicate. Their stories, along with those of the Technical Specialists, were more likely to repudiate the family than were the other types' stories. Among the pictures were two that sought almost pointedly to stimulate family associations. Yet eighteen respondents' stories gave the family passing reference or ignored them completely. This could be interpreted as nonverbalized rejection, since the family cue stands out strongly in the pictures. Technical Specialists and Underchosen were more likely to ignore the family than were the Stars and Social Specialists. The data are shown in Table H.8.

Table H.8

REFERENCES TO FAMILY:
NUMBER OF CASES WHERE THEME WAS PRESENT AND ABSENT

ROLE TYPE	FAMILY THEME PRESENT	FAMILY THEME ABSENT	TOTAL CASES
Stars and Social Specialists	21	6 (22%)	27
Technical Specialists and Underchosen	13	12 (48%)	25
Total	34	18 (35%)	52

Family Gratified Through the Hero's Personal Success

A fourth alternative for resolving a potential conflict between family and work was to omit the possible conflict from the themes in the stories and to assume that the family would be gratified and pleased through the hero's success. Proportionally more Technical Specialists expressed this theme than any other type, as shown on Table H.9.

Summary of Emotional Themes Related to the Family

The general theme of a need to provide for families characterized most of the stories. Stars and Technical Specialists were more likely to include this theme in their stories than were the other types (Table H.5). It was expected that since a potential conflict between work and family characterized the themes of many stories, particular emotional modes of resolving this potential conflict might be associated with the role types. The emo-

Table H.9

FAMILY GRATIFIED THROUGH HERO'S PERSONAL SUCCESS:
NUMBER OF CASES WHERE THEME WAS PRESENT AND ABSENT

ROLE TYPE	THEME PRESENT	THEME ABSENT	TOTAL CASES
Stars	2 (13%)	13	15
Technical Specialists	5 (50%)	5	10
Social Specialists	3 (25%)	9	12
Underchosen	2 (13%)	13	15
Total	12 (23%)	40	52

tional modes of resolution, and the types with which they were associated, were as follows:

(1) Table H.6: Feelings of guilt—Stars.
(2) Table H.7: The family as a support and anchor—Underchosen.
(3) Table H.8: Ignoring, rejecting, or repudiating the family—Technical Specialists and Underchosen.
(4) Table H.9: Gratifying the family indirectly through the hero's personal success—Technical Specialists.

Stars were more likely to see a conflict between success and family and were more likely to internalize the conflict with feelings of guilt than to externalize the conflict by rejection or depending upon the outside "object," the family. The other types were less inclined to recognize a conflict and showed disparate reactions when they did. Social Specialists tended slightly toward internalizing guilt, but in other ways were mixed in their thematic expressions. Technical Specialists tended to express an ignoring or rejection of the family, and/or expressed the assumption that the family would and should be gratified through the hero's personal business success. The Underchosen tended to express rejection of the family and to express strong dependence on it when it was mentioned in their stories.

SELF

Themes around the conflict of the family situation with work, and the uncertainty of the work system itself, shade into the thematic perception of self. The feelings and perceptions discussed under the previous headings mold, influence, and make up these feelings about the self. In both relationships, work and family, a tendency to express feelings of anxiety, guilt, and conflict emerged in the stories as part of self-perception patterns. In dealing with feelings centered around the self, it appeared that respondents tended to express an additional sense of failure and confusion of values in their stories.

Sense of Failure

The widespread expression of anxiety about the uncertainty of the business system of rewards, and the general hostility of the system, implied that the respondents might also have concerned themselves with failure. Fifteen out of the 52 expressed this concern, but in 9 of these 15 sets of stores, sense of failure was centered around interpersonal relations within the family and business world. Tables H.10 and H.11 present these findings.

Table H.10

OVER-ALL SENSE OF FAILURE:
NUMBER OF CASES WHERE THEME WAS PRESENT AND ABSENT

ROLE TYPE	THEME PRESENT	THEME ABSENT	TOTAL CASES
Stars	7 (47%)	8	15
Technical Specialists	3 (30%)	7	10
Social Specialists	2 (17%)	10	12
Underchosen	3 (20%)	12	15
Total	15 (29%)	37	52

Table H.11

INTERPERSONAL FAILURE:
NUMBER OF CASES WHERE THEME WAS PRESENT AND ABSENT

ROLE TYPE	THEME PRESENT	THEME ABSENT	TOTAL CASES
Stars	5 (33%)	10	15
Technical Specialists	1 (10%)	9	10
Social Specialists	2 (17%)	10	12
Underchosen	1 (7%)	14	15
Total	9 (17%)	43	52

Stars were more likely to be sensitive to failure, and especially to failure in interpersonal relations. Social Specialists dealt only with interpersonal failure. Technical Specialists who dealt with a sense of failure, did so only in technical terms, echoing a general tendency to ignore interpersonal relations. Proportionally fewer Underchosen expressed concern with a sense of failure.

Confusion about Values

Many respondents expressed doubts about what their heroes really wanted out of life. These heroes felt that they had been forced into decisions without an opportunity to build a coherent system of beliefs about what they wanted from life and felt this as a definite lack. Stars set the pace for the population in expressing more confusion about values in their stories. Proportionately more Underchosen expressed relative certainty of beliefs and desires. The results are shown in Table H.12.

Table H.12

CONFUSION ABOUT VALUES:
NUMBER OF CASES WHERE THEME WAS PRESENT AND ABSENT

ROLE TYPE	THEME PRESENT	THEME ABSENT	TOTAL CASES
Stars	8 (53%)	7	15
Technical Specialists	4 (40%)	6	10
Social Specialists	4 (33%)	8	12
Underchosen	2 (13%)	13	15
Total	18 (35%)	34	52

Over-All Conflict and Anxiety

In the initial reading, the stories were scored on conflict themes, where the criterion involved the presence of alternatives for action and/or an expressed need for making a choice. The results are shown in Table H.13.

Table H.13

CONFLICT:
NUMBER OF CASES WHERE THEME WAS PRESENT AND ABSENT

ROLE TYPE	THEME PRESENT	THEME ABSENT	TOTAL CASES
Stars	11 (73%)	4	15
Technical Specialists	5 (50%)	5	10
Social Specialists	5 (42%)	7	12
Underchosen	2 (13%)	13	15
Total	23 (44%)	29	52

The Stars' stories tended to be more conflict-laden, and the Underchosen participants' stories tended to be free of conflict, compared to the stories of the Specialists and compared to each other. A comparison of these findings with the results of the second and third readings' analysis of anxiety themes will help interpret both sets of findings as well as the theoretical relationship between conflict and anxiety.

The themes scored as anxiety-laden had to do with expressed or implicit feelings of failure; concern with chaos, confusion, and conflict; focused and unfocused fears; concern with death, loss, and embarrassment; concern with values, worth, and worthlessness; and general inconclusiveness, tentativeness, uneven terseness, and lack of imagination. These themes did not center around choosing or alternatives; they referred to emotional states independent of action or behavioral alternatives. The findings of the analysis of anxiety content are shown in Table H.14.

Table H.14

ANXIETY:
NUMBER OF CASES SCORED HIGH OR LOW IN RELATION
TO POPULATION AVERAGE SCORE ON ANXIETY CONTENT

ROLE TYPE	HIGH SCORES	LOW SCORES	TOTAL CASES
Stars	11 (73%)	4	15
Technical Specialists	4 (40%)	6	10
Social Specialists	6 (50%)	6	12
Underchosen	9 (60%)	6	15
Total	30 (58%)	22	52

The Underchosen tended to score high in anxiety while expressing relatively conflict-free stories. For the other types, anxiety and conflict themes apparently tended to occur together. This could mean that in the Underchosen members' stories, felt anxiety tended not to be associated with action alternatives while in the other types' stories anxiety and action alternatives did tend to occur together. When this interpretation is coupled with the previous indications from the Underchosen participants' stories— lower emotional involvement with work, perception of the work system as impersonal, dependence upon the family as a support

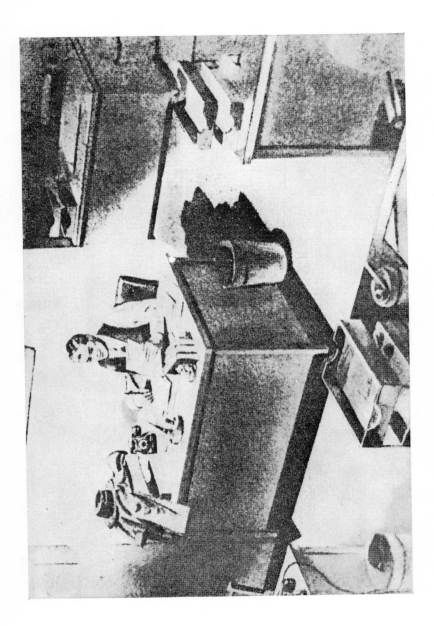

tended to be more insightful, less guarded, and more candid about psychological pressures than the stories written by the other types.

Technical Specialists

The stories these men wrote tended to stress the idea that if one shows competence and works hard, he will achieve a highly valued success, but they tended to minimize an underlying concern about achievement and expressed a feeling that the system was vaguely hostile. They did not express concern with interpersonal relations, which may explain their lack of concern about impersonal systems. They expressed little conflict between family and business success, assuming that the family will be provided for and satisfied vicariously through the central person's business success. If the family did appear to make conflicting demands, their tendency was to reject its demands on them. They did express a conflict between personal task satisfaction and external requirements, indicating that their heroes sought primary fulfillment through work. They appeared to express confidence in their heroes' ability to cope with the business world. It would appear that Technical Specialists guarded their heroes against themselves and others, and that a need to achieve was balanced against basic doubts and fears about other people, which was expressed in a diffuse anxiety.

Social Specialists

Social Specialists tended to describe the world as pleasant, happy, and favorable to the individual. They tended to describe the business system as hostile to the individual, but this hostile perception did not seem to include the idea that people within the system are cold and uncaring. While they expressed dependency on personal relationships, they did not seem worried about interpersonal failure, for they described individual people as helpful and pleasant. However, when the individual shaded into the large "they" it disturbed their general equanimity. The impersonal system might have thwarted their heroes' efforts to relate warmly to others. While they expressed anxiety, personal responsibility, and guilt, they were less likely than Stars or Technical Specialists to emphasize it, and they may have projected it onto the impersonal system which was impervious to close identi

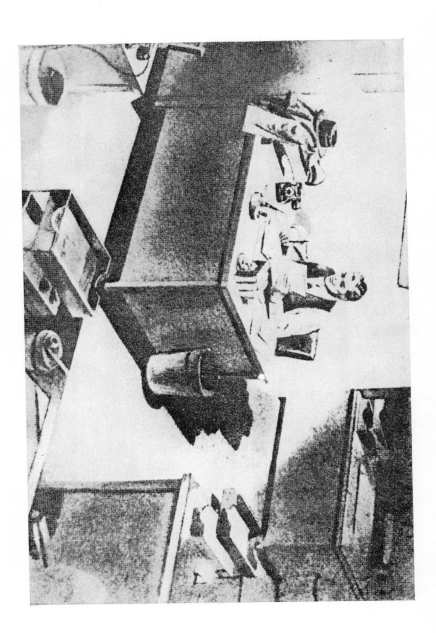

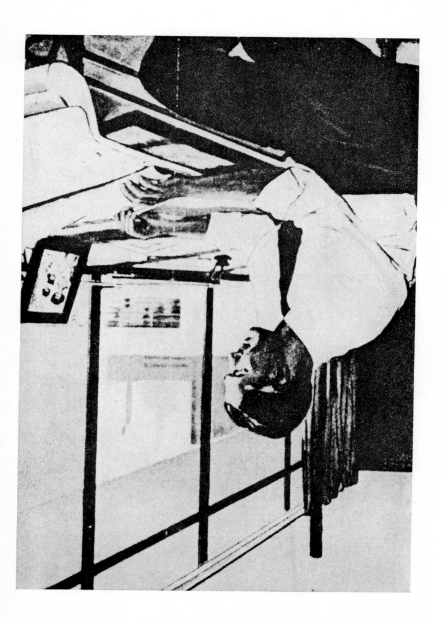

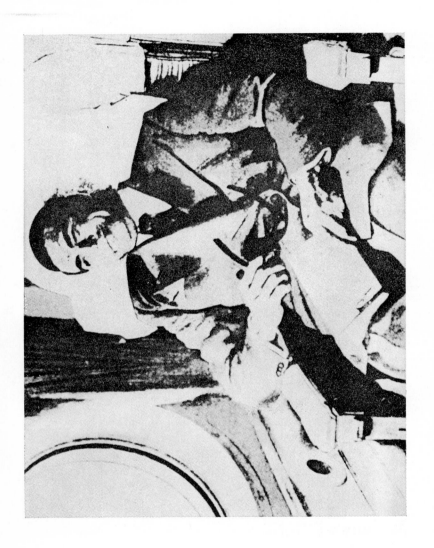

and anchor, and a tendency to repudiate the family—a characteristically different manner of dealing with anxiety is suggested. Instead of coupling the anxiety with a search for alternative ways of reducing the anxiety through action, as would be involved in the conflict themes, this mode would attempt to place the causes of the trouble in events and entities outside of the person, rather than internalizing the concern in the form of guilt and feelings of personal responsibility, as tended to be the case in the Stars' stories. The extreme alternative to internalization would be projection; the person would feel irresponsibly dependent upon external objects and forces, such as the work system and the family, and would feel incapable of influencing the course of external events. He would not feel guilty because he could not see himself as causing events outside himself. His behavior would be expected to be primarily expressive of his anxieties rather than adaptive or coping, which would imply searching for and testing action alternatives.

SUMMARY

The comments which follow summarize the TAT analysis data presented in this appendix, and include some of the TAT readers' more generalized clinical impressions of the stories written by the four role types. The analysis of thematic content which proceeded one theme at a time did not capture the over-all impressions made by the interactions of themes in specific stories. Hence, the following descriptions go beyond the quantitative data in some respects, having been generated in part by the over-all impressions of the complete stories.

Stars

These men were more likely than any other type to express conflict between family and business success and correspondingly were less likely to present happy endings to their stories. Their stories tended to be concerned with imperatives, providing for family, and giving family love, care, and concern. They tended to express more consciousness of failure, in terms of work and in dealing with people. At the same time, they were less likely to describe work as intrinsically gratifying and they did not express concern with growth through work. On the whole, their stories tended to be more insightful, less guarded, and more candid about psychological pressures than the stories written by the other types.

Technical Specialists

The stories these men wrote tended to stress the idea that if one shows competence and works hard, he will achieve a highly valued success, but they tended to minimize an underlying concern about achievement and expressed a feeling that the system was vaguely hostile. They did not express concern with interpersonal relations, which may explain their lack of concern about impersonal systems. They expressed little conflict between family and business success, assuming that the family will be provided for and satisfied vicariously through the central person's business success. If the family did appear to make conflicting demands, their tendency was to reject its demands on them. They did express a conflict between personal task satisfaction and external requirements, indicating that their heroes sought primary fulfillment through work. They appeared to express confidence in their heroes' ability to cope with the business world. It would appear that Technical Specialists guarded their heroes against themselves and others, and that a need to achieve was balanced against basic doubts and fears about other people, which was expressed in a diffuse anxiety.

Social Specialists

Social Specialists tended to describe the world as pleasant, happy, and favorable to the individual. They tended to describe the business system as hostile to the individual, but this hostile perception did not seem to include the idea that people within the system are cold and uncaring. While they expressed dependency on personal relationships, they did not seem worried about interpersonal failure, for they described individual people as helpful and pleasant. However, when the individual shaded into the large "they" it disturbed their general equanimity. The impersonal system might have thwarted their heroes' efforts to relate warmly to others. While they expressed anxiety, personal responsibility, and guilt, they were less likely than Stars or Technical Specialists to emphasize it, and they may have projected it onto the impersonal system which was impervious to close identification. They described little conflict between success and family, and like the Technical Specialists, they identified their heroes' satisfactions with those of the family, but they differed from the Technical Specialists in that this identification tended to arise out of a close relationship rather than rejection and distance.

Underchosen

These stories were relatively conflict free and generally ended happily. They expressed a positive concern for the family and perceived its members as sources of gratification and happiness. They expressed more dependence on families than any other type, referring to them as supports, anchors, and possible retreats from an impersonal system. At the same time, the Underchosen showed a tendency to reject and repudiate the family. They discussed obligation, but they tended to express less personal guilt and responsibility than any other group, choosing instead to project incapacities and inabilities on the machinations of the impersonal systems. The Underchosen tended to be less insightful, more guarded, more insecure, more vacillating, and more distant from and rejecting of work and family than the other types in the content of their stories.

BIBLIOGRAPHY

Abraham, K., *Selected Papers on Psychoanalysis,* London: Hogarth Press, 1927.

Adler, A., *Understanding Human Nature,* New York: Greenburg, 1927.

Adorno, T. W., Frenkel-Brunswik, E., Levinson, D. J., and Sanford, R. N., *The Authoritarian Personality,* New York: Harper, 1950.

Argyris, C., *Interpersonal Competence and Organization Effectiveness,* Homewood, Ill.: Irwin-Dorsey, 1962.

Atkinson, J. W., *Motives in Fantasy, Action and Society,* Princeton: D. van Nostrand Company, Inc., 1958.

Bales, R. F., *Interaction Process Analysis,* Cambridge: Addison-Wesley, 1951.

Bales, R. F., "The Equilibrium Problem in Small Groups," in Parsons, T., Bales, R. F., and Shils, E. A., *Working Papers in the Theory of Action,* Glencoe, Ill.: The Free Press, 1953, pp. 111–161. Abridged in Hare, A. P., Borgatta, E. F., and Bales, R. F., editors, *Small Groups,* New York: Alfred A. Knopf, 1955, pp. 424–456.

Barnes, L. B., *Organizational Systems and Engineering Groups,* Boston: Division of Research, Harvard Business School, 1960.

Benne, K. D., and Sheats, P., "Functional Roles of Group Members," *Journal of Social Issues,* Vol. IV, No. 2, Spring 1948, pp. 41–49.

Bennis, W. G., *Bureaucracy and Social Change: An Anatomy of a Failure,* unpublished paper presented at a meeting of the American Sociological Association, August 1962

Blau, P. M., *The Dynamics of Bureaucracy,* Chicago: University of Chicago Press, 1955.

Borgatta, E. F., Couch, A. S., and Bales, R. F., "Some Findings Relevant to the Great Man Theory of Leadership," in Hare, A. P., Borgatta, E. F., and Bales, R. F., *Small Groups,* New York: Alfred A. Knopf, 1955, pp. 424–456.

Bradford, L. P. et al., *Explorations in Human Relations Training,* Washington: National Training Laboratory in Group Development, 1953.

Bronfenbrenner, U., "The Changing American Child," *Journal of Social Issues,* Vol. XVII, No. 1, 1961, pp. 6–18.

Capra, P. C., and Dittes, J. E., "Birth Order as a Selective Factor among Volunteer Subjects," *Journal of Abnormal and Social Psychology,* Vol. 64, No. 4, 1962, p. 302.

Chowdhry, Kamla, *Executive Needs in Management Development Programs,* unpublished paper based on her pilot project exploring the selection of participants in the Program for Management Development at the Harvard Business School, 1962.

Christie, R., and Jahoda, M., editors, *Studies in the Scope and Method of "The Authoritarian Personality,"* Glencoe, Ill.: The Free Press, 1954.

Erikson, E. H., *Childhood and Society,* New York: W. W. Norton & Company, Inc., 1950.

Erikson, E. H., "Ego Development and Historical Change" in "Identity and the Life Cycle," *Psychological Issues,* Vol. I, No. 1, 1959, pp. 18–49.

Erikson, E. H., "The Problem of Ego Identity" in "Identity and the Life Cycle," *Psychological Issues,* Vol. I, No. 1, 1959, pp. 101–164.

Fenichel, O., *Psychoanalytic Theory of Neurosis,* New York: W. W. Norton & Company, Inc., 1945.

Foote, N. W., Cottrell, L. S., Jr., *Identity and Interpersonal Competence,* Chicago: University of Chicago Press, 1955.

Fouriezos, N. T., Hutt, M. L., and Guetzkow, H., "Measurement of Self-Oriented Needs in Discussion Groups," *Journal of Abnormal and Social Psychology,* No. 45, 1950, pp. 682–690. Condensed in Cartwright, D., and Zander, A., *Group Dynamics,* Evanston: Row, Peterson, 1956, pp. 354–360.

Freud, A., *The Ego and the Mechanisms of Defense,* London: Hogarth Press, 1937, 1954.

Freud, S., *Three Essays on the Theory of Sexuality,* London: Imago, 1949, 1952, first published in U. S. under title *Three Contributions to the Sexual Theory,* New York: Nervous and Mental Disease Monograph Series, No. 7, 1910.

Freud, S., *A General Introduction to Psychoanalysis,* Garden City, New York: Garden City Publishing Co., Inc., 1938. Earlier edition, New York: Boni & Liveright, 1920.

Freud, S., *Beyond the Pleasure Principle,* London: International Psychoanalytical Press, 1922.

Freud, S., *Group Psychology and the Analysis of the Ego,* London, Vienna: The International Psychoanalytical Press, 1922. Paperback ed., New York: Bantam Books, 1960.

Freud, S., "Analysis Terminable and Interminable," 1937, *Collected Papers,* Vol. V., New York: Basic Books, 1959.

Goodman, L. A., and Kruskal, W. H., "Measures of Association for

Cross Classification," *Journal of the American Statistical Association*, No. 49, 1954, pp. 723–764.

Hartmann, H., *Ego Psychology and the Problem of Adaptation*, New York: International Universities Press, Inc., 1958.

Homans, G. C., *The Human Group*, New York: Harcourt, Brace and Company, 1950.

Homans, G. C., and Schneider, D. M., *Marriage, Authority and Final Causes: A Study of Unilateral Cross-Cousin Marriage*, Glencoe, Ill.: The Free Press, 1955.

Homans, G. C., *Social Behavior: Its Elementary Forms*, New York: Harcourt, Brace and Company, 1961.

Hovland, C. I., "The Role of Primacy and Recency in Persuasive Communication," Maccoby, E. E., Newcomb, T. M., and Hartley, E. L., editors, *Readings in Social Psychology*, New York: Henry Holt, 1958, pp. 137–149.

Kluckhohn, C., Murray, H. A., and Schneider, D. M., editors, *Personality in Nature, Society, and Culture*, New York: Alfred A. Knopf, 1956.

Kubie, L. S., "Some Unsolved Problems of the Scientific Career," in Stein, M. P., Vidich, A. J., and Manning, D., editors, *Identity and Anxiety*, Glencoe, Ill.: The Free Press, 1960, pp. 141–168.

Lawrence, P. R., Bailey, J. C., Katz, R. L., Seiler, J. A., Orth, C. D. 3rd, Clark, J. V., Barnes, L. B., and Turner, A. N., *Organizational Behavior and Administration*, Homewood, Ill.: Irwin-Dorsey, 1961.

Leary, T., *Interpersonal Diagnosis of Personality*, New York: Ronald Press, 1957.

Lewin, K., *Field Theory in Social Science*, New York: Harper & Brothers, 1951, a publication of the Research Center for Group Dynamics, University of Chicago.

McArthur, C., "Personalities of First and Second Children," *Psychiatry: Journal for the Study of Interpersonal Processes*, Vol. 19, No. 1, February 1956, pp. 47–54.

McClelland, D., Wilkinson, J. W., Clark, R. A., and Lowell, E. L., *The Achievement Motive*, New York: Appleton-Century-Crofts, Inc., 1953.

McNemar, Q., *Psychological Statistics*, New York: Wiley & Sons, Inc., 2nd Edition, 1955.

Maslow, A. H., *Motivation and Personality*, New York: Harper & Brothers, 1954.

Moreno, J. L., *The Sociometry Reader*, Glencoe, Ill.: The Free Press, 1960.

Parsons, T., and Bales, R. F., *Family, Socialization and Interaction Process*, Glencoe, Ill.: The Free Press, 1955.

Rank, O., *The Myth of the Birth of the Hero and Other Writings*, New

York: Alfred A. Knopf, Inc., 1932. Available in paperback form, New York: Vintage Books, Inc. (cat. no. K-70), 1959.

Reich, W., *Character Analysis,* New York: The Noonday Press, a subsidiary of Farrar, Straus, and Cudahy, 3rd Edition, 1949.

Roethlisberger, F. J., and Dickson, W. J., *Management and the Worker,* Cambridge: Harvard University Press, 1939.

Rogers, C. R., *On Becoming a Person,* Boston: Houghton Mifflin Co., 1961.

Rokeach, M., *The Open and Closed Mind,* New York: Basic Books, 1960.

Sarbin, T. R., "Role Theory," *Handbook of Social Psychology,* Vol. I, Cambridge: Addison-Wesley, 1954, pp. 223–258.

Schachter, S., *The Psychology of Affiliation,* Stanford, Cal.: Stanford University Press, 1959.

Schutz, W. C., *FIRO: A Three-Dimensional Theory of Interpersonal Behavior,* New York: Rinehart & Company, Inc., 1957.

Sears, R. R., Maccoby, E. E., and Levin, H., *Patterns of Child Rearing,* Evanston: Row, Peterson and Company, 1957.

Selltiz, C., Jahoda, M., Deutsch, M., and Cook, S. W., *Research Methods in Social Relations,* New York: Henry Holt, 1960.

Siegel, S., *Nonparametric Statistics for the Behavioral Sciences,* New York: McGraw-Hill Book Company, 1956.

Slater, P. E., "Role Differentiations in Small Groups," in Hare, A. P., Borgatta, E. F., and Bales, R. F., editors, *Small Groups,* New York: Alfred Knopf, 1955, pp. 498–515.

Slater, P. E., "Parental Role Differentiation," *American Journal of Sociology,* Vol. LXVII, No. 3, November, 1961, pp. 296–311.

Vroom, V. H., *Some Personality Determinants of the Effects of Participation,* Englewood Heights, N. J.: Prentice-Hall, 1960.

Walker, H. M., and Lev, J., *Statistical Inference,* New York: Henry Holt, 1953.

White, R. W., *The Abnormal Personality,* New York: Ronald Press, 1948.

White, R. W., *Lives in Progress,* New York: Dryden Press, 1952.

Zaleznik, A., *Worker Satisfaction and Development,* Boston: Division of Research, Harvard Business School, 1956.

Zaleznik, A., Christensen, C. R., and Roethlisberger, F. J., *The Motivation, Productivity, and Satisfaction of Workers: A Prediction Study,* Boston: Division of Research, Harvard Business School, 1958.

Index